SIX
DEGREES
OF
PARIS
HILTON

SIX DEGREES OF PARIS HILTON

*Inside the Sex Tapes, Scandals,
and Shakedowns of the New Hollywood*

Mark Ebner

SIMON SPOTLIGHT ENTERTAINMENT
New York London Toronto Sydney

Simon Spotlight Entertainment
A Division of Simon & Schuster, Inc.
1230 Avenue of the Americas
New York, NY 10020

First Simon Spotlight Entertainment hardcover edition November 2008

SIMON SPOTLIGHT ENTERTAINMENT and colophon are
trademarks of Simon & Schuster, Inc.

For information about special discounts for bulk purchases,
please contact Simon & Schuster Special Sales at 1-800-456-6798
or business@simonandschuster.com

Designed by Gabe Levine

Manufactured in the United States of America

10   9   8   7   6   5   4   3   2   1

Library of Congress Cataloging-in-Publication Data
Ebner, Mark C.
   Six degrees of Paris Hilton : inside the sex tapes, scandals, and shakedowns of the new
Hollywood / Mark Ebner. — 1st Simon Spotlight Entertainment hardcover ed.
      p.   cm.
   Includes bibliographical references and index.
   1. Motion picture actors and actresses—California—Los Angeles—Social life and customs.
2. Celebrities—California—Los Angeles—Social life and customs.   3. Motion picture actors
and actresses—California—Los Angeles—Biography.   4. Celebrities—California—
Los Angeles—Biography.   5. Scandals—California—Los Angeles.   6. Sex customs—
California—Los Angeles.   7. Hollywood (Los Angeles, Calif.)—Social life and customs.
8. Hollywood (Los Angeles, Calif.)—Biography.   9. Los Angeles (Calif.)—Social life and
customs.   10. Los Angeles (Calif.)—Biography.   I. Title.

PN1993.5.U65E26 2008
302.230862'10979494—dc22   2008039000

ISBN-13: 978-1-4169-5934-2
ISBN-10:   1-4169-5934-3

In Loving Memory—
Ian Herbert Just and Fred "Mad Dog" Valis

CONTENTS

CAST OF CHARACTERS

Giovanni Agnelli—Film and TV producer (with Scott Bloom); nightclub promoter of Wednesday nights at the Belmont.

Tommy Alastra—Nightclub, TV, and event promoter.

Donna Estes Antebi—Socialite and charity fundraiser; Darnell Riley once worked as part of a security detail at her Bel-Air estate.

Heather Bernardcyck—Former dancer, club denizen, Jack Ninio's wife, and Kristen Williams' best friend.

Scott Bloom—Actor, TV and film producer (with Giovanni Agnelli); nightclub promoter of Wednesday nights at the Belmont.

Bolo—Early mentor for the teenage Darnell Riley.

Joe Carnahan—Film director (*Blood, Guns, Bullets and Octane; Narc; Smokin' Aces*).

Brandon Davis—Grandson of oil tycoon Marvin Davis and Paris Hilton's frequent escort.

Rick Doremus (also known as "Nas" or "Shrek")—Former drug dealer turned DEA informant.

Joe Francis—*Girls Gone Wild* mogul worth an estimated $100 million and victim of a 2004 home invasion in which he was forced at gunpoint to star in a homosexual-themed pornographic video, for which Darnell Riley is currently serving 10 years, 8 months in prison.

Ruben Hernandez—A former drug dealer, now born again.

Paris Hilton—Ubiquitous scion of the Hilton hotel family and the most famous reality star ever.

Timmy Iannello—Nightclub manager and comic. Hung out with Darnell Riley and Will Wright.

Rich Jardine—CEO of advertising firm Clear Media, owner of BeverlyHillsBookie.com, which employed both Darnell Riley and Will Wright, and contributor to WhoIsWillWright.com Web site.

Mario King (aka Mario Goode, aka Ocean)—Bolo's cousin, and a mentor to the teenaged Darnell Riley.

Detective Steve Koman—LAPD Robbery-Homicide detective and lead investigator of the Joe Francis break-in.

Frankie Liles—World Boxing Association Super-Middleweight boxing champion and Mixed-Martial Arts trainer who worked on a security detail for Donna Antebi with Darnell Riley; was one of Darnell Riley's closest friends.

Parrish Medley—Entrepreneur and financial analyst. Shared office space with Rich Jardine.

Jared Merrell—Owner of J Star Motors in La Habra, car dealer to Paris Hilton and her friends.

Erin Naas—Former Elite model, companion to celebrities, and ex-roommate of Will Wright.

Jack Ninio—Former sportsbook impresario and professional gambler who divides his time between Mexico and Costa Rica; Heather Bernardcyk's husband.

Ocean—*see* Mario King.

Chuck Pacheco—Nightclub impresario, film producer, co-owner of Villa, and a good friend of Rick Salomon's.

Charlie Pope—Anna Nicole Smith's former lover.

David Reich—Second-generation sports agent, one-time confidante of Paris Hilton, Hollywood raconteur.

Ron Richards, Esq.—Attorney for, at various times, Darnell Riley, Will Wright, Timmy Iannello, Erin Naas, et al.

Darnell Riley—Debt collector, drug dealer, thief, boxer, fight trainer, burglar, Lothario. Serving 10 years, 8 months in prison for the Joe Francis home invasion.

Jerry Rosenberg—Fight trainer, former gym owner, and friend of Darnell Riley.

Rick Salomon—Director and co-star of *1 Night in Paris,* Paris Hilton's film debut.

Donald Thrasher—Friend of Rick Salomon; entrepreneur.

Alex Vaysfeld—Russian bail bondsman, boxing manager, and friend of Darnell Riley.

Kristen Williams—Actress-model, dated Will Wright and Louis Ziskin.

Will Wright—Film producer, man about town.

Louis Ziskin—Ecstasy kingpin, now serving 30-year sentence; dated Kristen Williams.

SIX
DEGREES
OF
PARIS
HILTON

PROLOGUE

I've got twenty-three years sober.

I started drinking at eleven, was a full-blown pothead by high school, upgraded to coke and heroin in college, and was sharing needles two years later, which earned me a lifelong case of hepatitis C, a liver the size of a football, and a functional heart murmur. By the time I was twenty-three, I was living at the Tropicana Hotel in West Hollywood with a raging drug habit, no skills to speak of, no talent for crime, and an ass that, even in my delusional state, I could tell wouldn't draw market value out on Santa Monica Boulevard. I did what it took to get by, and I took out a long-term mortgage on shame, which I've been paying down ever since. Somehow, I found recovery, or recovery found me, and by the grace of someone else's higher power, I edged my way back from the crumbling lip of self-destruction.

In recovery, there's a concept they call "the bottom." It's a relative term, individually fashioned for the contours of each person's addiction, but basically it refers to that point which you cannot dig beneath. When you start to skid, your bottom is where you come to a stop. It's the personal endpoint on degradation and humiliation beyond which your vestigial self will not let you fall. Where you're in the gutter, looking up at the curb and imagining it an unassailable height.

The problem is—and I think a lot of addicts will tell you this—that after the dope wears off, after your particular high pales and its grandeur and myth have ceased to sustain you, the thing that rushes in to fill that vacuum is the bottom itself. The degradation. The sick, exquisite rush of seeing yourself in a new, furtive light among the emotionally homeless—those without interior lives who wear their resources on their persons, costumes stitched out of bluster and desperation and the reflexive con. Where everything is more colorful, more dangerous, more real—all the things you were missing that led you into dope in the first place. A lot of us come for the drugs, but we end up staying for the addiction.

For me, the drugs were the easy part to give up. They promised something they never delivered. They were a little less effective every day: one more scam you walk straight into with eyes open, because someone figured out what you were looking for long before you got here. So I kicked, and I found a fellowship, and I worked it and it worked. But the bottom always stayed with me.

Twenty years later, and it's the weeks just after 9-11. I'd carved out a living selling freelance articles to any magazine looking to juice their circulation with some celebrity exposé, something dark that settles over household names like radioactive dust. I was in New York taking my semiannual round of meetings with sympathetic editors—those whose continued patronage had not yet cost them more than they were willing to part with. But this time out, it was different. I was hearing an emerging policy line coming out of the mouths of hardened cynics and functioning alcoholics that did not favor my own jaundiced worldview:

"Ebner, we want *nice*," the senior editor of a major American film magazine—maybe the last—told me in a midtown Asian-themed restaurant fifty blocks north of a smoldering slagheap they were still hoping to pull bodies out of. "We're thinking about putting an American flag on the cover."

I'd spent five years as a regular contributor picking at the loose threads of the American Dream. "Are you sure that's the way you really want to go?" I asked. "I mean, shouldn't this be the time when we're asking questions?"

"They're just not going to go for it," the editor said, closing the book on our lunch meeting. I realized then that my days in print journalism were numbered.

Salmon swim upstream to spawn. The rest of us just resent those who float downstream with the current.

I needed a career change in a bad way. I had coauthored a book that became a *New York Times* best seller—an arch polemic called *Hollywood, Interrupted* that bit hard at the hand that fed me. I'd figured if I burned all my sources, it might finally force me to leave the rat's nest. Six months later I was literally living in my van next to a park in Santa Monica with my two pit bulls. Apparently, a best seller and a quarter will get you a cup of coffee in this town, except you'd better make it a soy latte and $3.75.

Then out of the blue I got a message from someone at American Media, publisher of the *Globe*, the *Star*, and their crown jewel, the *National Enquirer*—the holy trinity of tabloid journalism. An old-school tabloid reporter had given them my name ("Ebner, you should come join us—see the world!") and they wanted me to come to their offices in Boca Raton, Florida, and interview for a job. A plane ticket was on its way.

If it's not apparent to the layman, there is no lower job in journalism than working for the tabloids. They pay for stories. They use each other as sources. They employ a situational ethics of the most robust variety: subjects are excused for reprehensible behavior one day because of some cooked-up synergy with the home office and then persecuted the next out of sport or spite. Stupidity is pandered to, stereotypes are reinforced with a vengeance, and every story features a moral to be found in that lacuna at the perfect nexus where our lowest common denominator intersects with the lesser angels of our nature. The tabloids are where you book transit when you're not planning on coming back.

After checking into the deluxe, extended-stay hotel in AMI's football field–size office park and picking up my rental car—which I would never use—I walked across a central plaza to the pumping heart of the scandal universe. Everything was flamingos, palm trees, and aggressive pastels—it looked like the opening credits of *Miami Vice*. Escorted through a sprawling newsroom big enough to bring down a standing president, I was deposited outside the office of editor in chief David Perel, visible to me through a glass partition. The waiting area literature consisted of the latest *Enquirer*, which I discovered you can read from start to finish in approximately fifteen minutes, and the contents of which made my teeth hurt. I had just done the crossword puzzle—and think for a moment what kind of crossword might be published in the *National Enquirer*—when he rapped on the glass and waved me in.

"Ebner," he greeted me like we were old friends—or more probably, like he saw in us a common pathology. "I read all your clips. Good stuff. By the way—you finish that crossword puzzle yet?"

"Yeah," I said.

"Then you're hired."

And before I had time to second-guess, I was on a plane back to L.A. It was now January 2004. For the first time in my adult life, I was making a five-figure annual salary I wouldn't be embarrassed to see published in a daily newspaper. I had a health plan, a dental plan, an expense account, and a generous travel allowance. I had a corner desk in Santa Monica six blocks from the ocean. In one strange turn of fate, I was suddenly an adult, a tax-paying citizen, and a reenfranchised member of society. Because what they did produced rich bouquets and overflowing fountains of money—so much money that it even trickled down to people like me. American Media's combined circulation was 5.4 million; the *New York Times*, by contrast, was barely over a million. I felt like part of an elite military machine, and all I'd have to do to be a part of it was to kill someone with my bare hands.

On a typical day, I'd get into the office about 8:30. First thing I'd do was register the verbal memos about who had been granted immunity: We're not touching Sylvester Stallone—we're going to do a magazine with him; he doesn't get any coverage. It was all very pleasant.

Next, I'd see if they had me assigned to any story for the day. Let's say they've got a blind tip. "Attention: Elizabeth Taylor might be dying today." I'd get in my '69 baby blue Volkswagen bus with the hand-tinted windows and I'd drive up and park in front of her estate discreetly tucked into one of the canyons. I'd sit there all day recording license plate numbers for every vehicle that came in or out of her compound. Then I'd call them in to the office manager, who in turn would contact our mole at the DMV. One of the names that came back was actually one of our long-time stringers. Maybe they had a legitimate job inside and they just never mentioned it. But a more tantalizing possibility was that Elizabeth Taylor herself was controlling her portrayal in the tabloids. The Mossad guys who worked security for her—bullet-shaped Israeli ex–secret service agents who knew how to break all 206 bones in the human body—would come out and knock on my window and ask me what I was doing. I'd tell them, "I'm doing the crossword puzzle." I couldn't have been more obvious. That assignment happened more than once.

Or my bosses would send me over to the San Fernando Valley to Annette Funicello's house—Mouseketeer emeritas and television's first consensus pinup, now debilitated by multiple sclerosis. My assignment was to knock on the door and when someone answered, try to get a good enough look at her to assess her condition. As her thankless caretaker tried to maintain her civility for the fifteen seconds of our encounter, I spotted Funicello across the room from the back, shaking in a chair, excused myself, and reported back. Somehow, these people were always inches away from death, and yet they tended to live out their lives.

But the one thing I discovered was that I had an affinity for crime stories. However much a reporter from the *National Enquirer* is reviled in places like Los Angeles or New York, he is a rock star in the depressed midwestern states that make up his readership. In some small town, peeling a handful of C-notes off the Chicago roll in my pocket—with an unlimited amount I could have wired in on request—I could put food on somebody's table for months or satisfy the most vicious methamphetamine habit. I would troll the wire feed or atrocity Web sites or skim small-town papers for days on end until something caught my eye—"Fetus Snatcher," let's say—and then suddenly I was on a plane that night to Kansas City, Missouri, driving the next morning to Melvern, Kansas, population 429. And then, just like in *In Cold Blood*, I was walking down a farm road two weeks before Christmas, on my way to doorstep the farmhouse where Lisa Montgomery had returned two days ago, having crossed the state line into Skidmore, Missouri, and cut the living fetus out of the womb of twenty-three-year-old Bobbie Jo Stinnett, who died hours later. She had planned to raise the child here as her own.

When no one answered the front door, I walked around back. There through a gap in the chintz curtains, I could see the remnants of the family's postponed Christmas holiday: a forlorn tree, half-decorated, unopened presents, and stockings above the fireplace—one too many for the number of reported family members, the last one a tiny red bootie half the size of the others. An image at once maudlin and horrifying—*this* was my lede. While I was scribbling in a reporter's notebook, a haunted man in a faded pickup truck pulled into the driveway and rolled down his window.

"Can I help you?" he said firmly.

"Sir, I'm from the *National Enquirer*, and—"

That was all he needed. "Get off my property," he said, "or I *will* call the police."

I made the front page of the local paper the next day.

At a truck stop on my way out of town, an overweight convenience store clerk confessed to me that she had been pregnant a few years back when Lisa Montgomery had stared at her belly for an uncomfortable period of time. That became my follow-up story idea: "It Could Have Been Me." And her kids got extra presents that year.

Or take the BTK Strangler, half a state away in Wichita, Kansas. BTK stands for "Bind, Torture, Kill," a kind of how-to mnemonic offered by serial killer Dennis Rader in his taunting letters to the press between 1974 and 1991. After a fourteen-year hiatus, he picked up the correspondence again when his guilt presumably got the better of him. By the time we were onto it, Rader had been pretty well picked over by the national press corps. So my assignment? Make him gay.

Of course, this married father of two, Cub Scout leader, and devout Lutheran never exhibited the slightest tendency toward homosexual behavior. But this was not a problem for the resourceful reporter. First I went through his roster of known acquaintances until I found a woman at a local university who was a lesbian. Source One: Proximity to lesbians. Next I phoned the only gay bar in Wichita and asked the owner whether it was *possible* that Rader might have been there any time in the past. He answered, "Sure, I guess it's possible." Source Two: Locked. And for Source Three, I twisted the arm of a criminal profiler on call out of Alabama until he suggested that the BTK's father had probably molested him as a child.

One, two, three sources: Gay BTK. It wasn't quite the UFO beat, but it was something akin to investigative fiction; the trick was to see how much you could get away with without being sued, and the *Enquirer* had it down to a science. I wrote probably thirty bylined stories over the course of the year. I'm not even saying I was that good at it. I'd try for that sweet spot of the tabloid voice—overly solicitous, maybe even a little breathless, yet ultimately disappointed in the human condition—but I bet I hit it less than half the time. I suppose I could have gotten better if I'd stuck around longer, but for the most part it was the rewrite guy's problem. The old guys there didn't look like they were heading into a happy sunset.

I finally hit the wall in 2005 on the Dermot Mulroney-Catherine Keener bust-up. Two mid-level stars, both consummate actors, married with a kid, were filing for divorce, and on the strength of her left-field Oscar nomination for *Being John Malkovich* (her second was for *Capote*) and it being a slow news week, the story had some play. I had enjoyed Mulroney's Celtic rock band, Low and Sweet Orchestra, once at the Troubadour and spent a charming half hour with Keener at Sundance one year, and they both seemed like genuine people. But I dutifully put a comment call in to Keener's mother in Florida. She answered on the first ring.

"Mrs. Keener? Hi, this is Mark Ebner. I'm a reporter for American Media."

First rule of cold-calling: Out in the heartland you're from the *Enquirer*; with celebrities or their families you're from American Media. It gives you an extra second to wedge your foot in the door.

"I'm reading a report here that says your daughter and Dermot have broken up."

"Oh, really?" came a sad voice from the other end. "I was just there two weeks ago and they seemed really happy."

I told her how sorry I was.

"You know, you seem like a nice man," she said to me, the only person she had to commiserate with her. "I hope you do the right thing." I thanked her and hung up. Then I sat there for a long time. It was my moment of clarity: there was no reason to do this story. Even on a slow news week, it didn't make sense to me. These people had never hurt anybody. They weren't out there driving drunk with their kids or clamoring for attention. They were trying to get through a difficult situation with their dignity intact. Plus it wasn't going to sell papers. I called the publicist and told her I was off the story, and that I was burning the numbers and deleting my files.

"Mark, what's got into you?" the publicist asked.

It was just a matter of weeks before they let me go. They had their reasons. While on assignment, I'd taken pictures of me embedded with the Minutemen on the Arizona-Mexico border and posted them on an unrelated Web site. I gave an interview to the *Los Angeles Times* on comedian Dave Chappelle, who had disappeared (to Africa, it turns out), where I said, "He's my hero . . . If he stays far away from people like us, he'll be fine." Mainly, because this job came with a 95 percent burnout rate, they were trained to watch for early warning signs. I just manifested mine ahead of the curve. The day I saw the head of human resources gingerly making her way to my desk, I told her, "I've been waiting for you." My severance check had already been cut.

One of the last stories I filed in those early months of 2005 was when Paris Hilton's T-Mobile Sidekick was hacked and her phone numbers, T-Mobile notes, text messages, and private photos were released onto the Internet. My first instinct was that this was another "Oops, I Did It Again"

moment: butterfinger *ingenue* keeps bobbling sex tapes and salacious photos, gets tossed back into the briar patch of bright media flame. I was one of
the first reporters to see that material, and I filed the story for the *Enquirer*.
But if this was a setup—and I was of the cynical cast of mind that everything you see in the media is a setup—then it was a particularly boneheaded
one, since the private numbers of five hundred of her fellow celebrities and
privileged insiders were compromised in the balance. This was a security
breach on an order of magnitude above anything I'd ever seen: Limp Biz-
kit frontman Fred Durst with his erection in his hand and a caption that
read, "Miss me?" *Us* magazine West Coast editor Ken Baker making party
plans with Paris, and her reminder to herself to download her latest tidbit
of gossip to him. All part of the same celebrity-industrial complex.

As I was going through her T-Mobile notes and cross-referencing them
with her phone list, and then cross-referencing *that* with key dates in the
Paris Hilton chronology, one item caught my eye. On September 27, 2004,
at 12:58 p.m., there appeared the following listing:

> Allan
> Jewelry 510 336 3111
> Darnell Ryley

There wasn't an Allan in her phone list, but there *was* a Darnell Riley,
right between Rick (Salomon, her ex-boyfriend, and the infamous director
and costar of the *1 Night in Paris* video) and Andy Roddick, a tennis star
Hilton allegedly dated in October 2004, after first dating his best friend
Mark Philippoussis, Tara Reid's ex. Moreover, this date was the same week
a story had appeared in the Rupert Murdoch–owned British tabloid *News
of the World*, our major rival, featuring images from fourteen hours of videotape reportedly stolen two months earlier during a break-in at the home
Paris Hilton shared part-time with her sister, Nicky, in the Hollywood
Hills. Those tapes allegedly showed Hilton in various sex romps with former boyfriends Nick Carter and Jason Shaw, rolling and smoking a joint
(in possible homage to the Pamela Anderson-Tommy Lee honeymoon sex
tape) and, most controversially, using a racial epithet against two club kids
of color who tried to invite her to a fashion show hosted by the rapper/TV
star Eve.

The number following the word "Jewelry" dialed into a Bay Area company called Jewelry by Rosalina, whose owner/designer Rosalina Tran

Lydster was the daughter of a Saigon jeweler who relocated to San Francisco during the war, and who appeared to make high-end costume jewelry for a celebrity clientele that included Paris Hilton and her parents Rick and Kathy. But what would Paris Hilton, "heir to the $300 million Hilton Hotel fortune," as the spoken interlude to her reality show, *The Simple Life*, never tired of reminding us, need with costume jewelry?

If, as I believed, almost every story you see in a newspaper has been intentionally put there by interested parties, then a corollary to that belief is that in a field of famous names, it's the ones you don't know who signify the real story. My nose told me there was more there than met the eye, but I also had Christina Aguilera's and Eminem's private phone numbers to follow up on, so I let the matter drop.

Six months later, I got a call from *Radar* magazine to cover a court date that might be tied to a rash of high-profile, high-end burglaries. *Girls Gone Wild* mogul Joe Francis had suffered a bizarre shakedown in January 2004 when he was held at gunpoint by an unidentified African-American man and reportedly forced to make a premeditated, graphic, homosexual-themed pornographic video—certainly the by-product of someone's heightened sense of irony. The assailant had been arrested fourteen months later and was now scheduled to make his first appearance in court, and his attorney was threatening to enter the tape into evidence. According to Francis, a key break in the case had come from none other than Paris Hilton, and the tabloids were reporting that Francis's alleged assailant had also been a key suspect in the theft of the Paris Hilton tapes reported in the *News of the World*, as well as the ongoing crime epidemic attributed to the Bel Air Burglar, responsible for over two hundred burglaries in upscale Los Angeles over a three-year period.

The suspect's name was Darnell Riley.

"You mean the guy who was in Paris Hilton's phone list?" I asked.

My editors had no idea what I was talking about.

My planets had just come into alignment.

THE HUSTLER, THE HEIRESS, AND THE SOFT-PORN KING

The video is stark and grainy, its color garish, almost fluorescent, from one too many generations of unauthorized copying. A figure lies face-down on a bed, his eyes glassy, his mouth puddled in a stuporous grin, his pants pulled down around his ankles. There is a remote-controlled, multi-pronged pink vibrator resting along the crest of his buttocks, lazily whirring in a clockwise motion, like a rotating finger. A whip-pan stage left shows a driver's license pinned to a wall—a subtle parody of the count-less porn ingénues forced to comply with Title 18, Section 2257 of the U.S. Code, the federal record-keeping law passed in the wake of the Traci Lords scandal to make sure the adult film industry stays that way. Except nobody here is acting brazen or flirty or petulant or even just the slightest bit naughty. It's more like one of those hostage videos from war-ravaged Iraq, its subject disheveled, sleep deprived, and, just maybe, fearing something on the order of a live, on-camera beheading.

"My name is Joe Francis," he says over and over in a damaged mono-tone. "I'm from Boys Gone Wild, and I like it up the ass."

This blockbuster video, which you cannot buy through late-night TV ads or a vanity Web site, was to have been the centerpiece of what was shaping up to be the first Trial of the Century, an O.J.-size opus for the porn-drenched, fame-addled, meta-logical, proto-YouTube generation, slated for Los Angeles Superior Court in late February 2006. Police say Darnell Riley, now thirty-one, a Hollywood strong-arm enforcer, rough-trade Lothario, and now convicted burglar with an apparent taste for the good life, which he was willing to cultivate by any means necessary, planned to sell the tape back to Francis, thirty-five, the *Girls Gone Wild* impresario who parlayed a privileged Laguna Beach upbringing into a $100 million empire of ersatz sleaze—who for once would be playing the victim. The twist—the hook, as they like to say in Hollywood—is that the missing link in the case, in fact the Junior G-Girl whose phone call to police provided them with probable cause to execute a search warrant on Riley's Hollywood apartment, was none other than accidental porn star and heiress aberrant Paris Hilton, the most famous reality-TV star in the history of the world. (Francis says they "dated"; Hilton begs to differ.)

Or at least that was how I spun it in my feature article in the November 2005 issue of *Radar* magazine titled "The Hustler, the Heiress and the Soft-Porn King."

In the early morning hours of January 22, 2004, Francis returned home from a nightclub to his tony Bel Air mansion to discover the door unlocked, the houselights on, and a masked, light-skinned black man selectively placing his possessions into a Louis Vuitton valise "like he was on a shopping spree." Francis, soft and doughy, quickly dissolved into tears, while the diminutive intruder held him at gunpoint for more than six hours, all the while talking to someone at the other end of a two-way radio. According to Francis's police statement, after walking him from room to room looking for a safe, Riley removed a Sony DV camera and pink sex toy from a Nike backpack in what was obviously a premeditated act, telling his victim, "Don't get me wrong, I'm not a faggot," and forced him into a makeshift porn audition tape, for which Riley attempted to extort upward of $500,000 in ten subsequent phone calls over the next six months. As dawn broke over the serpentine hills, the terrified Francis was eventually bound with black zip-ties covered with duct tape and forced into the back of his Bentley GT, which his assailant(s) left at the bottom of the canyon. (Francis's Ferrari and Bentley, parked in the garage, can be glimpsed at the tail end of the handheld tape, and a woman's voice heard faintly in the background.) Francis claimed he was robbed of personal property totaling $300,000, although in court records, Riley's attorney, Ron Richards, put the figure at $14,800—a Rolex, a Sony video camera, a Picasso print worth $1,000, two pieces of Louis Vuitton luggage—and $15,000 in cash.

For the thousands of women who may have confused sexual empowerment with an alcohol-fueled lack of judgment when importuned to "show us your tits," Joe Francis's comeuppance at the hands of a twirling pink sex aid may seem like nothing short of poetic justice. Before his incarceration for contempt of court related to his legal troubles in Florida (and subsequent extradition to Nevada on tax fraud charges, which may have circuitously resulted from the preliminary hearing in the Riley case), Francis seemed to attract unwanted lawsuits and unwanted attention from the authorities on a more or less constant basis. At one time, he faced seventy separate charges stemming from spring break 2003 in Panama City Beach, Florida, when the mother of an underage girl claimed her daughter and three friends had been coerced by Francis and his professional entourage to appear naked and engage in sexual acts on camera, and to lie about their age. Francis was charged with racketeering related to prostitution, drug trafficking, and child pornography, and his private jet was briefly confiscated. The racketeering and drug trafficking charges were dismissed in November of that year when a judge ruled the hydrocodone and oxycodone pills seized in a raid on his rented condo were prescription medications.

At the time of the break-in, rape charges by two women, one a minor, had just been dismissed against Francis in a murky scenario in which he wore a wire in a meeting with opposing counsel, allegedly at the behest of the FBI, to prove charges of extortion. And in April 2004, just three months later, a Texas college student claimed Francis drugged and raped her in a Miami Beach hotel room. Francis responded by claiming the sex was consensual, and that the woman and a friend stayed through lunch, which they ordered up from room service the next day. The investigation was soon dropped, and Francis in turn filed suit against the woman for $25,000,036— the fractional amount to compensate for the price of the lunch. (That case has also been dismissed.) In fact, one anecdote then making the rounds in Hollywood circles was that actor Erik Palladino, who starred on *ER* from 1999 to 2001 and bears a striking resemblance to Francis, was constantly getting punched by irate women in nightclubs who mistook him for the amateur porn kingpin.

When police finally raided Riley's apartment on March 28, 2005, some fifteen months after the break-in, they discovered a VHS copy of the Joe Francis videotape (not the original) and numerous *Girls Gone Wild* master tapes, one of the Louis Vuitton bags (with an Oahu sticker on it from Riley's recent trip to Hawaii), and five handguns—one of which belonged to restaurateur Dipu Haque, co-owner of Koi, where the Hilton sisters were regulars, and another belonging to horror filmmaker Wes Craven. Police also found a Mossberg 12-gauge shotgun propped behind the door and, reportedly, sticks of dynamite. Riley was charged with two counts of first-degree residential burglary, two counts of kidnapping, and one count each of carjacking and attempted extortion—all felony charges; the kidnapping counts alone each punishable by life imprisonment. (Weapons charges were never filed, although the guns were not returned to him.) Bail was set at $1,050,000.

Understandably, the tabloids had a field day. With his name now connected to not one but two high-profile hillside burglaries (Joe Francis in Bel Air and the August 2004 burglary at the Hilton sisters' Hollywood Hills home that produced the fourteen hours of Paris Hilton footage), it was a short step to connecting Darnell Riley to the infamous Bel Air Burglar, thought to be responsible for some two hundred heists among Los Angeles's rich and famous zip codes, even if the prime suspect was already a middle-aged white guy captured on surveillance footage (he was later apprehended). The *Globe* speculated the Burglar was actually a ring that used an Elite model to gain access codes to the well-appointed addresses of credulous millionaires. A source in the Francis camp identified her to me as "lingerie model" Erin Naas, who appeared in (but did not actually pose for) the September 2004 issue of *Playboy* and who dated Francis in late 2003. In an e-mail, Riley's lawyer Richards claimed his client was also friendly with Naas, which explains how his fingerprints were reportedly discovered in Francis's Bentley, which Naas borrowed on occasion. (Naas denies being involved with any burglary.)

After Riley's arrest, the *New York Post* reported that Riley was blackmailing Paris Hilton for $20,000 a month to keep her stolen videotapes off the market. None other than Joe Francis claimed to have seen the tapes, and that their release would "ruin her career." Hilton told the *Post*'s Page Six, "Anyone who blackmails should be prosecuted to the full extent of the law." In an e-mail responding to my questions, Richards attempted to clarify the matter: "[Riley] recovered the tape from someone trying to sell it to Rick Salomon [on the strength of his *1 Night in Paris* tape]. That person knew Darnell and knew that Darnell knew Rick, so he contacted Darnell to get the tapes back to Rick . . . to give them to Paris Hilton." In the same e-mail, Richards claimed that "Darnell was sexually intimate with Nicole Richie," Hilton's costar in *The Simple Life*. Speaking from the red carpet at the Video Music Awards in Los Angeles, Richie answered, "I have never met that person in my life. I know he said that crap before, and he needs to stop lying."

Yet for someone accused of multiple felonies, Riley's career path wasn't all that different from all the other eager young hopefuls who show up in Hollywood looking to trade upward on their good looks, innate charms, and sexual prowess: he worked as an extra in films, went to the right parties, and rubbed elbows with an A-list crowd he thought could help him achieve his outsize goals. And when times got hard, he did things he may have regretted later.

According to a blind quote added to my story after I filed it, "a source close to Hilton" said, "Darnell knows some models and was on the fringes of that scene, but has no intimate contact with Paris, Nicole Richie, or Joe. If Paris had his number, it was some sort of business arrangement due to the tape." But in his e-mail, Richards said that he had a statement from Paris that read, "Darnell is a friend of mine and he never robbed me." In fact, even though Francis denied knowing Riley, Richards claimed the two had business between them. His client had attended a Halloween party in 2003 at the Francis home (actually held at a separate location). Richards also claimed that Riley had been hired to humiliate Joe Francis by the father of a young woman, and that Riley was negotiating a settlement with musician Stevie Wonder, on whose property he allegedly tripped and fell the same month he was arrested. And just to spice things up, Riley was reportedly prepared to testify, as a cornerstone of his defense, that he was having a sexual relationship with Francis, and that the bizarre Joe Francis vibrator tape was a consensual act.

While researching the *Radar* story, I got a tip from one of my sources—a Teamster—urging me to talk to a guy named Alex Vaysfeld, a Russian boxing manager/promoter, bail bondsman, and self-styled bounty hunter who was a regular at Hollywood Gym at Hollywood and La Brea.

Vaysfeld is a Russian immigrant who came to this country with $120 in his pocket and a handiness with his fists, which he managed to parlay into a brief boxing career as a 147-pound welterweight before starting Union Bail Bonds, his Los Angeles–based national bail bond chain. Compact and pugnacious, a Jew who answers his phone "Hey, Jewboy!", he still keeps his hand in the sweet science by managing professional boxers on the side, like the light heavyweight champion Roman "Made in Hell" Karmazin. It was at Hollywood Boxing where he met Riley, who used to hang around the gym, training and sparring with the pros in the hopes of trading body shots with some of the celebrity clientele, which included Mickey Rourke, Pauly Shore, John Stamos, Denzel Washington, and the

Wayans brothers. Despite his slight build—five feet eight and 165 pounds, with almost delicate features—Riley had something Vaysfeld may have recognized in himself, something the fight world calls heart, that would routinely see him hold his own against opponents who were out of his weight class or who had inches on him in reach. He's also not a man to mince words.

"Don't let Darnell's looks and stature fool you," says Vaysfeld. "He'd do collections work for some powerful people who didn't want to get their hands dirty. He referred clients to me. I deal with these fucking niggers day in, day out—he was a hustler but Darnell was faithful. Most of them think everybody owes them. He got educated in jail. He was good with computers, and when he got out, he started trading on the stock market. He did it well. Darnell was fascinated with glamour and all the Hollywood bullshit. He thought he would make it up the ladder in Hollywood somehow, but he was criminally minded. I tried to mentor him. Some days, he'd come to me and say, 'I'm so fucking broke I'm ready to knock off a 7-Eleven.' I'd toss him a hundred dollars every now and then."

Such was his appearance and demeanor that someone at the gym who said he knew Riley could still claim, "I honestly thought he was a successful young businessman."

Vaysfeld also further clouded the chain of provenance by introducing a third mysterious figure into the Paris Hilton/Joe Francis phone call that fingered Riley.

"Darnell had a celebrity confidant who will go unnamed," he says. "We'll call him 'Will.' Will and Darnell were good friends. Will was drunk one night and he told Paris Hilton about what went down with Darnell and Joe Francis. Darnell claims he was banging Paris and her sister, Nicky, before all this went down. [I think he means Nicole Richie.] Paris, who believes she was robbed by Darnell earlier, went to Francis and said, 'I know who hit you.' Francis picked Darnell from a photo lineup. Now the kid's life is completely screwed up. We probably won't see him for ten years. Last time we talked, he said he was willing to make a deal and take the extortion charge. In many ways, he was a fall guy."

Before I left, Vaysfeld told me one more story, one that I didn't put in the *Radar* article. At the time, it was too explosive for even me to go out on a limb for, and I only had the one source. Later, after an article ran in an August 2006 edition of the *Los Angeles Times' West* magazine where reporter Claire Hoffman described being slammed onto the hood of a car by a near-psychotic Francis attempting to demonstrate his treatment at the hands of Miami police, I changed my mind and dumped the whole thing on my Web site.

Through his contacts in Russia, Vaysfeld is a partner in the popular Moscow nightclub, Night Flight, known as a home base for expensive prostitutes. It was there that he met Francis and his entourage several years ago, presumably there on a fact-finding mission to gauge the relative wildness of girls behind the former Iron Curtain.

"Francis was staying at the luxury hotel Balchug in an eight-hundred-dollar-a-night suite with some friends," recalls Vaysfeld. "At the club, he said he wanted girls. I said, 'How many girls do you want?' and he said, 'As many as I can handle.' My club is one of the biggest pickup joints in Moscow, so that was easy. I got him five girls—my treat. I came to his hotel suite with them, and he and his buddies were popping Viagra like crazy. They were banging the girls—flip-flopping with them—and videotaping the sex. Then Joe asks me for some X [Ecstasy]. He banged all five of the girls, then he said, 'You know what I really want—right now?' I said, 'I gave you girls, dope—what else do you want?' He said, 'I want a twelve-year-old to fuck.' That's where I jumped off. Joe Francis is a sick piece of shit—a pedophile.

"I split, and later that night I got a call from Francis's hotel. He was on the phone telling me, 'My friend's money is gone. It was about three thousand dollars.' He was trying to accuse me of ripping his friend off! Obviously, I did no such thing. I fart three thousand dollars. But when I got back to Los Angeles, my friend the actor Mario Lopez told me that Francis was telling people that I stole money from him. Mario warned me, 'He's gonna put people on you.' "

Asked if he was worried about a powerful millionaire like Francis carrying a vendetta against him, Vaysfeld just laughs. "They never get to me," he says. "I get to them first. I'm licensed to carry a gun. If I see him or any of his people following me, he's liable to get shot and die. I know that prick is under indictment for things like rape and pedophilia. The second he brought up the twelve-year-old, he was finished with me. Now, I will tell everyone he's a pedophile."

I also tracked down Riley's mother, Azline Hibler, who was just then using the name Azline Washington. In fact, she had a whole host of aliases she revolved between—Washington, Hibler, North, Cox, Perez—collected through numerous marriages and inhabiting a police record that included embezzlement and numerous claims of domestic violence. Washington agreed to meet me at a Denny's in Palmdale, California, a dusty watering hole in the high desert noted for its Joshua trees and meth labs. She arrived early in a gold Cadillac Escalade and immediately ordered a steak. A large woman with a robust appetite who has studied the law and done paralegal work, in addition to working as a Hollywood extra, Washington chose to open the conversation by noting, "My son is facing the possibility of life without parole and there wasn't a bruise on Joe Francis's body." She systematically discounts most of the stories swirling around her son as so much urban legend. "Darnell wants it known, 'I may be a lot of things, but I'm not the Bel Air Burglar,' " she states emphatically.

As to charges that he was blackmailing Paris Hilton for compromising videotapes, Washington claims her son was a frequent guest in the Hilton home.

"My son was with the Hiltons a week before his arrest," she says. "If he was extorting her, what was he doing at a function at the Hilton family home?" Besides, she says, "My son and I are very close. If he was getting twenty thousand a month from Paris Hilton, I would know about it. When he has had money, he's always helped me out. Whatever he had from Paris Hilton, she gave it to him."

Washington claims she has five other children, one of whom was shot in a still unsolved murder. She describes Darnell as a polite kid who got his associate in arts degree and a culinary certificate while incarcerated, and who has turned his life around since he got out.

"I'm not saying he's one hundred percent innocent," she says. "But if there's a tape out there with her saying the N word—what's up with her? The reason these people are setting Darnell up is because there are tapes of Paris saying 'nigger' and having sex, and things about underage girls and boys and Joe Francis that may get out. A lot of people caught up in that Hollywood scene are cowards. I want him to come home and finish his life and give me a grandchild."

At a preliminary hearing in August 2005, Riley was brought into court in a regulation-blue county jumpsuit and sat quietly at the defense table, asking occasional questions in a barely discernible voice. His close-cropped hair and the thick beard beginning at his sideburns still couldn't obscure his Roman nose, Arabic or Hispanic features, olive skin, and piercing brown eyes set in thick palm-frond lashes, nor the implacable calm and extreme confidence that reportedly served him well in Youth Authority.

This is the prison system for minors where Riley served a six-year bid from ages fifteen to twenty-two for a double homicide, the details of which were sealed by court order. Richards emphasized that his client had no prior adult record, but then, in all fairness, he hadn't had much time to acquire one.

Outside the L.A. County courthouse after the hearing, I blindsided Richards and asked him to let me see the infamous videotape—mostly in jest. Instead, he told me to meet him at his office at the Sierra Towers, a multistory mostly residential building that anchors the western end of the Sunset Strip. There, he screened the forty-five-second clip for me, as well as some of the *Girls Gone Wild* master tapes confiscated from Riley's apartment, which showed Francis barking orders at a bevy of volunteer models like somebody's dad coaching girls' softball, and at the end, manually stimulating one of them to his professional satisfaction.

Richards most resembles a Jewish Fred Flintstone—slimmer, but with soft jowls and a pronounced beard line—and his bespoke suits and wire-framed glasses make him look like he's still chasing the dream of *Miami Vice* from the mid-eighties. He has represented a number of high-profile clients, including John Rutter, the photographer accused of attempting to illegally sell topless photos of Cameron Diaz, and John Gordon Jones, the so-called Limousine Rapist, acquitted in 2001 of drugging and date-raping a series of women he met at nightclubs. Richards also specialized in Ecstasy cases—at least according to his Web site—and more recently served as an on-air legal analyst for NBC in the Michael Jackson trial.

"I tend to represent underdogs and rougher clients," Richards tells me. "They're more interesting and more colorful. By and large, celebrities are prima donnas. With Darnell, the business model is that a lot of people know him in town and feel favorably toward him, whether out of fear or respect, and so I get kudos by defending him. And then, just so many people hate Joe Francis . . . He's a pedophile scumbag."

However, he bristled at the suggestion, made in the *National Enquirer*, that he had marketed the Paris Hilton videotapes in partnership with Riley.

"I would never go into business with Darnell Riley," he states categorically. "Think how insane that is."

The other shoe finally dropped on why Richards was being so accommodating to me at the next court hearing, held September 14, 2005, the Honorable Marcelita V. Haynes presiding. Haynes is an intimidating

African-American woman in her forties or fifties who rules her courtroom with an iron hand, and you were free to talk to it all you wanted. She wore reading glasses on a chain and stared down over the top of them imperiously, as if from a great height, and with Richards refusing to bring his client out due to a beef with my photographer, she was the one thing I had to look forward to. At an earlier hearing, when a gang-banger in a wheelchair tried to bargain her down on some legal point, she told him, "You remember what you told me the last time you were here? You said if it weren't for people like you, I wouldn't have a job. Now, you want to go back there again?" He quietly shook his head no. Another time, after she had to separate the attorneys like a boxing referee, she turned to me in an aside and said, "I don't want you magazine folks to get the wrong idea— I'm shy and retiring."

Richards and Deputy District Attorney Hoon Chun were in the midst of one of their endless procedural squabbles over whether to enter the video in the court record—thereby making it accessible to the media in attendance but ostensibly violating the rights of the victim. All had agreed to table the matter for the time being—or thought they had.

"Doesn't the defense get to respond to this?" Richards asked after one particularly brutal exchange.

"I'll tell you what, you run the show and I'll sit here," said Haynes.

Finally given the floor, Richards began his argument, then motioned me to the railing. Raising the videotape to make some point, he turned and handed it to me. I heard the judge scream "No!" but I kept my eyes on the bailiff, who had dropped to a crouch and was deliberating whether he should shoot me just to be safe.

"I was given this tape with no order," Richards said. "I wanted him— the media—to have standing to litigate the issue."

"Would you please return that to him?" Haynes instructed me. I handed the tape back to Richards. "So now you've made a whole other issue that I have to deal with. You did it underhandedly, in open court, in a very dishonorable way in my opinion. It's exactly the opposite of what I ordered you not to do. I'm just aghast."

After my story ran, a couple of things happened. One is that a guy named Rich Jardine e-mailed me and told me to take a look at a Web site called "WhoIsWillWright.com" (since taken down). Jardine was the CEO of an advertising company called Clear Media in Beverly Hills that had shown up in the Joe Francis police report as one of half a dozen burglaries to which

Riley might be connected. He was also, I would find out later, the owner of Beverly Hills Bookie, an online sportsbook gambling site Darnell did collections for and claimed to have equity in; Wright's one-time best friend and the author of the WhoIsWillWright.com site; and a confidential informant who told the LAPD, "I was with Will when I got robbed and he actually sold my stolen paintings back to me!" Inside, beside a photo of a skinny white kid with a wandering eye in b-boy drag (Nike sweatshirt, gold chains, a hoodie that read "Don't Ask Me 4 Shit") with the caption "Will Wright: Compulsive Liar," I found the scarcely believable story of a Washington State pot dealer with a manic spiel who had bum-rushed Hollywood with the best of them.

According to his personal mythology, conveniently collected in would-be press releases for a proposed film based on his life, to be directed by Joe Carnahan (*Narc, Smokin' Aces*) and financed by FilmEngine, an L.A.-based film production company just then flush with cash, Wright was an academic prodigy and star high school athlete who was scouted by the Seattle Mariners, and who at seventeen managed to build a $70 million drug empire in the Pacific Northwest before serving nine years in prison. But from the story painstakingly laid out in legal documents pertaining to his Washington court case, as well as comments from victims of his numerous instances of alleged fraud, Wright is revealed as a pathological liar who forged documents to prove his storied exploits and made Sammy Glick look like a weekend warrior.

Wright was introduced to young Hollywood society—people like Paris Hilton and Brandon Davis—by ex-girlfriend Kristen Williams, an aspiring model-actress, who in a heartfelt mea culpa on the Web site maintains that Wright convinced her to sell the engagement ring given to her by former fiancé and convicted Ecstasy dealer Louis Ziskin, worth $250,000, for which she received $90,000. Wright claimed to be investing the money for her in a series of commercial ventures, all confirmed by financial documents. In reality, she says he created the documents in Photoshop and used the money to charter private jets, pay hookers, and buy bottles of Cristal champagne and expensive gifts for the celebrities and wealthy elite he sought to impress and emulate.

"He was very charming and knew the right things to say," she says in her statement. His last communication with her was a threatening text message on the eve of her first interview with me; it read, "Darnell is going to be out sooner than you think."

In court documents, Joe Francis identified Wright as the voice at the other end of the walkie-talkie Riley held the night of the home invasion, and Wright also emerged as the hypothetical "Will" who Vaysfeld said had dropped a bug in Paris Hilton's ear. Coincidentally, his lawyer was Ron Richards. I eventually condensed much of this into a story for my Web site Hollywood, Interrupted ("How a Cast of Royal Screwups Took Down A-List Hollywood," April 2006) that later became the basis for "The Paris Hilton Tapes" episode of NBC's *Dateline*, where I appeared on camera as a reporter and served as a consultant for the story.

I was even contacted by a drug dealer named Rick Doremus, better known as "Nas" or "Shrek" (between the metal plate in his head and his years of rough-and-tumble in the drug trade, he really does bear a disturbing resemblance to the affable green ogre), who said he could tell me more about Will Wright than I would ever want to know. Doremus had his own epic tale—not the least part of which involved his recent career change as an undercover agent for the Drug Enforcement Agency, which he judiciously employed to settle unresolved scores from his days in the life—and I later profiled him in *Maxim* ("Rat," April 2007). Also from Washington State, he could tie Wright heavily into the drug trade.

VH1 called and told me they were doing a documentary on "Hollywood Blackmail," and they wanted to make the Joe Francis story the centerpiece. They sent out a producer in his late twenties and we scheduled one full day of interviews, starting with Ron Richards at his office. We staged on the sidewalk outside, where I told him, "This is going to get hairy." When we walked off the elevator into Richards's apartment-cum-office with our camera crew, a figure suddenly emerged from around the corner in the kitchen who I recognized as Will Wright—shaved head, shorts, and a T-shirt—working it to look menacing. I said to my producer, "This is a setup."

So I immediately went on the offensive. I said, "Will, what are you doing here?"

Ron answered, "He's my client."

"Who are your sources?" Will said, swaggering up to me.

I told him, "I'm here to interview your lawyer; I'm not going to get into who my sources are. But if you want to go on camera, I'll interview you right now."

He said, "Naw, I'm not really a TV guy. And besides, I'm on federal probation; I can't do any interviews."

Bullshit. I said, "I've interviewed plenty of people on probation. It's your constitutional right." He pressed me for my sources again, and I told him they were none of his business.

"Well, then you're a punk-ass bitch," he said, squaring off. I could see Richards over his shoulder, and it became clear he was trying to bait me. I just laughed at him. The producer looked shell-shocked, or at least like this was above his pay grade. When we finally got Richards on camera, he declared that Wright had nothing to do with the Joe Francis break-in, and if we reported anything to the contrary, he would sue us.

Outside, waiting for the valet, Wright switched into his "charming" mode. He volunteered that they were making a movie of his life, and that Joe Carnahan would direct. "Oh yeah?" I told him. "Joe Carnahan's a friend of mine." He dropped the subject. When I mentioned I was going to New York, he told me he kept a place there. I could see that upstairs, he was the cornered rat lashing out; down here he was just the "successful businessman," waiting for his slate-gray Escalade, on the way to his next meeting.

When it became clear that the talking heads out here came with their own threat level, VH1 asked me to conduct the Joe Francis interview myself. At his sleek Mantra Films offices at the high-end Water Garden in Santa Monica, a seventeen-acre complex with Versailles-styled fountains and a man-made lake, Francis sat down in front of a black backdrop in a corner of the shipping and receiving bay and described his ordeal. On camera, his eyes kept wandering all over the place, and I had to keep reminding him to focus on me. After the interview, as he reclined at his massive desk, framed against a row of three or four Andy Warhol dollar bill canvases, I mentioned that I had written the *Radar* article. Suddenly, he was on his feet and swearing up a blue streak.

"Motherfucker, I can't believe you did that!" he yelled into my face. "You cost me the cover of *Architectural Digest*! I was looking for a way to sue you guys." His publicist froze. I told him to calm down. "Fuck me once, it's on me; fuck me twice, it's on you," he said, his voice a threatening growl. Or at least I think that's what he said. His whole demeanor was totally erratic—he was up and down, his eyes kept shooting off; he was prone to fits of anger one minute and then making up with you like he was your best friend the next.

For the *Dateline* special ("The Paris Hilton Tapes," broadcast September 23, 2006, on NBC), they put me on camera and again I wrangled some interviews for them. We filmed Will Wright's ex-girlfriend Kristen Williams and her friend Heather Bernardcyck, who had flown in from Las Vegas, at Kristen's Sunset Plaza apartment. This is the same complex where Kristen had lived with Will Wright; where Erin Naas had lived (Will moved in with her when he lost his own apartment, and then both were evicted Christmas 2004 when Will threw furniture off the balcony); where nightclub manager Timmy Iannello "was over so much he pretty much lived there"; where club promoter Chuck Pacheco had lived and shared an apartment with actor Lukas Haas; where Darnell's girlfriend Ruby lived before he met her; and where Darnell himself lived platonically with an Austrian model named Simone (with whom he also shared a New York loft) from 1999 to 2001, with Rick Salomon crashing there from time to time. It was their own little *Melrose Place*. "Mark Wahlberg lived there!" said Kristen when I asked her about it. "When I dated Mark ten years ago, he lived there." She and Heather hadn't seen each other in a while, and they were giving me an animated rundown of their exploits, stripped down to their underwear in Kristen's walk-in closet, doing shots to calm their nerves and trying to find something to wear while I did my best to get them pumped up for the camera.

Afterward, on-camera interviewer Keith Morrison (Matthew Perry's stepfather) took us to lunch at Caffe Med on Sunset Plaza, which was walking distance from the apartment. We were barely seated when both girls flitted off to another table to talk to a gaunt character in a knit skullcap with piercing eyes, there with his friends, who kept shooting glances over at me as they explained to him what they were doing. When they returned to the table, both seemed slightly flushed.

"That's Rick Salomon," said Heather, who had spotted him first. "We've known him forever."

A few days later, Morrison's producer told me they had just gotten Will Wright on camera at Ron Richards's office. "You know, you didn't make any fans over there," she confided to me.

On the broadcast, looking sketchy and evasive, Wright presented his theory of Hollywood: "In Hollywood, celebrities, you know, party on the fringes of people who are in the gray and in the dark. You know what I mean? It's a very interesting crowd. It's like, celebrities mix with people who sell drugs for a living or commit crimes. I mean, Hollywood's weird like that."

No doubt.

But long before this rich stew of characters and connections could come to a satisfactory boil, Darnell copped a plea. As a testament to Richards's lawyering skills, after the preliminary hearing—a de facto two-day trial—he turned over all sorts of rocks in Joe Francis's sub rosa business dealings and argued that Francis was incapable of telling the truth, even under oath. The D.A. dropped burglary, carjacking, and the two kidnapping charges in exchange for Riley pleading guilty to extortion and robbery with a gun enhancement and agreeing to serve ten years, eight months. At his sentencing, asked if he understood the terms of his deal, Riley smiled and gave the judge a thumbs-up. As far as Darnell was concerned, of all the crimes he had ever considered or committed, this seemed among the least likely to put him away for most of his thirties. Without any new charges slipping down the pike—and from the little I knew about him, Darnell was up in a whole mess of things—he'd be out by the time he was forty. And the circus closed up shop.

Then a week before the *Dateline* show, I got an e-mail in the comments section of my Web site. It was from Darnell. I'd been logging periodic posts on the subject, some of them at his expense—at one point, I called him Dildo Dude—because, well, really, why not? He wasn't going anywhere.

Now it seemed that Darnell was unhappy.

2

THE POPE OF THE SUNSET STRIP

It has taken me a lot of time and thought to come to a point of being able to care about dignifying the many outlandish, somewhat mythical and comical stories that have been attributed to my 5'8" frame. All 165 pounds of me has been burning to debunk the urban legends that have caused friends of mine in Europe to question who it was they were partying with.

Apparently, the *Dateline* special awakened a slumbering beast. Eighteen months after his arrest, a year and three-quarters after the crime itself, and Darnell Riley was finally breaking radio silence with a missive to me. In his mid-October post to my Web site, he labeled the *Dateline* special "fluff," which he contrasted with the "brave investigative journalism" of Dan Rather's famous comeback line to Richard Nixon. (Nixon, after Rather's name drew applause at a press conference: "Are you running for something?" Rather: "No sir, Mr. President—are you?") To prove the scope of the conspiracy against him, Darnell accused Joe Francis of modifying his testimony on the gun that was used to terrorize him: "a blue steel semiautomatic (a 9mm)" at the time of the first police report versus "a stainless steel .357 revolver" by the time of the preliminary hearing. These are "at the far ends of the spectrum," according to Darnell (maybe in your world), and my failure to notice this just further demonstrated my own dereliction. Me he pegged as a *National Enquirer/Star* magazine hack destined for the outskirts of legitimate journalism who had fallen under the spell of an It girl with a knockoff Louis Vuitton handbag, who if I had half a brain I would know was "a porn actress . . . riding the waves of a society that is so fed up with its bleak existence [it] would rather cling to a chick with huge duck feet and a humpback." Joe Francis he called "a sexual deviant smut purveyor who is one arrest away from overdosing on Vicodin, pornos, coke, and anal lube." Don't hold back with your opinions.

Darnell also hyped the book he was shopping, *The Pope of the Sunset Strip*, which would set the record straight on whether he had blackmailed Paris Hilton, the sordid truth behind the Joe Francis break-in, and the rumor that he had the Beverly Hills offices where Hilton conducted her colon cleansings wired for audio/video, which he would be releasing on the Internet in conjunction with his book release.

"I took a deal," reads Darnell's letter. "My deal was not my admission of guilt, it was my way of saving my life. I am a gambler, and I know when to hold 'em and when to fold 'em. The risk of losing at trial was too much to play with. With the compromise (the plea-bargain deal), I get to live again. I'm sure you could understand my position."

He signed off, "Ciao, D. Riley."

I wrote him back—gingerly—and tried to establish a dialogue. He'd started out by insulting me; I didn't need to be poking him with a stick. To my surprise, the letters started flowing—over seventy of them before we were done, more than seven hundred fifty pages in all, handwritten in pencil in a tight, run-on scrawl on white or yellow legal sheets, both sides filled, margins crammed with footnotes and asides and second thoughts. And a fantastic story began to emerge, one filled with a riotous cavalcade of hard-boiled character types right out of central casting: scions of wealth and tabloid fodder in their unvarnished natural states, hard-case megastars who crumble at the first flash of danger, shady art dealers, feral waifs, five-star sex dolls, meth- and press-addled lawyers, gullible film directors, predatory gigolos, and six-figure hipster dupes, just for a start.

It was like my own private cable series, unfolding in real time.

Darnell claimed he had spent his time in prison productively. An intelligent observer, one who earned an associate's degree during his first stint in prison, he had taken a six-year run at Hollywood and managed to pack more living into that brief controlled burn than most people do in their fifty years of adult life—more than enough to tide him over until he got another shot at it. Along the way, working at a class disadvantage, he was careful to take copious notes, as perhaps his only insurance for the future, and now his only means of settling the score with those who had turned against him. This presumably included "two-bit punk criminals . . . half-ass socialite porn queens and dildo-loving media moguls. I guarantee you that there will be several indictments on all the yet-to-be-charged conspirators/associates/crime partners."

He claimed to be counting down the minutes on what crimes he could and could not talk about: "There is more that I left out than I've put in. Some that the statute of limitations hasn't ended on yet, and some where the statute of limitations doesn't exist (if you follow me)." Sometimes his rage could be quite elegant: "Adjusting back to this lifestyle and dealing with this world took up a lot of my energy and focus, but now I'm ready to deal. Some have described me as the agent by which Karma is delivered. Karma is a weapon that may be delivered from a bullet, a sword or even a whisper." And he described his book as *"Fear and Loathing in Las Vegas* mixed with *The Confessions of St. Augustine,"* which would explain in detail this world of the hyper-rich in the Hollywood fast lane and their dangerous flirtation with thug life—a closed world, governed by access, a mash-up of unearned privilege and the indelicate lure of street knowledge, where everyone wants the thing they don't have and status is determined by degrees of separation from Paris Hilton. He quoted F. Scott Fitzgerald ("Show me a hero and I will write you a tragedy), Honoré de Balzac ("Behind every great fortune there is a crime"), and Jean Renoir's *The Rules of the Game* (". . . everybody has his reasons"). And he described his place in this rarely plumbed milieu, the by-product of social Darwinism and centuries of inbreeding, as the black pearl inside a giant clam.

"Let me explain my relationship with [Joe] Francis and a lot of other privileged Hollywood trust-fund babies who burn their bridges, fuck over someone who is connected and then come running to me for help," says Darnell in one of his letters. "It never fails. They always seem to forget that I've got dirt on them. It may be in the form of a video of them smoking crack, [using] racial epithets or giving someone a blowjob. Then again, it may be something much more obscene."

If Ice Cube was right that "life ain't nothing but bitches and money," then here was the real-world counterpart—or at least its de facto purser, keeping careful account of every folly and indiscretion and setting it in reserve for some final judgment. When his manuscript arrived, a cursory read through the first few pages indicated we were in for a florid ride—lots of bombast and braggadocio, Old Testament by way of Hemingway, that deep trough around Proverbs and Ecclesiastes and into the Song of Solomon.

There on the first page, Darnell tells a story from *Lawrence of Arabia*:

"Peter O'Toole played Lawrence, and said, 'For some men, nothing is written.' Lawrence goes back into the Nefud Desert to save a comrade. His friend Ali, played by Omar Sharif, insists the comrade's fate 'is written.'

After rescuing the comrade, Lawrence later executes the man he saved to keep peace among the rival tribes. 'What ails the Englishman?' asks Auda abu Tayi, played by Anthony Quinn. 'That man that he killed is the man he brought out of the Nefud,' says Ali. 'Ah,' says Auda. 'It was written.' "

The implication was clear: all those who Darnell spared just to bring this far were his alone to sacrifice as he saw fit, as long as it made for a better story. And the story he told in his book was a wild one: he was "The Incredible Mr. Riley," the man who made Paris Hilton a legend, who brainstormed the *1 Night in Paris* video, and who liberated the porn star inside this pampered princess—a Mob-connected criminal mastermind whose decade inside the juvenile criminal justice system instilled in him a ruinous longing for the good life. From his early forays into South Central L.A. and the boxing gyms where he met Rick Salomon, second-generation movie royalty Scott Caan, and Getty heir Balthazar Getty, to his indoctrination into the criminal arts at the hands of charismatic local toughs, his early promise was cut short by the violent jewelry store heist for which he took the fall. It was here that his formal training began.

Back in the world at twenty-two, Darnell gravitated back to the gyms, where he fell into collections work for Hollywood high-lifers who weren't constitutionally up to the challenge and started plowing his way through the throngs of well-appointed club honeys with a taste for danger who sprouted like mushrooms wherever the heat and the damp intersected. He also reconnected with Rick Salomon, now dating a physically tiny, little-known socialite who allegedly stood to inherit the Hilton hotel fortune with her sister, Nicky—a myth they parlayed into soft-core magazine spreads, a *Vanity Fair* article, and journeyman careers as paparazzi bait and nightclub shill. "Paris was stone cold wasted, a train wreck" the first night he met her at Salomon's hotel room. When Salomon quietly explained that this mysterious newcomer had killed two people, Paris instinctively responded, "That's hot."

Darnell was linked with Rod Stewart's ex, Rachel Hunter, and dated Nicole Richie. Meanwhile, Darnell says he quickly moved to set up some drug deals with connections back east and found partners in crime in various runway models. In between his legitimate bank job in international finance, he would ride shotgun—literally—on drug deals over his lunch break, crouching in the back of an SUV with an AR-15 assault rifle or backing down career drug dealers when a difference of opinion arose. He befriended various offshore gambling interests eager to exploit his growing knowledge of how to structure deals and hide assets. Through his boxing world connections, he tattoo-branded fighters with the logos of such online betting sites as Goldenpalace.com, in effect inventing a new medium for advertising and product endorsement (and infuriating ESPN in the process).

In between his storied exploits, Darnell runs down the club scene, the network of favor-based lawyers, and the elaborate trade in compromising secrets that informs most transactions in his world. "When you know the owners of certain massage parlors and strip clubs, you sometimes have the goods on people," he noted. Along the way, there are affairs with fashion models and Playmates, trips to Europe and Russia, surreptitious work as a fixer for Joe Francis, a showdown with Mark Wahlberg's Funky Bunch Crew, not to mention the entire saga of Will Wright and a series of home burglaries targeting Hollywood's wealthy party crowd, often when Will was out with them in the clubs. Darnell claims he helped Marvin Davis's grandson Brandon Davis settle his prodigious gambling debts. He describes banging club hotties side by side with Mickey Rourke at the Le Montrose hotel just off the Sunset Strip. (Rourke, one of the few Hollywood types who stood by Darnell throughout his criminal proceedings, gave him the nickname, "The Pope of the Sunset Strip," and showed up at one of his court appearances, making the boxer's sign of a fist over his heart in support.) And this being Hollywood, there are endless reels of sex tapes, not all of which feature Paris Hilton.

Typical of these claims is an early letter in which Darnell addresses the encumbrances of fame and its demanding proximity, even as he tosses out household names like rose petals in his wake:

"I don't know how many times I've been introduced to people, and the person doing the introduction prefaces the conversation with, 'This is Martina Jones—you know, Quincy Jones's daughter.' What—am I fucking Quincy Jones by touching her up? So the love, the relationship, becomes a love of possessions. It's like leisure society is a new form of [existence], driven by finance and speculation. If I bang Martina, does Quincy automatically give me the keys to the castle? Does everyone that I meet know that I'm in with Quincy because of his unknown, noncelebrity daughter? So as much as I've prided myself on being the self-made man, the materialism has always been a lure. The duplicity of me; the duplicity of Hollywood . . .

"But I finally analyzed how people viewed me when I went to brunch with Heavy D, the rapper-producer-actor. We had two other buddies with us. We went to the Griddle on Sunset, a nice hole-in-the-wall spot—all Hollywood types hanging out, a couple of looky-loos, plenty of 'producers' handing out business cards. You know the scene. While we were waiting for the other two guys to come in to order, Heavy D said to me in confidence how he's been hearing things. My name has been connected to a lot of shit. 'The streets is talking.' I knew why he was saying that. He knew it also, but respectfully just tugged at my coat to let me know to take control of my life. Our buddies came in and he killed the conversation and started to talk about how Jay-Z used Biggie Smalls' ghost on one of his tracks ('A Dream' on Jay-Z's *Blueprint 2.1* album). With the lyrics, I knew he was still telling me to check myself and not let others tell my story.

"Heavy D and I would jog to his Beverly Hills condo whenever we had free time in 2002–3 and early 2004. He was on a serious mission to drop weight in a healthy way, and he did—he lost over one hundred pounds. But one jogging session we were leaving his place on Santa Monica and he started telling me how he had just talked with Puffy (Sean Combs), who was a protégé of his . . . He was hyped about getting a role on Tracy Morgan's (*SNL* alum, now on *30 Rock*) new comedy show. He said he called Puffy to give him the good news and Puffy shit on him and busted his bubble. Puffy said, 'Nigga, you happy about that chump shit role? That ain't shit. Sean John did $300 million last year. Don't be satisfied with peanuts, fool. Do your own shit!' He says that's how they motivate each other . . .

"Heavy D knew I was ready for a clean break and he was ready to go full force into producing films and wanted to team up with me. I was honored. He reminded me that my name was still ringing bells back east, then he told me it was in circles where the only roads are to Marion, Sing Sing or Attica. Without getting into my personal business, he said to let him know when I was ready to take control of my name. He said, just like Puffy shit on him and it woke him up, he was giving me the juice to move forward and not settle for the names and titles that people want to attribute to me. Write my own story if I want it told correctly."

I kept thinking about the last quote in the *Radar* piece, from Bill Horn, Joe Francis's PR flak, about Darnell's claims that he knew Francis before the break-in: "[Attorney] Ronald Richards can claim that Lee Harvey Oswald and Joe were friends, but that doesn't make it true." I started combing back through my notes, looking for clues into exactly who this enigmatic character was—completely silent for his entire moment in the sun and now gushing like a Brooklyn fire hydrant on the hottest day of July. I came across an e-mail from my *Radar* editor that I didn't remember seeing before, which contained that quote about Darnell existing on the fringes of the Paris Hilton crowd. The quote was from a blind source that had come from Brenda You, the West Coast editor of *Star* magazine and a redheaded spitfire who had once posed for Playboy.com. The magazine had lifted the only direct quote in her e-mail for my piece, but You's setup was infinitely more telling.

"My source says Darnell was on the edges of the club scene, nothing more than a con man and definitely not a friend of Paris, Nicole or Joe Francis," she wrote. "My source, who is black, says none of those people have black friends other than himself, so if any other black person were at one of their parties or at their club table, he'd definitely know him or introduce himself."

Now this was troubling. The one potential source I'd found who actually knew Darnell—the one source who wasn't a known criminal—identified him as a confidence man. I called a friend of mine who was still back in the tabloid world to see if I could track Brenda You down. Maybe her source could shed some light.

"Oh, didn't you hear?" my friend asked. "Brenda You killed herself."

I called a mentor of mine, a guy who'd worked the tabs like I had but was now a respected investigative reporter. I told him my dilemma.

"Mark, there is no worse source than a convict sitting in prison," he told me. "Those guys got nothing but time."

I remembered my early years in Los Angeles, living in Venice out near the beach, which was still a gang stronghold back then. The illegally converted garage I lived in with a patch of grass for my pit bulls had security gates on all the windows, as did most of the places in the neighborhood. But junkies would climb up in the windowsill with a screwdriver, away from a street or alley view, and sit there all day painstakingly taking the gates apart. It's there I learned one of the guiding tenets of my profession: never underestimate the criminal element. Some of those guys had a work ethic like you wouldn't believe.

I couldn't help but think this tale owed more than a little to John Guare's 1990 play *Six Degrees of Separation*, albeit with a hip-hop gloss, where a silver-tongued con artist from the inner city talks his way into moneyed society, exploits its liberal deference to race and the noble savage, and feasts on its banquet of privilege and sex until finally someone gets hurt. The film version three years later made Will Smith into a serious actor and Kevin Bacon into a parlor game.

In the play (or at least Fred Schepisi's film version), Will Smith, playing Paul, is ushered into the Central Park West penthouse apartment of Flan and Ouisa Kittredge (Donald Sutherland and Stockard Channing), having convinced the doorman he was the son of actor Sidney Poitier and a friend of their children from college. He claims to have just been mugged on the edge of Central Park, and the only copy of his master's thesis stolen. After they've gotten him cleaned up, the Kittredge's dinner guest, played by Ian McKellen, asks Paul the topic of his thesis. There is a long pause, as if we've finally come to the end of this mildly diverting charade. Instead, Paul launches into a masterful exegesis on J. D. Salinger's *Catcher in the Rye*, which he pronounces a book about paralysis, and how it has become a secondary bible to our disenfranchised youth and cultural assassins—John Hinckley, who shot Ronald Reagan and Mark David Chapman, who murdered John Lennon:

"The aura around this book of Salinger's, which perhaps should be read by everyone *but* young men, is this: it mirrors like a fun house mirror, and amplifies like a distorted speaker, one of the great tragedies of our times— the death of the imagination. Because what else is paralysis? The imagination has been so debased that imagination—being imaginative—rather than being the linchpin of our existence, now stands as a synonym for something outside ourselves, like science fiction or some new use for tangerine slices on raw pork chops . . . The imagination has moved out of the realm of being our link—our most personal link—with our inner lives and the world outside that world, the world we share. What is schizophrenia but a horrifying state where what's in here doesn't match up with what's out there? Why has imagination become a synonym for style? To face ourselves—that's the hard thing. The imagination—that's God's gift to make the act of self-examination bearable."

This is echoed in Ouisa's final meditation on the experience: "Everyone is a door opening into new worlds. Six degrees between us and everyone else on this planet."

The play was based on the real-life escapades of David Hampton, a teenaged hustler in the late eighties who swindled wealthy New Yorkers out of several thousand dollars before being apprehended by police and serving twenty-one months in prison. After the film made him infamous, he dined out on it for a decade, phoned Guare incessantly until the playwright took out a restraining order, sued him unsuccessfully for copyright infringement (for a reported $100 million), and, by all reports, remained an unrepentant hustler and con man for the rest of his life. He died on June 16, 2003, at thirty-nine in a New York City hospital of complications from AIDS. At roughly the same moment, Darnell claims the FBI had followed him to Saint-Tropez on the French Riviera, where he rented a yacht with a claque of models, and Puffy Combs—by now answering to P. Diddy—applauded them as they passed his own smaller yacht.

Whether my raising the specter of doubt created a butterfly effect in the planetary ether, raised red flags on the part of a finely attuned student of human nature, or actually launched a chain reaction through six degrees of separation, I got a call from Shelly Wood, a paralegal and pro bono legal services volunteer who knew Darnell in Youth Authority, was close friends with him in civilian life, and remained an advocate for him after his most recent incarceration. She told me Darnell wanted me to have his cell phone. True to her word, a FedEx package arrived three days later with an off-the-shelf model Verizon Wireless phone inside with eleven phone messages, thirty-five text messages, and 191 separate names loaded onto it. Darnell's voice mailbox was long ago deactivated, and according to my P.I., the phone messages were unrecoverable, as Verizon dumps their stored messages every six months or so. A quick survey of the names revealed numbers for Paris Hilton, Mickey Rourke, Scott Caan, Balthazar Getty, Martina Jones, Rick Salomon, Heavy D, and Carol Aye Maung, the *News of the World* reporter. Numbers for Hilton spokesman Elliot Mintz, Erin Naas, Will Wright, and Joe Francis matched the numbers on Paris Hilton's purloined T-Mobile Sidekick II (Naas shows up as "Knass"), although all had been changed since Hilton's little stunt.

Darnell's text messages run from roughly October 12, 2004, to March 28, 2005, the day of his arrest, when an outgoing message to his girlfriend six hours before police raided his home reads, "Let's push 4 !0pm" (exclamation marks are routinely substituted for Arabic numeral 1s, perhaps as a security measure), and she replies, ominously, "Okay I'm so nervous." There are texts to ESPN Russell Racing, an "open-wheel formula racing" school; Cartoon Bank, an online cartoon replica merchandiser; and Skycorp and Marquis Jet, both charter jet companies. There are two messages from someone named Melissa M., who Darnell later identified as a friend who works for designer Marc Jacobs, through whom he met many of the models he knows. The first, on February 14, 2005, Valentine's Day, at 6:13

p.m., reads, "Amanda Moore . . . ex jessica stam and tasha tilberg." All three are models repped by IMG. The second occurs on March 18 at 9:40 a.m. and reads, "Haha!! Palm Springs for a ladies night. [A New York number] graces number. Love u too. Be back tomorrow!!!"

And there are fifteen text messages both to and from Paris Hilton, more than any other single person. They are sent to and received from the phone number and e-mail address widely disseminated as Paris Hilton's, and all of them occur before the February 15, 2005, date when Hilton's Sidekick was hacked and those numbers were made public. (Although there are ways to forge incoming calls—spoof cards allow you to substitute the source number of your choice—they would have to have been made on the dates in question.) Hilton's messages are chatty, but they also provide a de facto travel itinerary:

- October 12, 6:36 p.m.: "Yeah, I'm good. Just working on my movie. I'm so fukin sick of Miami" (*Pledge This!*, released in 2006, was filmed in Miami.)
- November 2, 12:38 p.m.: "I'm in fukin new jersey doing the simple life." (On Season 3 of *The Simple Life*, Episode #19: "Mechanics," airing January 26, 2005, and #22: "Mortuary," airing February 9, 2005, were filmed in New Jersey.)
- November 11, 4:55 p.m.: "No, Maryland." (Episode #26: "Zoo," airing March 16, 2005, and #27: "Bakery," airing March 30, 2005, were filmed in Baltimore.)
- November 20, 6:19 p.m.: "I'm in ny" (Episode #31: "Firefighters," airing April 20, 2005, was filmed in Atlantic City, New Jersey.)

Also, November 20, 2004, was a Saturday, and if you cross-reference this with Hilton's own T-Mobile notes, under a listing for November 18, Thursday of that week, you'll find Manhattan numbers for Ron Perlman (either the actor or financier Ron Perelman—given her customized sense of spelling), "Jennifer Goldman in ny for weekend" (an L.A.-based event planner), and "Nicole lenz in ny" (the *Playboy* Playmate and Hilton's former roommate).

And their final exchange is nothing if not intriguing. On January 3, 2005, at 11:17 p.m., Paris asks, "Why were u in Japan?" (I will learn that Darnell spent New Year's Eve 2004 in Tokyo with boxer Frankie Liles, who trains Mixed Martial Arts fighters there.) On January 8, 2005, five days later, Darnell's greeting at 5:04 p.m. is aggressively familiar: "what's up rockstar, what zipcoada r u in?' Paris responds "10022" (Manhattan between 50th and 60th Streets east of Fifth Avenue). She follows up at 10:31 p.m.: "I start the simple life again on mon for a couple of weeks. what's the name of ur spot?" At 11:51, Paris continues, "What's a bug and how is it in his ass?" At 11:59, she writes, "That's hot :P." And at 12:06 a.m., Darnell writes back, "He likes 9's or better. big purple plum pops. ha ha. I brought him a pocket pussy—but from japan. he luvs it."

I called the Paris Hilton number, but as I imagined, it had been disconnected. I called Darnell's girlfriend Ruby to the same end. I found a Melissa M. on Darnell's phone list, but those numbers weren't working, so I tried Grace's number from her text message. Surprisingly, a woman answered. I explained that I was a writer looking for Melissa, who she said was living in Europe, but she could forward a message. Then I asked her about Darnell. There was a long pause, like she was debating whether to answer or not. Then Grace gave me this quote:

"Darnell will always be available, and there will always be someone that needs him. He is very smart, very charming—you cannot be stupid and do what he does. But he has claimed his identity, and he is not about to change."

That's the last I ever heard from either of them.

On a whim, I dialed the number for "Heav D." Somebody picked up on the first ring.

"Is this Dwight?" I asked, using Heavy D's given name of Dwight Myers.

"Yeah," said an affable voice. "Who's this?"

I said I was writing a book, and did he know a guy named Darnell Riley.

"Yeah, I knew Darnell from Bomb Squad," says Heavy D, dropping the name of a West Hollywood gym at Gardner and Santa Monica Boulevard where Darnell worked out. "I knew him around the gym."

I ran through the claims in Darnell's letter.

"Everything Darnell said was true," he says. "We met at the Griddle for breakfast, I told him about what I'd been hearing on the street, and we talked about working on some things in the future. But that's just me: when someone reaches out to me or asks for help, I respond. That's just how I am.

"You know, what happened to him doesn't surprise me. You can tell he had a little street in him, and I work in an environment where this is commonplace. But what I did know about the kid, I liked him. I grew up with a lot of cats like Darnell. Darnell never tried to hustle me. Unfortunately, people like Darnell only know how to get money one way. I would guess that his father probably fell victim to the same circumstances. Did you know that Darnell was straight? No drugs, no alcohol. He was like me."

I told him about Darnell's juvenile history, the double homicide, which he didn't know anything about. "I'm sure Darnell wasn't the only person in that gym that killed someone," he says. "He was fourteen. He was a baby. How can you possibly judge that? That's between him and God."

About this milieu that Darnell claimed a part of, the rich and famous he supposedly walked among, Heavy D took a more nuanced view. "Darnell is not their reality," he says. "Their reality is an imagined safe haven. For Darnell, that's called 'making a living.' For Paris, karma is king. Darnell had little or no respect for that type. He knew they had no respect for him, so his attitude was 'go get 'em.' But remember, as far as Darnell is concerned, even the worst kind of people are good people. And this is the sick part about Hollywood, and your story: it's not tragic enough. That's sick, but that's Hollywood.

"I never thought of Darnell as being particularly violent. It would not surprise me if he had to slap someone around or something, and in prison he's probably thinking, 'One day I may have to lay one of these guys down,' but Darnell's future all depends on where they drop him off. I know he tried the college thing, and the Golden Gloves fighting. If they drop him off at Harvard, you're going to get a completely different person. If they drop him back to the clubs, *anyone* in that environment can flourish. Without change, he'll hustle again. I just pray that he decides to do the right thing."

Heavy D also left me with an ominous remark about the constellation of characters Darnell surrounded himself with:

"The Feds don't shoot in the dark."

3

IN THE TOOLIES

It's a two-and-a-half-hour drive to Corcoran State Prison in Kings County, California, about an hour north of Bakersfield. You stay on Interstate 5, the main drug corridor connecting Canada to Mexico, until you hit State Highway 99, right where the San Fernando Valley gives way to the San Joaquin. This is Steinbeck country, with small towns with names like Mc-Farland, Delano (home to its own pair of prisons), Earlimart, and Pixley, or at least it was back in Steinbeck's day when the wide expanse of farmland rising away in forced perspective would have been filled with convicts in prison grays, stooping from the weight of cotton sacks. At Tipton, you take the farm road west for the final ten miles, past a smattering of cornfields, rows of rusted milking machines, overbuilt farmhouses offset by ram-shackle barns, and a lone threshing machine abandoned mid-crop. The dust picks up and mixes with low-slung cirrus clouds to blot out the sun in patches. Save for the occasional palm tree, this could all be central Kansas, where the Clutter family awaits nightfall, and its fitful dreams, and their sudden interruption.

On the last stop sign before I turn onto state property, gang graffiti have been stenciled in white and then painted back over in red, leaving their outline in an uneasy pink, a last flash of colors and pride before institutional submission. As you enter the visitor's parking lot, with an electrified fence running the perimeter, "California State Prison at Corcoran" has been written in river stones, its giant letters visible by air, no doubt in hopes of one of those last-second helicopter breakouts half remembered from the movies. There's a formal city of Corcoran somewhere past the prison, but you'll never see it unless you go looking for it.

Corcoran State is a maximum-security facility built in 1989 to hold three thousand inmates that currently houses twice that, and a tent city off to the left fills several acres. The prison was built on the western reaches of what was once Tulare Lake, the largest freshwater lake west of the Great Lakes during the nineteenth century, but emptied to reclaim its six hundred square miles of rich bottomland in the most fertile agricultural region in the country. Tulare Lake was named after the Spanish word—in turn stolen from the Aztecs—for the bulrushes or giant cattails, known as tules (or "toolies"), that once proliferated along its shores and the vast border marshes that were drained after the Civil War. As a consequence, the phrase "in the toolies" came to mean an area both remote and isolated—"out in the boonies"—and in Spanish the phrase "in deep toolies" took on a darker cast, meaning in trouble—"up shit creek"—or specifically, in trouble with the law. Earl Rawley, the oil wildcatter played by Richard Farnsworth in *The Two Jakes*, the sequel to *Chinatown*, uses the term in lecturing Jack Nicholson's Jake Gittes on how oil has supplanted water as the commodity of the moment:

"Without my oil, you got no automobiles. Without automobiles, you got no road construction, no sidewalks, no city lights, no gas stations, no automotive service and no [Jake] Berman subdivision stuck out in the toolies, because nobody can get there. Then Mr. Berman's out of business, before he even gets in business. The name of the game is oil, John."

On a scale of toughest places to wait out a ten-year bid, Corcoran is no picnic—on the far end of the spectrum from your country-club prisons. It's where Charles Manson has come to rest, and where he'll probably die, transferred from San Quentin as a marquee name when Corcoran first opened. Sirhan Sirhan is a neighbor in the Protective Housing Unit, as is mass murderer Juan Corona, convicted of killing twenty-five Mexican day laborers in 1971. And in 1998, eight prison guards were indicted for staging inmate "gladiator" fights for the amusement of the prison population, where at least one participant was shot and killed when things got out of hand.

I visited Corcoran in the dead of August. Months earlier, a letter had arrived summoning me.

"There is a lot I would like to talk with you about, but I would prefer at visiting, as I am not one for the finality of my words on paper in regards to some sensitive info," Darnell wrote. "It's a good thing I took my deal and the Joe Francis incident can no longer affect me. But there are others that are at my mercy . . . Of course, I'll have death threats, but I wouldn't have it any other way. It'll let me know I wrote some powerful shit."

The letter rambled on, in some places familiar, almost jovial, in others barely concealing a prodigious anger served atop a sub-zero dish of revenge, and full of the kind of forced laughter that makes things go quiet in a crowded bar. Near the end, Darnell's argument swung through current events and the Bush administration's lack of accountability. "I'm debating talking too much shit about Bush, being that I'll be asking for a pardon as he leaves office," he wrote. "You think I got a chance?" He signed off, "Shalom."

Darnell was well into the third year of his 128-month term, and I couldn't imagine that sitting up here behind bars would have improved his demeanor any. *The Pope of the Sunset Strip* was a bust—by all accounts too angry and bitter for publishing houses—and I didn't much cotton to piling on my rejection in person. Nobody likes to hear that their work doesn't measure up, me included, and I've never killed anybody. Of course, Joe Francis had begun what would ultimately amount to a year in jail—first in Panama City, Florida, on contempt and later contraband charges, and then when that proved too rigorous, in Reno, Nevada, on federal tax evasion charges, where he voluntarily remained incarcerated to avoid extradition back to the harsher Florida conditions. For that matter, Paris Hilton had served half a forty-five-day jail sentence for repeat-offender DUI. So maybe that had cheered him up.

Before I left, I took a look at the Corcoran Web site, which helpfully offers a list of Inmate Visiting Guidelines: be there by 3 p.m.; change machines are located in the lobby (apparently vending machine treats can take on an outsized dimension to those in custody); bring a picture ID; no hats, wigs, or hairpieces; no sunglasses allowed unless they're prescription. Shelly also sent me a crib sheet outlining the strict dress code for visitors: no blue jeans; black is okay, including sweats; no red, blue, green, or orange; and no backless shoes. Blue jeans were standard work attire for inmates. The color embargo I assumed was to not enflame gang tensions—red and blue for Bloods and Crips or Sureños and Norteños, respectively; green (according to the LAPD's own Web site) designating a neutral gang member or drug dealer; and orange widely used throughout the prison system (i.e., easier to spot tunneling out of a prairie dog hole in the mid-distance). Why no back-less shoes, you got me.

After emptying my pockets and having my reporter's notebook confiscated ("Prohibited Items: Writing materials or books, unless approved prior to entering the Visiting Room"), I passed through a metal detector and was directed into a closed wire-mesh cage twenty feet square, then buzzed onto the grounds of what looked like a colorless junior college on spring break. Well-marked arrows led me down a sidewalk lined by flowerless flower beds and into a large holding room designed for crowd control, and then into the Visiting Room, which was about the size of a double classroom. A row of vending machines occupied one wall, and a carpeted area in one corner held a raft of toys and an army of kids to play with them. Two uniformed officers sat at an elevated front desk like in a police station, their unflinching glances sweeping the forced reunions before them like a lighthouse beam.

I filed my paperwork and took a place at a corner table. During my fifteen-minute wait, I studied the twosomes and threesomes around me hunched over the circular tables, leaning together without touching, as if warming themselves over a fire, who communicated far more in unbroken stares than in the occasional small talk that interrupted them. And then, before I even recognized him, Darnell was upon me.

"Mark—hey, thanks for coming."

I stood and shook hands with him—short, maybe five feet eight, slight and rendered almost invisible by the black reading glasses riding down the bridge of his nose. Gone were the shaved head and full beard that made him look like the Devil's second string; he'd let the sides grow back, emphasizing his male-pattern baldness. But most striking were his hands—tiny hands, almost delicate, dwarfed by mine. He seemed like a jailhouse stockbroker, were the authorities ever foolish enough to allow hardened criminals day-trading accounts. Taking a seat across from me, he seemed almost solicitous, anxious to offer me what little he could pull from the hospitality of his surroundings. I offered instead to buy him a sandwich with the mountain of loose quarters I'd brought as a makeshift tribute. He accepted the gesture with a practiced grace.

"How's Charlie doing?" I ask, referring to one of the few bigger celebrities in here than him. Darnell grins.

"I have a meeting with Charlie soon," he says. Apparently, you had to get on a waiting list. "I've turned into a journalist in here."

He had the eye for it. He showed me how a foursome playing dominoes got a pencil and paper from a trustee, and one of them took minutes of the meeting while pretending to keep score. "Look over there," he says, nodding at a nearby couple lost in longing and desire. "In a second, she'll get up to go to the bathroom. When she comes back, she'll be ready to go. Inmates and visitors can kiss only when they meet and when they part. In the bathroom, she'll take out a packet of drugs wrapped in plastic she smuggled in her pussy and put it in her mouth. When they kiss good-bye, she'll spit it into his mouth and he'll swallow it, then dig it out of his shit in the morning. That's how drugs get into prison." As he spoke, it happened exactly the way he said it would—the long sexy walk to the bathroom, the purposeful return, the deep soul kiss followed by a hasty departure. (His comments here and throughout are mingled with my notes, jotted down on the fly, as well as his letters and frequent phone calls, which would invariably circle back around to our caucuses with the benefit of reflection. But if I quote him, it's his words, not mine.)

From what I gathered, Darnell spent his days reading—both books and the endless magazines he subscribed to—as well as listening to music on his CD player and watching TV on the tiny portable in his cell. Consequently, he was a human repository of popular culture, which he was able to handicap with an insider's firsthand knowledge. At one point, as a gesture of imagined solidarity I suppose, I quoted the one hip-hop line I know by heart, and also the most severe—Eazy-E off the first N.W.A album, *Straight Outta Compton*: "What about the bitch that got shot? Fuck her! / Don't give a damn about a bitch—I ain't a sucker." If I was looking for props, I got instead a lecture on how Darnell didn't listen to too much rap, and certainly didn't subscribe to the rappers' fuck-a-ho attitude. To demonstrate, he ran through a checklist of his CDs in current rotation: aside from the obligatory Jay-Z and Biggie Smalls, there were also U2, the Rolling Stones, Madonna, Fleetwood Mac, John Mayer, Nirvana, Paul Oakenfold, Coldplay, and Tony Bennett. Okay, here's something new: Darnell Riley has the musical tastes of a dentist's office.

Darnell's chronic insomnia allowed him to keep up a robust correspondence (not just with me), as well as author children's books, brainstorm inventions or Web sites, practice calligraphy, and fire off the occasional letter to the *Los Angeles Times*, usually whenever they ventured an editorial or series on prison reform. He ticked off the books he had read recently: *Brutal* by Kevin Weeks, *The I Chong: Meditations from the Joint* by Tommy

Chong, *Confessions of a Video Vixen* by Karrine Steffans, *Underboss* by Sammy "The Bull" Gravano, and *The Last Party* by Anthony Haden-Guest—by implication contrasting the Irish Mafia, Taft Federal Prison, the backstage hip-hop milieu, the Gambino crime family, and Studio 54 in its prime with the various worlds he has inhabited and chronicled, and finding the others lacking in comparison. His speech, easygoing with a natural flow, was an odd mixture of the anecdotal and the academic. Describing prison life, he imagined using the Ring of Gyges from Plato's *Republic*—which carries the power of invisibility—not to operate with impunity, as in the original, but rather to restore the simplest dignities: "stuff like being able to take a crap without five other inmates sitting next to you, or continuously being made to show the cops your brown eye (the one that stinks, not the one that winks) every time you're strip-searched. This shit is crazy."

And here and later, he took great pains to place his story in a literary context—his "Incredible Mr. Riley," a third-person homage to Patricia Highsmith's *The Talented Mr. Ripley* (or was it Don Knotts's *The Incredible Mr. Limpet?*), quoting Harper Lee's *To Kill a Mockingbird* on the justice system, railing against "mendacity" straight out of Tennessee Williams and *Cat on a Hot Tin Roof*. He repeatedly saw himself in the tradition of Melville's *The Confidence Man*, Twain's *Huckleberry Finn*, and, most vaingloriously, Fitzgerald's *The Great Gatsby*—the trickster rogue passing between worlds, the allusions hanging off him like so much ice-encrusted bling.

"Like Jay Gatsby, I've always been the one on the scene that everyone wonders where he came from," he says. "Self-made? Family money? Some knew bits and pieces, but most were left with more questions than answers. None ever knew how I traded in my old self for a new one."

Just as everyone in the privileged world he once occupied imagined themselves gangsters or psychic outlaws, right up until the moment it actually cost them something, so Darnell imagined himself a literary hero.

Or else this was all for my benefit. He claimed the police were following my moves carefully, and were hoping that any book I might write would detail his alleged crimes enough to lead to additional indictments. "Imagine how much extra publicity will come from that?" he asked. His words put another pair of eyes on my back.

As he spoke, and as his innate intelligence and natural charm put me more at ease, I began to notice some things I hadn't at first. First of all, his biceps were enormous underneath his royal-blue standard-issue prison jumpsuit. And then, not just his upper arms, but also the contours of his chest showing through his white cotton T-shirt seemed to be rippling with tattoos. I asked him if they were gang tattoos. He didn't seem taken aback by the question, and in fact gave the impression of total transparency, as if this was all just some expositional mix-up, sorting out the mysteries of his life. He claimed to largely avoid the racial superstructure of prison gangs by associating with the Others, a freeform alliance of Cubans, Puerto Ricans, South Americans, Asians, and South Pacific Islanders—particularly the Samoans, who typically balance a gentle spirit with enormous dimensions. "We generally are neutral in matters," he says.

Darnell claims to speak both Spanish and Arabic. "I'm Cuban to all these guys," he says. "My granddad's mom was from Cuba. His dad was of African-Dominican background. His mom's family came to America in the late eighteen nineties. They didn't speak English and they looked odd. They were neither black or white in appearance. So they blended in with the Native-Americans. My granddad's father inherited the name Riley from his granddad, who bought the name (literally) on a trip from the Dominican Islands to England. My grandmom was French-Dominican, and my mom's family are Dominican/African-American."

He gave me a makeshift guided tour through the ink covering most of his torso. "The object on my left arm is an *asura* (Ap-sa-rat), which may be known as a pixie, like Thumbelina in western fairy tales. The *asuras* in Buddhist or Hindu teachings represent the duplicitous nature of man, and are paid to go out and do his bidding. Although the *asuras* are one level below human beings, we share in the effects of our individual characteristics: happiness within suffering or suffering within suffering. Humans realize that enlightenment may be obtained by degrees, or it may be sudden, and delusion as well can be compounded in many different ways and with many degrees of intensity. The point of reaching nirvana is in recognizing the difference between delusion and enlightenment, and the difference in attitude. In essence, the mind remains the same. The *asura* does my bidding. She is like the Balinese dancer—charming onlookers with the eerie look on her face, seducing them with her charm and grace. She's my girl.

"I have a dragon going down my right arm, symbolizing power. In the party scene, you know we chase the dragon. Well, I caught it. On my left chest, I have a dragon in a cloud of fire facing another dragon that wraps around the right half of my body like a chest plate, warrior style. The dragon on the right is ascending out of water, with a koi fish for prosperity circling it. So I have fire, water, earth, and wind—the four elements for balance. My guy who did it is an artist and owned his own shop. He doesn't work on many people anymore; all his pieces have a spiritual meaning to the subject. It was three months of two to three hours a day—three days on, four days off to heal. The only other thing I'll get in the future is the Mea Culpa prayer in Latin on my upper arm. I have a couple of fifth-century Latin prayers down, and my favorite is the Mea Culpa: 'Mea culpa, mea maxima culpa' ["through my fault, through my most grievous fault"]. But no time soon. Although I was thinking about a phoenix coming out of fire on my back."

I ask Darnell what he thought the world owed him.

"Unequivocally, I can say the world owes me nothing," he says, quoting a long passage from the opening lines of *The Great Gatsby*, which his father used to read to him:

> In my younger and more vulnerable years my father gave me some advice that I've been turning over in my mind ever since. "Whenever you feel like criticizing anyone," he said, "just remember that all the people in this world haven't had the advantages that you've had." . . . In consequence, I'm inclined to reserve all judgments, a habit that has opened up many curious natures to me and also made me the victim of not a few veteran bores. The abnormal mind is quick to detect and attach itself to this quality when it appears in a normal person, and so it came about that in college [the college of hard knocks, he pointed out], I was unjustly accused of being a politician, because I was privy to the secret griefs of wild, unknown men.

"The world does not present itself to us in morally transparent terms," Darnell explains. "We live in a world in which propaganda and self-deception are rife. I've gotten off the straight and narrow, the path Walter set me on. That's my earliest memory of being taught what ethics was: 'Doing what is right, even when no one is looking.' That's how Walter explained it to me."

I asked him to elaborate on his father, but he was quick to correct me. "When I speak about my granddad, Walter, I sometimes call him my dad," Darnell says. "My sperm-donor dad—my granddad's son [Darnell Riley Sr.]—has had his share of drug and gambling issues, and the rest is twenty to thirty years of drama. Since I've been an adult, we've worked through a lot, and I understand him and his issues; he's a good man. But he's an ad-dict. (Later on, Shelly would tell me a story: Darnell's father was passing through LAX on his way somewhere else, and Darnell asked Shelly to come to the airport with him for support. When his father came off the plane, he said, "Hello, son," and shook Darnell's hand. And that was it. The whole encounter took less than fifteen seconds. About his mother, Darnell says, "I love my mom, but you've met her—she's certifiably nuts." His parents were divorced in 1990 when Darnell was thirteen.)

Contrary to what I imagined, Darnell didn't grow up in South Central L.A. He lived with his mother in Koreatown (not Sacramento as I had re-ported) until he was ten, and once instability overtook her, with Walter in Larchmont, one of central L.A.'s handful of actual neighborhood commu-nities. Walter Riley had been a surveyor and mapmaker for the Los Ange-les County Road Department (now the Department of Public Works), and he reportedly owned six thousand acres of timberland in East Texas that he inherited from his father, estimated at $10 million ("Timber as far as the eye can see, a developer's wet dream," is how Darnell puts it, although his financial estimates sometimes tend to waver across several decimal places). Walter's brother Herman was a Tuskegee Airman, is rumored to have worked for the government as a spy, became an influential Bay Area Epis-copalian priest and wrote a book called *Po' Boy!* (under the name Herman C. Riley), and another brother worked at JPL. By then retired, Walter held weekly poker games every Friday night for his friends and their mistresses where Darnell would mix drinks for tips and wash cars for more serious money. Walter taught him cards and the stock market, and took him along on gambling trips to Las Vegas or Atlantic City where, left to his own de-vices in the casinos, Darnell learned how to hustle.

"He always said out of all the family, he knows I'll be alright," says Dar-nell. "Of all the jewels that got handed down, I remember a sketch for a painting called 'The Thankful Poor.' It's of an old black man at the dinner table; his son across the table has his hand on his head in disgust at the meal, but the old man has his hands folded in prayer in thanks for what he does have. My granddad has the sketch now, and that is all I would want as an inheritance." If I was still on the magazine beat, that would have been my lead. (In a year of knowing and interviewing Darnell, the only favor he ever asked of me, including going off the record on sensitive matters, was that I not upset his family, which meant not interviewing Walter, who lived in the high desert around Palmdale and whose heart had been broken by

Darnell's fate. I checked out all the family details above, but I agreed to that. Shortly before this book's publication, Walter succumbed to cancer. Darnell was unable to attend the funeral.)

Darnell played Little League baseball at Ardmore Park in Koreatown and high school football at Inglewood High until he broke his femur and was put in a body cast. He was a Dodgers fan ("Kirk Gibson and the gimp, Bulldog Orel Hershiser"), a Raiders fan ("Bo knows everything"), and a Lakers fan (Showtime, Vlade Divac, and Magic). His team doctor was also a team doctor with the Lakers, and Darnell rubbed elbows with the players at his office and sat in on practices at the Forum. He also found his way to Broadway Gym, a legendary boxing gym at 108th Street and Broadway in the heart of the hood, where patriarch Bill Slayton had trained world heavyweight champion Ken Norton and a host of others. "Out of all the drama that the gangs have going on, the boxing gyms are a sanctuary— off-limits to the bullshit," says Darnell. A bus dropped him off right outside, and he remained largely oblivious to his surroundings. That was where in late 1990 he met Rick Salomon, the son of a Warner Bros. film executive who also had something to prove.

"Rick and I hit it off cool," says Darnell. "I liked him because he was one of the only white dudes going into the hood to box. I was way out of my zone on 108th and Broadway, too. But I had a passion for boxing, like Rick did, and in L.A. the Broadway Gym was the place to be. It was natural for us to gravitate to one another."

Then in 1992, the year of the L.A. riots, while attending Reseda High School, Darnell was discovered with a gun on school grounds and permanently expelled, despite being a Police Explorer and an A student. (He claims he planned to sell it to another student.) In juvenile hall while dealing with the gun case, he met and befriended future actor Scott Caan, son of James Caan, who also eventually found his way down to Broadway Gym. Banned from the L.A. Unified School District, Darnell first attended Garden Gate Community School, a special "probation school" at 41st and McKinley on the grounds of Johnson Middle School (since torn down), and then Walter put him in New Horizons, a "continuation school" and putative art school for social misfits that Darnell terms "a private school for fuckups," in the heart of Hollywood at Highland and Franklin Place, just north of Hollywood Boulevard. There, he met Balthazar Getty, another chronic underachiever, somewhere in line for the immense Getty fortune.

"Balthazar was already a kid actor-junkie and not fit for regular high school," said Darnell. "He fucked up big time and got caught on a film set with a needle in his arm. He had just been in *Young Guns [II]* with Emilio Estevez. Here was this royal fuckup and me. We clicked immediately.

"He was banging Drew Barrymore [also a New Horizons alumnus], and he had heard that this boxer dude in town had fucked her. Balt wanted to find out who he was. Well, it didn't take much before we found out it was Rick Salomon. I brought Balthazar to the gym, but he didn't come across Rick until the Drew Barrymore debacle in mid-'92."

That year, Darnell got his first taste of Hollywood, meeting and hanging out with Barrymore, Juliette Lewis, River and Joaquin Phoenix, Leo DiCaprio, and Leo's childhood friend Chuck Pacheco. He also met two older characters, cousins, whom he still would identify only by their street names, Ocean and Bolo. Walter warned him to stay away from them, but it didn't take.

"I listened to all the talk from Walter on his business dealings, and I listened to all the talks from Ocean and Bolo—tough-guy shit—and I saw men in control of their own destiny," says Darnell. "Whether legal (Walter's) or illegal (Ocean's/Bolo's), it was theirs, and then the seduction happened."

I asked him if he knew whatever became of Ocean and Bolo. I was surprised when he answered me.

"Ocean—we went our separate ways," he says. "Since I've been in, he's reached out through connects. When I was in L.A. County, his people wanted the go-ahead to visit Joe Francis. But I'm careful in what I ask for. And Bolo is actually doing a seven-year beef in Delano. But the cops want him real bad on some other shit."

"What did he do?" I ask.

"Well, allegedly, a woman burned him on a drug deal," says Darnell calmly. "He's supposed to have set her on fire."

In twenty years of reporting, Ocean and Bolo are also the closest I think I've come to witnessing consummate evil. And they wound up having a more profound effect on Darnell's destiny than anyone he had met, before or since.

4

WILD, UNKNOWN MEN

Darnell uses the term "reservoir dog" to refer to the various members of his crew—names on his phone list like Bo and Jiggy and T-Bone and Doc, who have since retired to suburban enclaves or been shipped back to their simpler origins as walking liabilities, and whose numbers are disconnected. Although vague about their qualifications or pedigree, the impression he leaves is of soldiers in a sub-rosa army, ready to suit up in batting gloves and bulletproof vest at the drop of a dime.

Reservoir Dogs the movie was released in mid-October 1992, the story of a bungled jewelry store heist in which several people were accidentally killed, all of which took place largely off-screen, and the ongoing existential conflicts between the criminals in the bloody aftermath who attempt to extract their fate from circumstances beyond their control. According to the *New York Times*, it was filmed "in a stopped-in-time shopping strip in Highland Park, a modest passed-over community between downtown Los Angeles and Pasadena."

Four months later, on February 25, 1993, a real-life Pasadena jewelry store heist ended in similar bloodshed and chaos, and the criminals involved or implicated conducted their own postmortem to control their fate. The official record is sealed, due to the age of the designated triggerman, Darnell Riley, then fifteen, but as detailed in a high-profile court case five years later, Darnell's various reflections, press accounts, and the recollections of participants, unanswered questions remain.

"One of my cousins got me into boxing, and he also ran numbers out of his buddy's bar/strip club," says Darnell. This was where he met Bolo, who ran the local gambling trade—"six foot three, two hundred fifty pounds, proficient in boxing and judo," he "looked like Mean Joe Green." Bolo means an uppercut punch in boxing, a shotgun shell with multiple slugs connected by wire that becomes a flying guillotine, or a particularly vicious Filipino machete, not to mention standard police shorthand for "be on the lookout," and any one of them could have given him his street name. When Darnell was twelve, he began to accompany Bolo on his rounds—whether it was shady collections or administering a "beat-down"—and hanging out at the strip club, where he was invariably the youngest person in the place. He sold Polaroids of the strippers to the other kids at school, and eventually lost his virginity to one dancing girl in particular—professional name Anna Banana (he's got all the details if you want to hear them)—whom he offered a hundred dollars on a slow afternoon.

But while Bolo was his ticket into this parallel world, one that Walter never suspected and his straight As and Bs bought him the freedom to explore, it was Bolo's cousin Ocean, "six feet, two hundred fifteen pounds, and built like a gazelle," who became Darnell's mentor. Whereas Bolo was all swift and terrible power—"You try to play him: dead. You try and stiff him on a debt: dead. Let him think you got over on him on a debt, you'd wish you were dead"—Ocean represented finesse, strategy, and how to apply your innate intelligence to a criminal problem as an advantage over those not so fortunately endowed.

"These two introduced me to the dark side," says Darnell. "I went on pickups from thirteen or fourteen, on the bus. I'd get tossed some wise guy's car keys every now and then, and Ocean let me drive his Mercedes. Bolo gave me a Jeep Cherokee when I was about to turn sixteen. In a weird way, Bolo and Ocean complemented one another. Not too many dudes wanted to cross either one's path. Since my weight around town was handed to me by these gangsters, I knew I couldn't drop the bucket and fuck up. Clearly, I didn't pose a threat to anyone, but those who I was connected to did. I didn't abuse the implied power."

Ocean taught him the art of collections work, where he first observed the spectrum of humanity in all its intensified colors, and where he saw firsthand the value of leverage on an immovable situation, learning how to weigh his target, opportunity, and exposure in a momentary calculus. According to Ocean, "The cops got a lot of chances to fuck up, we only got one." Since criminals have generally slipped the bonds of family, religion, and community that instill order in regular society, such criminal lore and lessons may be the only thing that keeps anarchy from rushing in to fill this moral vacuum like dark water, and it was Ocean who laid it out for him like a graduate seminar in survival.

Darnell tells of a Brentwood plastic surgeon with an expensive coke habit that exacerbated his gambling habit, or maybe it was vice versa. Ocean was sleeping with the doctor's wife behind his back, and he took some photos to prove it. He had also introduced a stripper to the doctor, for a fee—as a value-added service and an inexpensive insurance policy—and he had the photos to prove that. When the doctor fell behind on his payments, Ocean had Darnell drop off a package at the doctor's office. In it were Polaroids of the doctor and the stripper, with a note that said the debt had now escalated.

He had Darnell make a similar delivery to the doctor's wife, with photos of her and Ocean together. Then he turned off his pager and his cell phone—the early clamshell model with a chip that would clone any number that passed within a hundred feet—and they drove to the beach to get a slice of pizza. After a half hour, he had unanswered messages in double digits. Not just guilt and humiliation, but the implied interruption of the couple's delicate balance, did his work for him. When he finally called the doctor back, his money was waiting for him.

It was at a party at the couple's house where Darnell got his first taste of celebrities operating in their own private world. Amid the general eighties-era revelry, Darnell reports seeing one of the Pointer Sisters snorting coke and Charlie Wilson of the Gap Band swinging from the chandelier (with Bolo there as his guest). Whatever this life had to offer, it was laid out before him like a banquet. He took the chorus of "God Bless the Child"—not the Billie Holiday version, but Ella Fitzgerald's 1982 cover version from his grandfather's collection—as a motto to live by:

"God bless the child that's got his own."

"I believe my magnum opus came when we were on a mission," says Darnell. "I had pulled off a string of cat burglaries, collections, hired gun shit—all strengthening my back for the bigger shit that was to come. But up until this point, I had only been used as a decoy or a lookout, or sent out to do recon work, being that no one would suspect a kid going about his day with a backpack and an innocent face. They had an inside job to pull off. It was almost like what I went down for in '93. An associate of theirs owned car lots, and he owed cash from gaming debts. He couldn't pay, so he had a great idea: he also owned several cleaners/laundromats, and on his pickup day, he would have all the cash at one spot. He and his wife would be at the cleaners. She had a Gibraltar of a rock on her hand and all the shiny jewels of a pampered wife. The job was simple. Bolo would go in at closing time, draw down on the lady at the register, take her jewels as a cover, and Ocean would conveniently stumble upon the pickup cash. The other two people involved in my '93 jewelry store case were in on this one also—a criminal couple who turned evidence on us all—Bonnie and Chris. We had it all laid out, but Bolo's back went out. He had nerve damage from hoisting humans up all his life. So the deal was probably on hold.

"I was just going to be on the cover car, to follow behind the main car carrying the gunmen and the loot and provide cover if the cops got on the trail. But with Bolo in limbo, I stood up and said I'd go in with Ocean. I saw eyes light up. People were impressed. Up until this point, I had gone on collections and busted up a couple of knees, but to be dealing with civilians, so to speak, was uncharted territory. If a gangster got out of hand, or someone who fucked you over on a deal, you could whack him up and not feel bad, chalk it up to occupational hazards. But when dealing with civilians, it's uncomfortable. There has to be a level of professionalism at the forefront—no room for mistakes.

"I played Bolo and it went off like clockwork. We all met up [afterward], and I was somewhat fully vested in the crew. It wasn't like they were treating me as a charity case. It's like all the grooming and seduction that went into our daily interactions came to a boil when I stepped up, versus being asked to do it. I drove Ocean's Camaro home that night, and like all the other times that I drove a car home, I parked it down the street and walked to the house, like I had just gotten off the bus, making my dad [Walter] none the wiser. The next day, I got a nice payday—six thousand dollars. I don't know if I was getting shortchanged, but it didn't matter. I got my ring, so to speak. I don't know who they told about my big, ballsy moves, but I noticed others treating me differently at the strip club/bar. The bar was a mix of Latin dudes from Central and South America—El Salvador, Nicaragua, Belize; Cubans, Puerto Ricans, Jamaicans. This was the eighties crew who had come to America with *Scarface*-Tony Montana dreams. Tons of coke was floating around L.A. Many of these guys had survived civil war in their homeland, and L.A. was the big pie to be chopped up. I'd kick ass in soccer with the guys, play dominos, and I knew when to shut up. Out of all my ballsy moves, that's probably the one that propelled me the furthest—I knew when to shut the fuck up.

"The day the shit hit the fan, I did what I always do: I went to school and checked in with Ocean afterwards. He had already told me about the Pasadena job. Chris's connections had hired us. I wasn't privy to all the ins and outs. I got to the spot and got my orders."

Darnell claims the jewelry store heist was an inside job as well—or at least that's what he was told. After it all went wrong, he was given a revised version: although someone involved with the Asian jewelry store was "supposed to be in on the job," negotiations between the parties broke down, and by the time Darnell got there, they'd hired a security guard "who had no idea we were coming in." As he writes in the manuscript: "Some older cats had been pulling these jobs with a couple"—Bonnie and Chris—"and these older cats needed a patsy that had no connection to them." Hence Darnell became the designated fall guy, who hopefully would be shot or killed. Darnell was first through the door and fired when the shopkeeper pulled a weapon ("the place jumps off like the Fourth of July"). He claims he hit the deck and fired repeatedly at the ceiling. By his count, there were over twenty shots scattered around the store, even though his firearm held a nine-shot clip and the store owner's held seven shots. Both the storekeeper's wife and son were killed in the shootout; without denying ultimate responsibility for the deaths, Darnell claims the only person who could have logistically shot the son was the father. Darnell also claimed a fifth person was involved in the heist, and has steadfastly refused to identify him for fifteen years. "As far as who was the unknown associate on my juvenile crime—well, he remains unknown . . . I kept my mouth shut and never ratted on anyone."

When they rendezvoused later that night, Darnell's cohorts argued that he was the best one to take the rap, since he was a minor and the system would go easier on him. "Ocean and Bolo knew I would be at a disadvantage because I didn't belong to a gang and was on my own," says Darnell. "When I took the lives of the two people, I didn't have time to reflect and grieve. All I knew was fear. I didn't have time to fear for what I had done, I only had fear for what was to come next. Immediately following the murders, I was shuffled around town by Bolo and Ocean. They cut my hair and began to run me down on all the what-ifs that we knew were inevitable. Ocean had checked in to see what the Pasadena cops had on the crime. I knew from my time working with the Police Explorer Scouts and working the phones at the [police] station that the LAPD released news reports to reporters on the status of crimes/investigations, so after getting the skinny on the investigation, we knew they didn't have anything: no prints and grainy videos. Several witnesses in and outside of the jewelry store had conflicting statements. So Ocean prepared me for the possible arrest. I was under sixteen at the time (in 1993), and you had to be sixteen to be tried as an adult . . .

"So Ocean and Bolo prepared me for the journey. Simply put, they gave me the tough-guy blueprint. The possible nine years that I would spend— I was almost sixteen, and my max would be until my twenty-fifth birthday—was a bit unnerving. I kept a stiff upper lip. Ocean kept close ties on me. I knew it wasn't all about how much he cared for me, but more about him wanting to make sure I wouldn't roll over on him if I was touched. We stayed in the boxing gym. Ocean kept giving me lessons in the form of stories that spoke to my upcoming journey. One story that resonates was from *The Art of War*: 'Do what is big while it is still small.' That was to be applied to every facet of life. If I had a problem with a guy, kicking his ass wasn't an option; stop the problem before it gets to be a problem, and if it's too late, break his fucking neck before it comes to a fight. That was one way he told me how to apply the lesson.

"Chris and Bonnie turned evidence and took a deal on a double murder. Bonnie was one of the gunmen with me. Chris was in the first getaway ride. But the D.A. wanted Ocean badly. So from '93 until '96, Ocean was out while they worked on a deal with Chris and Bonnie. I was in the Youth Authority. Ocean was finally arrested in '96 and they went for the death penalty for him for being the mastermind. By now, I had the feel of the system, and I had a lot to chime in on to help Ocean out. I told Ocean's lawyer not to call me as a witness for him. I wanted to have the D.A. call me. That way, if I was caught in lies, it would help Ocean out. I'd be an unreliable witness. The D.A. had already paraded Chris and Bonnie on the stand, who by this time were about a year away from getting out. Mind you, they were in their thirties and active participants in the crime; they wanted Ocean bad to cut these two a deal. I was pressured with being held in contempt of court if I didn't testify. I started crying. [Several jurors said] they thought I was being used by the D.A.

"And then they put me on the stand, and I'm dressed in a bright orange prison jumpsuit, shabby hair and beard, looking the urchin who is being used to send this other minority away to the gas chamber. Ocean's lawyer played the race card—Bonnie and Chris were Caucasian. They didn't have Ocean on video at the scene, only Bonnie and me and the confidence man, who Bonnie didn't know and I've never named. The two big questions were

'Who gave you the gun?' and 'Who gave you the orders?' being that they had Ocean as a mastermind, not as an actual participant in the shooting. On the stand, when the question was asked who gave me my orders, my answer wasn't Ocean. The D.A. was livid. So I played the part: not guilty. I was the only one who took responsibility and the only one who got punished."

According to Darnell, Ocean was immediately tried on another case, acquitted yet again, and then sued the city for somewhere between $200,000 and $2 million (his accounts differ), dumped it all into real estate, and went legitimate. Darnell served six years in juvenile confinement, which he terms his amateur days, and as a reward for his "loyalty and sacrifice" he had a sizable sum of money waiting for him when he got out.

"Once I got out, I sat down with the heads that [Ocean] dealt with and got an envelope and I walked. I have their respect and support, if I call on it. But as you've got the feeling, these guys are some real reservoir dogs. If they get called in, it's grave-digging time."

Bolo also cycled back through Darnell's life on occasion. One of the guns confiscated during his arrest in the Joe Francis matter, discovered to have been stolen from horror movie director Wes Craven, was reportedly a gift from Bolo. "How he got it, who knows?" asks Darnell. I asked Darnell if he would identify Bolo and set up a meeting. At the very least, I've never talked with anyone who had set somebody on fire.

"Hell, no, you can't meet," Darnell says. "You'd be opening a can of worms, and it would put a target on your back. As of right now, he isn't charged with that situation I told you about, so he wouldn't talk with you— even in the hypothetical. I hold the keys to his freedom. He wouldn't have anything to say regarding what I disclose to you in a book, and he wouldn't speak to you either."

Darnell spent 2,190 days inside the California Youth Authority, considered the most violent in the nation—first at the Nelles Youth Correctional Facility in Whittier, then the Ventura Youth Center near Santa Barbara (where he got kicked out, he suggests, for sleeping with a female guard). He was moved to Chino ("The real gladiator zone; it was all gang wars, twenty-four seven"), back to Ventura for college, then to Chad (N.A. Chaderjian Youth Prison, near Stockton, earmarked for CYA's most violent inmates). Darnell claims he ran a lucrative sports book and black-market cigarette trade, finished his associate of arts degree, held workshops for cops and inmates, organized fundraisers for victims' programs, and conducted a voter registration drive for the League of Women Voters (via one of his visiting UCLA instructors). He also worked as a supervisor of the round-the-world desk as part of the TWA Free Venture program, an outside-the-box outsource program whereby juvenile offenders served as reservation agents for the then employee-owned airline (including handling credit card transactions), and which was later the subject of exposés on ABC's *20/20,* CBS's *60 Minutes*, and elsewhere.

"While in YA, I continuously found ways to keep all of my growth confined to education," says Darnell. "I wasn't in control of my emotions, or open to the growth that would later come. I knew I felt bad. I knew what I had done was wrong. I knew I wanted to make it right, but I was in a world that preyed on vulnerabilities. I had six-plus years of psychiatric therapy and a thousand hours of groups on social interactions, AA, anger management, child growth and development. I've taken the MMPPI, the MMCI, and a host of other personality inventory tests. I looked at the gang bull as a waste of time and energy, and with time and confidence it wasn't a threat to me. I could always fight. I knew I could beat ninety-eight percent of the institutions I was in, but personal growth took a back seat to my survival concerns.

"My juvenile crime undoubtedly was my fault. Although there were other shooters, a slimy scam from the beginning, and just an all-out mess, I caused it. Maybe it would have happened had I not been involved, but I was. I am the cause of the lost lives, without any spinning to fit my position. I can't blame anyone. Yeah, I was seduced by the life. I was used as a kid, but I do accept the responsibility."

And then suddenly our time was up. Four hours had passed in a blink, and visiting hours were over. We said a cursory good-bye and I drove the three hours back to L.A. in a twilight state. Darnell had presented me with a kind of legend, designed to be passed along to others as part of an oral history. With his court records sealed, and the characters in his story largely answering to aliases, his recounting was rendered insular, true only to itself. I took it on tabled faith, and I went back to my reporting.

Then months later, talking with an Ecstasy kingpin named Louis Ziskin (Kristen's ex) doing his share of a thirty-year sentence in Taft Correctional Institute (a federal prison southwest of Bakersfield, less than an hour from Corcoran), I happened to tell him Darnell's story, passing it along the jailhouse telegraph as a means of introduction. Ziskin remembered a white guy in his forties named Chris Lynch whom he once shared a bench and swapped stories with for a couple of hours in L.A. County.

"Chris Lynch got busted driving a minor to a Pasadena heist," he tells me. "I think his father owns an Orange County Mercedes dealership." With a last name, I quickly located a Christopher Lynch, forty-seven, with a rap sheet that included robbery, burglary, and counterfeiting. His probation report identified him as a successful car salesman with a degree in economics whose life was destroyed by cocaine addiction. He didn't call me back. From there, I found Bonnie Doreen Knoll, forty-three. A relative told me she had gone away for a while—thirty-six months for writing bad checks. From there, it was a short hop to extensive coverage in the *Pasadena Star-News* of the 1998 trial of Mario Devorya King, better known as Ocean.

The abortive jewelry heist occurred at City Jewelry, located at 445 East Colorado Boulevard in downtown Pasadena. Owner Ling Yu came here from Cambodia in 1980 with his wife Kim "Anna" Yu, who was killed in the holdup, along with their eleven-year-old son Johnny. Ling Yu testified at Darnell's trial but refused to attend the Mario King trial. He has consistently refused press entreaties on the subject ever since.

A month after the heist, on March 21, 1993, Darnell, Chris Lynch, and a friend of Lynch's named Murray Benton were arrested following the late-night robbery of a Kinko's in El Segundo. Benton was in possession of twenty-five counterfeit Wells Fargo traveler's checks, and they allegedly planned to steal a color copier to create additional checks worth up to $1 million, but it was too bulky to load into Darnell's Jeep. When they were spotted by a passing patrol car, Darnell wrecked the Jeep trying to flee. King (aka Ocean), who was supervising the operation, took off on foot and got away. In custody and looking for leverage, Benton told authorities he had overheard his sometimes roommate and Lynch's girlfriend Bonnie Knoll discussing the jewelry heist with King, whom he identified as Ocean. Also involved were Lynch, Darnell (who he didn't know by name), and Bolo, who he believed to be the shooter. He identified them as a gang responsible for several area robberies, all orchestrated by King. Lynch, Knoll, King, and perhaps a fourth black male were subsequently identified by witnesses as having visited three other jewelry stores on the day of the robbery. (This would seem to call into question whether the original heist was an inside job.) At the preliminary hearing, Knoll testified she had been coerced into participating and initially thought they merely intended to fence stolen jewelry, but began to fear that a robbery was imminent as the day wore on. She said she overheard King say he wanted her to "get in the mix." She also identified an additional participant as "Bubba," who matches the general description of Bolo. There was no mention of a security guard, and both Ling Yu's niece and a police investigator testified that Mr. Yu never discharged his weapon. (Forensics were sealed as part of the court record.)

Darnell was convicted at trial of double homicide, and Lynch and Knoll were charged with multiple counts of murder and conspiracy, eventually pleading to sixteen and eleven years, respectively, in exchange for their testimony against King "as many times as necessary." (Their sentencing was postponed more than twenty times as a consequence. A codefendant in the original indictment, presumably Bolo, passed an eyewitness lineup and was released. Darnell is adamant the man named was not Bolo, and that Bolo was not the mysterious fifth man Darnell refuses to name to this day.) But before the case against King could proceed to trial, in a bizarre twist, Bonnie Knoll was accused of having had sexual liaisons with courthouse bailiff Walter Surowiec, who was eventually convicted of having forged paperwork for false trial dates to meet with her thirteen times between November 1995 and June 1996 in the Pasadena Courthouse lockup. In exchange, he allegedly provided her with unidentified contraband. Knoll and another Sybil Brand Institute prisoner filed separate $10 million lawsuits against the county. At trial, King's defense attorney, Franklin Peters Jr., claimed the trysts allowed Knoll to pass messages to Lynch, and in turn coordinate an alibi and devise a conspiracy against King. Despite facing twenty-six separate felonies, Surowiec pleaded guilty to just one misdemeanor count of consensual sex with a prisoner and received three days in jail and three months' probation, and was forced to resign.

According to press reports, Darnell confirmed that King, his stepfather's cousin, recruited him to rob the jewelry store. As described in a September 17, 1998, *Press-News* story by reporter Howard Breuer, Darnell was at first reluctant to testify, and "seemed to change his mind only after he talked for several minutes with his mother, who kissed and embraced him at the witness stand as the jury waited outside the room." Darnell also testified that King drove the second getaway car. However, he claimed that prosecution witness Lynch gave him the gun, even though Knoll claimed she saw King hand Darnell what she feared was a gun in a sock.

"[Riley] did not go in there to shoot anyone," said Deputy District Attorney Sterling Norris in his closing statement, as reported in the *Star-*

News. "He was fifteen, he panicked. Sending an armed teenager in to rob a jewelry store is like throwing gasoline on a fire, and King threw the gasoline here."

The jury disagreed. According to the foreman, there were too many inconsistencies in the testimony of Lynch and Knoll. Darnell, by contrast, they found perfectly credible as a witness.

King was immediately tried again for a Santa Monica home invasion that occurred on December 22, 1992, two months before the Pasadena jewelry heist, in which he and two female accomplices allegedly entered the home of Herbalife executives Constantino and Jill Garcia, bound their hands and mouths with duct tape, and stole a Rolex, jewelry, and other valuables, escaping in the victims' car. (Sound familiar?) He was acquitted by an Alhambra jury on July 17, 2000. As for King's settlement with the city, I could find no official record, and police investigator Thomas Delgado says, "I never went to any deposition or was in trial based on that, and I would have been one of the primary persons involved in that."

Norris ran twice unsuccessfully for District Attorney before joining Judicial Watch, a controversial judicial advocacy group active during the Clinton administration that has since gained the reputation of an equal-opportunity partisan watchdog. A decade later, Norris, sixty-seven, remembers practically every detail of the King trial that he prosecuted.

"He was a *nasty* guy," says Norris of Mario King. "It was very much a racial verdict. The Nation of Islam was in the courtroom. Mario's wife was a very rabid Muslim. King wasn't. He used her, too. He went along with her to be religious when it helped him."

During the trial, Imam Saadiq Saafir and a dozen members of the Masjid Ibaadullah mosque in Crenshaw, including King's wife, showed up in court every day in support of King. (Further research turned up someone by that name who was affiliated with the influential Bay Area hip-hop collective Digital Underground, had a small part in the film *Menace II Society*, and had once been roommates with Tupac Shakur. When I finally tracked him down, he knew nothing of King or his namesake, but he did know all about Darnell. He asked me to save him a part in the movie.)

This was also in the wake of the Rodney King verdict and particularly the O.J. Simpson acquittal, a tension that Norris feels his opponent Peters deftly exploited.

"He was very cunning," Norris says of Mario King, "especially in his relationship to the black jurors. I had those problems before, but this was something more. I talked to some of them afterward. It was amazing how they viewed him as someone who represented them. There's a difference between that and downtown, where there was a straight black versus white thing. King was very handsome. He appealed to the black women on the jury. I had a real problem. Two participants who I had given a deal to were white. And then came a third guy who was a white bailiff [Surowiec]—and somehow he was involved, because she [Bonnie Knoll] had sex with him. I was thinking, 'I'm in big trouble'—I had just passed two whites, and now I had to call the bailiff. I knew I was on a sinking ship then . . . He had a good lawyer—a black fellow who exploited my immunity for the others."

"It doesn't happen every day that you get a not guilty on a death penalty case," Peters was quoted as saying following the verdict.

Both Norris and Delgado are adamant there was no security guard, no shooter besides Darnell, and no possibility of an inside job. (Delgado is also emphatic that Darnell rolled over on Mario King on the stand.) But Darnell, Norris remembers favorably.

"King set him up, knowing that Riley would not be charged as an adult," says Norris. "What really annoyed me was that we had pictures of the girl and Mario King at the shop. We had all of these photographs, and the jury still wasn't convinced that we had them together . . . Mario King had a similar criminal history where he set someone else up similarly.

"We got very favorable reports on [Darnell] after he went to prison. Someone went to see him when he went to prison—King maybe, or his wife. He was concerned, and he called me. We tried to set something up with the authorities. He was concerned that he was going to get hit for his testimony. King had a great influence over him, and I would not have put it past him going back to work with King because of that Svengali influence."

For someone who imagines himself the Great Gatsby, Darnell seems equally cast in the role of Nick Carraway: observer of wealth, confidant of the dark and dangerous, and one of only three people who attends Gatsby's funeral. It's Carraway who is privy to the secret griefs of wild, unknown men:

"Most of the confidences were unsought—frequently I have feigned sleep, preoccupation, or a hostile levity when I realized by some unmistakable sign that an intimate revelation was quivering on the horizon; for the intimate revelations of young men, or at least the terms in which they express them, are usually plagiaristic and marred by obvious suppressions. Reserving judgment is a matter of infinite hope. I am still a little afraid of missing something if I forget that, as my father snobbishly suggested, and I snobbishly repeat, a sense of the fundamental decencies is parceled out unequally at birth."

5

THE GOOD THIEF

*I*n the first weeks of putting in calls, I learned something that F. Scott Fitzgerald could have told me eighty years ago: the rich are different from you and me. One of those ways is their judicious use of human shields. Picture the temples of privilege these people live in—hillside compounds with security consultants, Gothic fences, electrified moats, armed patrols, and packs of Dobermans roaming wild on their estates. Now translate that into waves and phalanxes of representatives—lawyers, publicists, planners, schedulers, agents, managers, and corporate crisis experts—standing two and three deep, ready to catch a spear from the oncoming Visigoth horde storming the castle keep. The Manson family still has these people shook up.

Typical is this response from Nicky Hilton's flak-catcher, Paul Fisher—actually one of the nicer ones I got: "Thanks for the request but I don't see how Miss Hilton gains anything from making a comment for your book." What about ending the victimization of celebrities by predatory interlopers who somehow got inside the party, and once and for all peeling the target off their backs? I suppose to them, that describes me in a nutshell.

I met with Detective Steve Koman of LAPD Robbery-Homicide at the House of Pies in Los Feliz (my choice). Koman was the lead investigator on the Joe Francis break-in, one of two cops who had debriefed Darnell when they first brought him in and whose daily log in the months leading up to the arrest shows the same procedural frustration I was just now becoming familiar with. For Koman, this was ancient history; four years is more like forty in cop's years. Stocky, crumb-catcher mustache, seen-it-all battle glaze, he was nevertheless missing that just-the-facts condescension I'd seen in cops before—a post-Watergate, post–Rodney King article of faith that assures them reporters aren't so much necessary pests or even colleagues they could share a drink with, but rather a class of people they would just as soon shoot on sight, if the press would only agree to conduct their interviews in vacant alleys. Although Koman didn't give up much, he did seem intrigued to see what stones I might turn over.

"Darnell is not stupid," Koman tells me. "He knows the statutes [of limitations]. Could he be counting the days? Yes, he could. And if I had enough evidence to charge Darnell with those additional crimes, I would have done it already.

"Now, there are several issues of people that just don't want to cooperate with law enforcement. And that is more problematic than actually putting the case together. Putting the case together was not that tough. Going through four or five different attorneys just to do an interview. I mean, a burglary where somebody in the nosebleed atmosphere loses a hundred thousand dollars—that's something they carry in their wallet. It's more of an inconvenience for them to come down and talk to the police. Especially if their names are going to be in the newspaper as witness to a crime. Even exposing themselves to this bad element and what they perceive these guys have access to: 'If I testify against them, it don't matter who I am, they're going to get me because they're in the community.' It's the same sense of fear people living in South Los Angeles have—it's just at a different level. And they have the ability to lose a lot more than the people in South Los Angeles do. So I can door-knock a place, but unless I have a search warrant, I'm not going to force my way in to talk to them. I can't force victims to testify. Everybody knew the problems that these guys were creating on the street, but nobody wanted to step forward to deal with it."

I ask him about Will Wright, and about Timmy Iannello, the club manager who was rumored to have been mixed up in the Joe Francis business.

"We know that Iannello was somehow involved because they were a threesome," Koman says. "You have Will and Timmy and all these other guys that are dealing in the hundreds of thousands of dollars, but would sell their mothers out, in my opinion, if it means not going to jail. [Timmy] was never arrested, never interviewed on the case. And it's the same scenario as Will Wright: Will says that I interviewed him and cleared him on the case, and that's totally bogus. Will did every possible thing he could to avoid me. Every possible thing. But as far as Timmy was concerned, I didn't do a whole hell of a lot with him, because we went with what we had. And what we had was Darnell.

"Now, do I believe that Will Wright and Timmy Iannello were involved in the Joe Francis thing? Yes, I do. But only one person went in the house, and I have no witnesses who can put Will Wright or Timmy Iannello at the scene. The only thing that I have is Darnell. And Darnell—as charismatic as he is—has major credibility issues. He's a charming young man, with a lot of panache. I've interviewed him in prison a couple of times, and he sits there and looks me in the eye—almost like he's talking to his father. Darnell won't admit to too much. He may admit to some of the stuff, and probably a lot of it is sensational, and for your book. He will give you a lot, but he'll minimize his involvement considerably. So utilizing his statement, you have to evaluate his motives and why he's saying what he's saying. To take time off for him? Take the light off him? That's where you have to be leery of Darnell, because he looks at everything like a transaction—how it's going to benefit him.

"Darnell is in an extremely precarious situation right now. He's got another, whatever, eight or nine years to serve, and unfortunately, he's the only one who took the fall on the case at this point in time. You know the other individuals involved, I know the other individuals involved, but you can only go on what you have to prosecute these individuals. And, although the investigation is not done on that aspect, the bottom line is—until something significant comes up—none of those guys are going to get arrested . . . Everybody gets their just deserts at some point in time, and Will Wright is going to be no different."

I ask him if he thinks Darnell's got a shot at redemption when he gets out. He weighs this one internally before he speaks.

"I would say yes. Obviously, the jury is still out on him. He has a lot of amends to make. He's hurt a lot of people, and how he deals with his own personal insides is how people are going to base their opinion on him. He's done a lot of bad things—what has he done to try to rectify that? When you look at him now, is he sitting in custody finding the Lord? Is he trying to contact different individuals to apologize to them? Is he helping the police? What is Darnell doing right now to make amends for all the stuff he's done in the past? Now, in my opinion, there is nothing you can do to make up for killing two individuals. Nobody gets away with that . . . But when crime has been your source of income for the last fifteen years, he could be like, 'Well, I've got some money coming, maybe I'll just reinvest in this, and see if I can turn two hundred fifty thousand into a million five.' He's losing a lot of the prime of his life. He's been in jail since he was sixteen— almost half of his life. It's a horrible existence. Making fifteen bucks an hour as opposed to making fifteen million on a transaction—all of that is that attraction. But he's the only one that can overcome it. Unless he's willing to do so, this is going to be his life."

At one point, down some dead-end street trying to make a point, I end up telling him, "I try and live the straight and narrow, but I'm attracted to crime and writing about it."

"You've got a real interesting cast, I tell ya," he says. "You live on the edge."

Okay, now he's making fun of me. Still, he's the closest thing to Yoda I'm liable to get. We agree to stay in touch. The burger combo is on me. Try the pie.

On the night he was arrested, Darnell gave Koman a list of people he was friendly with in Bel Air—the Davis family (Brandon and his brother Jason), the Hilton family, the Toddmans (Tripp), the Johnsons (Casey), the Antebis (Donna and her son Steven Jr.), Joe Francis. That last name is the one they were looking for, so they stopped there. But Donna Antebi was his unofficial ticket in and out of the neighborhood: through boxer Frankie Liles, one of Darnell's closest friends, he was working as part of a four-man security team to guard the Antebi family estate in a tony cul-de-sac of Bel Air Canyon along with Morgan Carey (Mariah's older brother, who Frankie supposedly knew from having dated her on and off for years) and Robert, a retired Army captain and Frankie's cousin.

Donna Estes Antebi is a professional socialite who devotes much of her time and means to charity. She is the chair of COACH for Kids—Community Outreach Assistance for Childrens' Health—affiliated with Cedars-Sinai Medical Center, which provides mobile health clinics to the inner city. Her husband, Steven Antebi, was a limited partner and managing director of Bear Stearns for twenty years before founding his own venture capital group. She confirms the couple gives away as much as $5 million a year. (They were separated during the time that Darnell worked there, placing the burden of protecting the family largely on Donna, although they appear to have reconciled.) Like a lot of rich families, the Antebis had beefed up protection in response to the Bel Air Burglar, responsible for an estimated 250 burglaries in the hills north of Sunset for calendar year 2004. Somehow, Darnell had seemed the perfect fit. (Antebi's immediate neighbors, *The French Connection* director William Friedkin and former Paramount head Sherry Lansing, were burglarized over Christmas 2006 while on vacation in Italy and filed suit the following August against security company ADT, on whose watch a statistically high number of these burglaries seem to have occurred.)

I decided to pay Antebi a visit. If nothing else, at least I could breathe the air up there for a few hours, clear my head. But if you thought famous people were hard to get hold of, try dropping in on the überrich. The problem was that Darnell claimed to be privy to her personal and financial dealings, proprietary things that she denied and that she was pretty clear she didn't want to see discussed in a public forum. He also claimed that she had contacted a psychic—Kim the Psychic, he called her—who told Antebi that she and her family were in mortal danger. Antebi admitted to knowing Kim the Psychic, but claimed she was trying to help her develop a TV show. Darnell was just as adamant that what he told me was the truth; his buddy Frankie would back everything up. (Frankie Liles, then and now, refuses to comment for the book.) Over the course of our dialogue, which stretched to several weeks, Antebi explained to me that she was a private figure; her personal business didn't have any place in my book and she was most definitely lawyered up. Noting that my publisher was a division of Simon & Schuster, which was owned by a company that was controlled by Sumner Redstone, she told me, "I don't go to parties for Sumner Redstone, Mark, I *host* parties for Sumner Redstone." We finally reached a truce: I'd keep her private business private, and she'd tell me what she knew about Darnell.

As I was buzzed through the looming security gates and made the long approach up to the main house, the first thing I noticed was a flowing waterfall against one wall and a circular fountain of waterspouts, like a home version of the Bellagio, and the ocean view clear to Catalina. I was greeted by a handsome young man who introduced himself as Antebi's godson, a British chap clearly on his way out to tennis by the way he was dressed, and one of half a dozen handsome young men—her son, Steven's nephew, their friends, well-bred strays—who seemed to have the run of the place. Maybe this is how rich people keep from growing old: by making sure they're never more than arm's length from perpetual youth. It's got to be cheaper than monkey gland shots, or those vampire transfusions Keith Richards used to take in Switzerland.

I was shown into a spacious study where it looked like an art bomb had gone off: a Robert Graham sculpture in the entryway, de Koonings staining the walls, Picasso shrapnel in the far corner. These canvases were way too big to be smuggled out in a stolen Louis Vuitton bag, that's for sure. Just when I'd about gotten settled in, Donna Antebi made her entrance: petite, slender, tight designer jeans, and expensive sweater, she was of an indeterminate age—mid-forties I'll guess, but very pretty, extremely well tended, and lit from within with the glow that apparently money *can* buy. She gave me a quick tour of the ground floor and the ground floor art, including her daughter's paintings, which she noted had been exhibited in the Louvre. Her daughter is eight. As we chatted, a nanny trundled through with a scrum of schoolgirls in private-school skirts, and her husband's voice boomed through the intercom in occasional bursts from upstairs, like he was trying to find his way back to the main part of the house.

According to Darnell, the house was worth $15 million and cost $150,000 a month to run, and their security team had been paid $5,000 a week—figures that Antebi didn't dispute. She did venture that the art collection was rated by *Town & Country* magazine as one of the twenty most important in the city. At twenty-two, Antebi had started a product placement company called International Film Promotions, whose clients included Eastman Kodak, Bombay Gin, and Clairol, which she gave up once she had her first child, Steven Estes Jr., now eighteen, by her first husband. In late 2004, with her neighborhood under assault and her maternal instincts on high alert, Antebi did what persons of resources usually do: turned to the professionals.

"They were hired to secure the property, and that's what they did," says Antebi. "They helped me install a security system around the house. I thought they were all extremely professional—all of them. I had interviewed a proper security company, and their estimate to give us coverage around the clock was like sixty thousand dollars a month, which was just ridiculous. Every time I'd go somewhere, I would take all my jewelry out of the safe and hide it all over the house. I eventually put everything in the bank, because they would come in and take the safes. These guys were coming down off the mountain, burglarizing your home, and then slipping back through the mountains. So I put together a private security team. I already knew who the other guys were, and they brought him on. I didn't dig any deeper. We just needed more people to rotate shifts around the clock. I don't think Darnell was here for more than a few weeks.

"I just remember thinking, my first impression, that he was a very nice guy. I found Darnell to be so humble, kind and polite, and yet also so charismatic. I know we thought he looked a little bit like the Rock, a smaller version. I saw a picture of him that was like a modeling shot, and he's a handsome young man. I remember one day I rode with him, and I was so impressed because he was such a conscientious driver. And this particular drive, he was talking about what he was going to do in the future: he and his buddies were getting ready to open a bar or a nightclub on Sunset Boulevard. He was part of the Hollywood scene, so I gathered. He showed me the area, between Sunset Plaza and Crescent Heights. And we were talking about that, and I thought that was great, and assumed that he and the other guys were just doing this because this is what people do: you take regular jobs while this is happening. While you build your American dream. And he told me that he had a bit of a difficult time in his childhood, or some difficult years. But then he went to college and he studied business in school, and now he was going forth with his life, and I just thought that was fabulous. I wouldn't have been surprised if he had opened one restaurant, and then another, and gotten involved with bigger and better things. I really thought that he was on the track to fulfilling his promise. I just found Darnell incredibly respectful, and conscientious, and there on time. And then one day he wasn't."

I asked her if she ever felt, thinking about it afterward, that Darnell might have had designs on robbing the place—if he was the ultimate inside man.

"I have to say, that is what just takes your breath away," she says. "It's so crazy and so ironic that he ends up being a prime suspect in the Bel Air Burglar [cases], when that's what you hired him to do. That you are hiring the burglar to be in your home! Can you *imagine*? I still didn't believe it for the longest time, because even when I found out that he got arrested and I heard about the Joe Francis tape, I still did not believe for a second that he had anything to do with the other burglaries. I let everybody go about two weeks after Darnell went away because one of these Bel Air Burglar guys—a guy by the name of John Vlagg—was arrested, and he got something like sixteen years in jail. I was buying into—outside of what he did with Joe Francis—that he's a good guy. The irony of the situation was not whether he did the burglaries or didn't do the burglaries, it's that he was arrested and his face was plastered everywhere—all over the news, all over the Internet—as the Bel Air Burglar. 'The Bel Air Burglar Captured!' We hired someone to protect us from the Bel Air Burglar, and they called him *the* Bel Air Burglar! I just thought, oh . . . my . . . God! Frankie brought this guy to me, and now I'm dealing with *this* kind of stuff?

"I believe that maybe there is a trust situation with Frankie that Darnell wouldn't cross. Frankie was doing a job. He was helping me out, and he was Darnell's friend, so I believe he was also helping out Darnell. I mean, Frankie brought his family over here; his daughter came over to play. So I don't believe that Frankie would have brought somebody to me that would harm me. But I could be wrong."

I thanked her for seeing me, and opening up about a breach in her carefully tended perimeter that obviously still troubles and confuses her. At the door, I told her, "I want some of your art."

"There are cameras on you from several different angles," she says, pointing them out to me. "There's a camera right there."

Darnell says he had one more encounter with Kim the Psychic. "I go over one night and pay her a visit, and she gives me a reading," he says. "She told me some shit about my dead brother that none of my buddies knew, and nothing that she could possibly know. We sat drinking tea at three a.m., and she further blows my mind with all the shit she's telling me that she shouldn't know. Made me a believer. Later, she told me that she had a vision that a friend of hers whose birth sign was Taurus was in trouble with the law. She didn't think of me—she had no idea I had a shady side—but once I was incarcerated, she gave me a play-by-play on meetings and conversations that were going on, that once again she shouldn't have known about. She continuously told me not to take a deal, to wait it out, that I wouldn't get convicted, that Joe was going down for a long time. But once the deal came by, I couldn't pass it up. For nearly a year, all the way down to me taking the deal, Kim called everything."

So I called Kim the Psychic. As I expected, she wouldn't talk about Donna Antebi, which she attributed to psychic-client privilege—something which, for future reference, I feel better knowing exists. But she did volunteer some thoughts about Darnell.

"Basically, the way that I work is, I see every walk of life without judgment," Kim tells me. "I get information channeled in, and then I forget it. But if he says that I told him not to take the deal, then I must have told him that. It doesn't matter who you are—if you're a killer or whatever. In the spiritual realm, there's not a lot of judgment . . . But I do wonder why Darnell went against what I said."

She also told me that my career was "about to shift"—and not a moment too soon—and also that I had been married twice. Oh, well—who needs to predict the past when you can predict the future?

Having clocked Darnell's place of business, I decided to take a spin by his last known residence, where he lived with his girlfriend Ruby and English bulldog Spanky for about eight months prior to his arrest. He kept what he called a crash pad in Hollywood, on Whitley, where it dead-ends three blocks north of Hollywood Boulevard into a maze of side streets and switchbacks that Darnell preferred because he could game out his getaways. His apartment was in back, and on the day I stopped by, I caught the owner of the units, Duncan Foster, overseeing some workers remodeling one of the apartments. Foster is an Ivy League–educated musician from New York who picked up some real estate out here, which affords him a comfortable living and the contemplative life. Fortunately, he had followed the Darnell Riley saga in the papers, and was here when the cops took him down in the driveway that runs along the side of their buildings, and he was anxious to trade information. He was also in a unique position to observe Darnell, in that he had turned over all financial matters regarding tenants to a property manager and posed as the live-in superintendent to save himself some headaches. He describes Darnell as generally dismissive of the help.

"He had charisma," says Foster. "A sociopath has charisma to everyone, I guess, but he was a prick to me. Darnell definitely has a self-aggrandizement disorder."

He quickly confirmed two cornerstones of Darnell's myth—the money and the women. "Darnell showed my property manager a stock portfolio to get the lease, and he would pay the rent six months in advance," Foster says. "And he always had smoking-hot girls over—supermodel types. I remember one time I stopped by about something, and he had a little bookshelf with maybe a couple of shelves of books, and this really hot bleached blonde asked him, 'Have you read all these books?' He had a Miro, I think [he probably means Picasso sketches—all limited prints] and a cash-counting machine with a scale on it. He said the scale was for weighing coins."

Foster recounts how Darnell drove a souped-up Chevy Nova sold to him by two dubious characters who turned back up as soon as he got arrested and tried to repo it, with mixed results. These turned out to be Darnell's friends Jerry Rosenberg and Doc Holliday, as well as all the evidence we need of honor among thieves.

"They were two white dudes," Foster says. "One was older, in his fifties, kind of scruffy, and one was younger with a shaved head. They were like the kind of guys you see working in a chop shop"—or a boxing gym, he agrees after prompting. "They came to take the car, and they couldn't get it running. It took them an hour to get it out of here. The battery kept dying, so they had to leave and go get a new one.

"When the cops came [on the day Darnell was arrested], they showed up early. They were U.S. Marshals in black Suburbans. They said, 'We're looking for this guy, nothing serious—he's a witness in a bar fight that took place down in San Diego. He was profiled on *America's Most Wanted*.' When Darnell drove up in his SUV, the black Suburbans and two cop cars rushed in behind him. He jumped out, looked like he was about to run, and the cops yelled, 'Don't even fucking think about it!' When they opened his hatchback, there was a brick of shrink-wrapped cash about the size of an air conditioner. After he was arrested, he told Ruby that it was fake money he was using to make a film."

In the weeks after his arrest, Foster reports that Darnell's mother and siblings came and rifled through his possessions for anything of value, which Darnell claims they're still holding for him. Foster also said that Paris Hilton, Nicky Hilton, and Nicole Richie had all supposedly called Ruby to offer their sympathy and say that what happened to Darnell was unfair and that they were going to try to help. He also attributed this quote to Ruby in the wake of Darnell's arrest:

" 'Darnell forgot that he was black.' "

I put in a call to Ruby, which turned into ten calls, then twenty e-mails, more legwork tracking her down, and finally a midday drive out to Baldwin Park, where she lived with her mother. This was in the nicer part of East L.A., that quadrant of Los Angeles above Interstate 10 and east of the 105 where ethnic, largely Hispanic neighborhoods of color are controlled and contained, in anticipation of the next riot. There were groups of young men hanging out on her block, talking about sports and cars and keeping an eye on the single neighbor lady who lives with her single daughter, and my blue VW microbus-as-makeshift-surveillance-van parked across the street for hours wasn't going to pass unnoticed. You don't need Elizabeth Taylor to tell you that.

I finally left a note on the front gate and eased my vehicle through a gauntlet of angry stares. Ruby called back in a couple of days, and she couldn't have been sweeter. I'd been told she had hundreds of Darnell's photos, his Rolodex, lots of financial and gaming records, and various valuable artifacts and that she could corroborate much of his story for the months leading up to his arrest. She agreed to meet me for coffee the following week. Outside of the message she left apologizing for standing me up, that would be the last I ever heard from her.

I made an appointment to go see Shelly Wood, who was the official keeper of Darnell's archives, and who could presumably document parts of his story. In one of his letters, Darnell states, "Simply put, Shelly is my conscience. She has renewed my faith in humanity." She and her immediate friends seemed to be some sort of respite for him from the pressures of his day job and who knows what other psychic violence. "They were/are my balance," he says. "Of course, they knew nothing about my extracurricular activities. They knew I was involved in gambling, but not all the extra stuff."

Shelly had known Darnell for seven years, from the age of twenty-three or twenty-four, working with Athletes and Entertainers for Kids (AEFK) on a program sponsored by Shaquille O'Neal for victims' rights that involved young people with violent pasts just out of Youth Authority. This soon expanded to events with Tyra Banks and Kathy Ireland and elementary school presentations. Darnell helped Shelly write a $10,000 Verizon grant called "Follow the Yellow Book Road," a phonetics-based afterschool reading program further subsidized by the National Council of Jewish Women. Shelly was familiar with the fight world: she manages Sytel Wilburn, at one time number two in line for the Olympic team, before he spent some time in jail. (He recently turned pro.) They also ran 5- and 10K marathons together, including one for APLA (AIDS Project of Los Angeles) sponsored by Paris Hilton, at the behest of Shelly's friend Ludo Vika, a comic stage actress whose nephew Angel had been born with AIDS, and who finally succumbed to it in 2005. Darnell continued to volunteer with APLA, transporting water to the races and training participants, including for the Hawaii Marathon in December 2001, and helped Shelly mount fundraisers for both APLA and the Lymphoma-Leukemia Society. Meanwhile, Darnell helped stage several plays with Ludo and her husband David, and was instrumental in bringing a lot of people to their shows—including, he claims, Paris Hilton and Nicole Richie. (This was before their fame, certainly before their respective infamy, and neither Ludo nor Shelly can confirm this part for certain.)

"He would do it all: production work, lighting, promotion, schlepping," says Ludo. "My play was called *Under the Mango Tree*, and he would make sure that key people were invited. I did see him there surrounded by recognizable people, and I was going to get close to them, but I can't say that I knew who they were . . . I don't know how he got into what he did, but I know the good side of Darnell. He was always there to help anybody. He was good to my nephew; he treated him like a person."

Darnell also befriended the special-needs teenage son of Shelly's ex-assistant, Laura Wilson, and the two became inseparable; Darnell taught him left from right and attended his baseball and soccer games.

"Nathan is fourteen, my only child—I'm a single mom," says Laura. "He's a victim of domestic violence; that's why he's considered special needs. I was kicked while pregnant with him, and he suffered brain trauma. Different diagnoses: moderate mental retardation, mild-to-moderate autism, and mild cerebral palsy. As any mom would be, I was hesistant, but they hit it off right away. Darnell was always supportive. He'd say, 'Oh, Laura, he'll be able to do this and that' when I thought otherwise. It's sad to say, but he had more faith in Nathan than I did. We traveled a lot together—Palm Springs, Catalina Island, Detroit. And Nathan loved Darnell. Everything was 'Darnell' to him. They called each other 'my buddy.' I know he did whatever he did, but Darnell is Darnell. The day he gets out, I really want him to come back and be part of Nathan's life. I know he would never hurt Nathan."

Darnell helped Shelly move numerous times and helped with her fledgling clothing company, setting up fashion shows and facilitating models. In turn, she helped him enroll in college, including the University of Phoenix's Woodland Hills campus, where she still teaches various criminal justice courses, and where he all but completed a degree in business administration. (In 1995–7, while still incarcerated, Darnell attended Ventura Community College's satellite campus on Youth Authority grounds, maintaining an A-B average. Later, he took exchange courses at Degendorf University near Munich, Germany, during at least one summer—he says to keep Walter happy—and briefly played football in 2001 for Antelope Valley College in Lancaster, forty miles northeast of Los Angeles, playing two games as outside linebacker before he quit.)

She also helped him find employment at Washington Mutual Bank in 2001, where he says that after pitching an electronic check transfer system at a job fair (which later became the internal "e-trieve" intranet system), he was hired and quickly moved to a fast-track junior executive program, where he studied international banking, worked on the acquisition teams for Great Western Bank and Dime Savings Bank of New York (both acquired during his tenure), learned how to structure businesses and hide money (later an asset in his work with online gambling companies and others), and made $70,000 a year with stock options by the time of his last semester in college.

Quick to master the new systems before him, and equally quick to feel the crushing weight of ensuing boredom, Darnell reveals that during his lunch hour, he would prowl college campuses, massage parlors, strip clubs, or any place else he might make up for lost time with female companionship. Over lunch one day, according to his manuscript, he secreted himself into the rear compartment of a friend's SUV, wrapped in a fetal crouch around an AR-15 assault rifle, ready to spring into action when three hapless drug suppliers got caught in a sham buy. He relieved them of four kilos of product worth $14,000 on the street in L.A. but $19,000 a key back in New York, and left them sitting in a parking lot as he drove out of sight, the red dot of his laser scope still dancing on their chests and foreheads, wondering whether they'd just been played by the cops or crims. "That deal was payback for my boy getting done wrong on a deal," says Darnell. Eventually, forced to make a lifestyle choice, he followed some of his fellow WAMU employees out on stress leave and took a severance package.

(All internal records of Darnell's employment are considered proprietary by Washington Mutual, which will only confirm the dates of his employment—October 22, 2001, to April 1, 2003—and his last position, "telephone banker.")

And this being Los Angeles, Darnell also imagined a place for himself in the film business, the world destination for hustlers, especially hardworking ones. He tried his hand at acting, as a football player in a cameo that was cut from the *American Pie* sequel, *American Wedding*, and with a recurring role as Josh Brolin's assistant on *Mister Sterling*, Lawrence O'Donnell's *West Wing* spinoff, which aired for nine episodes (a tenth was filmed) on NBC in 2003. Having studied both closely, I can attest that there is a scene with numerous black football players in uniform in *American Wedding*, although Darnell cannot be identified as among them, and that there is a recurring extra who resembles his general features and body shape visible in frame at various points during the season of *Mister Sterling*—at 11:05 in the first episode, 32:07 in the second, 11:54 in the sixth, possibly 9:15 of the ninth, and 5:36 of the tenth—although it would be premature to call that acting. (Yet what are we to make of the unaired tenth episode, "Sins of the Father," written by *Crash* author Paul Haggis, which contains the character of "Mr. Riley," a bagman who reemerges after twenty-five years to implicate Mister Sterling's retired-governor father, played by James Whitmore, in a series of long-buried scandals? Or dialogue like: "Who's this Riley guy?" "Don't know. He's just somebody who started talking" or "This guy Riley—he's got dates, he's got places"?)

But the constant waiting and putting your fate in the hands of others made acting even less conducive than banking to Darnell's plans. At one point, reiterating how he is anything but starstruck, Darnell notes that no less than Denzel Washington tried to steer him into acting: "Me meeting Denzel Washington at my boy's gym was no big deal . . . We met through a mutual friend—Terry Claybon at Hollywood Boxing Gym. He wasn't Denzel the actor. He was D. the ma'fucka who bummed a quarter off me to put in the meter. Or D. the dude that clowned me when I got my ass handed to me in a sparring session. Or Cedric the Entertainer, who practiced his comedy on all of us at the gym. He and others probably enjoyed my company because I didn't ask them for anything. I wasn't trying to attach my name (or theirs) to a project. Denzel asked me once if I was going to get into acting. I had a good look, he said, just making small talk. I hope I didn't sound like a dick, but I remember saying something like, 'Instead of playing a corporate titan, I'm just going to be one.' " (Claybon frequently trains actors for films, including Matt Damon for *The Bourne Ultimatum*, Shawn and Marlon Wayans for *White Chicks*, and Denzel Washington for *Hurricane*, released Christmas 1999. He also played welterweight/middleweight champion Emile Griffith in the latter, and Washington was at least at one point a fixture at his gym.)

Darnell claims to have interned as a PA (production assistant) on the cable series *The Best Damn Sports Show Period* on Fox Sports Network and worked as a segment producer on *Life in the Fast Lane with Steve Natt* on the Fine Living Network through his friend Susan Yannetti, the director of PR for Vivid Video and a friend of both Timmy Iannello and Frankie Liles. (She now works closely with porn megastar Jenna Jameson and appears on camera in *Porn Star: The Ron Jeremy Story*, where she observes of its subject, "I think he is a sensualist for what life has to offer.") Darnell shot spec commercials for his director's reel: one for Adidas, shot at the track of a Pasadena high school, featured Maurice Green, just deposed as the fastest man in the world, who had secretly broken his leg in a motorcycle accident in 2003 and was looking to up his profile and regain his title.

Darnell formed his own film company, called Mero Mero Films (which means "main man" in Spanish), and set about redefining himself as creative talent—a framed poster from the movie *Chaplin* is signed: "Darnell, Write me a screenplay. For real.—Robert" (aka Robert Downey Jr., a gift from Jim Epstein, Downey's attorney). With Shelly's help, he mounted and shot a docudrama on drug smuggling that has yet to be edited. And Darnell says he holed up in a luxury hotel in West Hollywood over Easter weekend 2003, where he says he lived for most of the calendar year, laid in cases of Red Bull, and ordered "cheesecake after cheesecake," and wrote his hyper-violent crime script *Scrapbook* in just three days.

Shelly's friend Jim Epstein is an attorney and one-time Stanford athlete who Darnell says is "like a mentor to me." Epstein, who planned to become involved if Darnell's case had gone to trial, is the son of legendary screen-writer Julius Epstein, who with his twin brother Philip (and Howard Koch) wrote *Casablanca*. The two attended Dodgers and Clippers games and watched the World Series and Super Bowl together; Darnell showed him and Shelly the Paris Hilton sex tape months before it was leaked onto the Internet. Says Epstein: "Darnell was a young man who gave the im-pression of having a tremendous amount going for him. He was good-looking, he was extremely charismatic. And apparently he just wanted it all right now, and he wasn't willing to wait for it."

Epstein is also best friends with Sean Cunningham, the creator of the *Friday the 13th* series, and Darnell called in a favor.

"When I finally finished the screenplay, he had a producing buddy read it, and when Sean got it he told me that they both said it was one of the sickest screenplays that they'd ever read, but there was something about it that wouldn't allow them to put it down. At that point, I realized that I was going to finance and distribute the film myself. I figured if the creator of Jason said something like that about my screenplay, as sick and twisted as Jason is, I had something. I was going to do it in Japanese *animé* style."

Darnell envisioned Mickey Rourke as the "sadistic-sexual deviant," Ni-cole Richie as his sidekick, Casey Affleck as his lead, a Russian Mafia hit-man—all of them, he claims, friends or acquaintances, and all done in voice-over. "So I disconnected myself at the end of 2004, cashed out from all my illegal dealings, and I went completely legit," says Darnell. "2005 was supposed to be my year. I was legit, but [Assistant D.A.] Hoon Chun didn't get that memo."

Reached in South Africa, where he and original director Wes Craven were producing a remake of Craven's *Last House on the Left* (which Cunningham originally produced), Cunningham writes, "I'm sorry, I have no recollection of *Scrapbook*. I remember Darnell asking me to read his screenplay and I remember it was predictably dreadful. (Why do people think writing a screenplay is so easy?!!!) But I'm afraid I can't help you with the content. Sorry."

Shelly also remembers Darnell doing collections work and being involved in gambling, always busy the day after major sports events, and she remembers odd bounty being given him in lieu of payments—three mink coats, or a souped-up Mustang, which they sold on eBay and shipped to Sweden. He told her he was working after-hours parties as a security guard, the muscle outside the room, but he would never let her come to one of them. Mostly, she remembers him involved in endless deals that were always on the verge of breaking big—billboards and exporting bananas and nightclubs on the Sunset Strip—without ever quite paying off.

"I questioned it, but I didn't really think about," says Shelly. "And then the more I did think about it, the more I knew something didn't feel right."

The pair were finally estranged in July 2004 when she discovered plane tickets to Germany and Prague that Darnell couldn't adequately explain. They argued, and she distanced herself, only to reconnect with him following his arrest.

"When I heard he was at Wayside [County Jail, since renamed Pitchess Detention Center/Honor Ranch], Frankie took me over to see him, and I realized he was facing a double life sentence plus seventeen [years]," says Shelly. "When I saw him, it just confirmed that he was desperate and had nothing to hold on to, that he was isolated, and that regardless of guilt or innocence, I was going to do whatever I could to give him some hope to look forward to. It was unconditional, and I made a personal choice to be there for the long haul, in spite of all the advice I was given by my friends, some of whom could not understand why. I'm an all-or-nothing kind of gal. I can only do me. I just realized that if I could prevent him from going off the deep end, then that was what I was going to do."

Shelly seems mystified by much of the story he tells, if only because she weathered it yet never witnessed it directly. "I think that that world took care of him, in many ways, because he was willing to do stuff that they wouldn't do," she says. "They would take him to Neiman Marcus and set him up so that he could play the role when he needed to play the role. When he was with me, he was wearing dirty shorts, the same red shirt—he was just a casual guy. He picked me up one time in a black Mercedes. I never questioned it. He said it was Timmy's. I don't know if it was Timmy's and he was taking care of Timmy's car, or it was something that they borrowed."

On one of our drives back from Corcoran, I asked her if she thought Darnell was a sociopath. The question seemed to catch her off guard. "I don't know," she says finally.

In his manuscript, Darnell sometimes refers to himself as the Good Thief, who was crucified at Calvary at the right hand of Christ, which he imagines to be some sort of Robin Hood character or instrument of a swift and terrible karma—stealing from Peter to feed Paul, maybe; administering justice as necessary. With the luxury of hindsight, his one unlimited asset now, he tries to apply his analytical skills to a strategy that seems not to have served him well, gaming out what might have been.

"Yeah, I could've been all legit and stuck with banking, but without cutting ties with the criminal element, I would just be any one of the guys at Enron," says Darnell. "I'd be that Kozlowski guy with Tyco, or the Rigases with Adelphia. We ain't no different. There ain't much difference in the methodology a crack dealer uses to justify his actions or a corporate scammer cooking the books. So now that I'm back to the overbearing reality check, with these bars closing in on me, I'm talking on the yard with a guy who used to be a lawyer, who scammed corporations and got caught, and he's mixing with a guy who lives a couple doors down who was a construction hand, who lives next to a kid who used to sell bootleg CDs. When we get searched, we all get butt naked, spread our cheeks and cough in a cadence like a chorus. We're all equals when we lay down on these hard-ass cots and wrap up in these itchy-ass blankets. So here I am in all my glory, as naked and vulnerable to the world as when I came into it. I have stewardship over my ship. I've never been a brute or a bully. I've worked within the parameters of whatever field I played in. I tucked my ethical position to get to the next point, no different than George Bush's buddy Scooter Libby, or the buddy he eulogized at his funeral, Ken Lay.

"I still wasn't finished with the fast life, so when I got out and saw all that some of my friends had going on, I wanted a piece. I wanted to make up for those six years I lost, and I was seduced by the nightlife once more. The self-deception that allowed me to get involved with the bullshit and rationalize my way through the many crimes was that I told myself that I wasn't robbing civilians. All the guys I jacked up or fleeced were in the life. They put things into play. They fucked someone over on a deal, so they knew what was possible by fucking someone over on a deal. I rationalized my way through it all in large part so I could sleep at night. I didn't really believe the bullshit, but I tucked the real me to get to the next level. It doesn't mean that I won't beat someone down if a motherfucker crosses me. I'm still a man."

ILL WILL

A s Darnell was settling into Youth Authority and inheriting the tainted spoils of his brief life of crime, a high school student in Blaine, Washington, on the Canadian border, was finding his own way off the straight and narrow and onto a path that would ultimately lead him to Hollywood and the VIP rooms of the most exclusive clubs, access to the most exclusive parties, and the secret interiors of the most desirable women—using only the weapons of impetuousness, mendacity, and blind stupid luck. Such decisions are made in a second, and predestined more than made. But at the point he set out for it, knowingly or not, all of it was merely a radioactive glow somewhere over the horizon—a red, infected Oz.

According to court documents, from September 1994 to the end of 1995, William Samuel Wright operated as middle management in a drug smuggling operation that included enticing his fellow students to walk backpacks full of hydroponically grown British Columbian weed, the finest in the world, from Canada into the U.S., past the giant Peace Arch built in 1921 to commemorate the friendship between the two countries, right where I-5 plugs Mexico into Canada, a billboard for free trade. Like Billy the Kid or Dillinger (or Darnell, for that matter), stories about Will Wright still abound in the area, having long ago settled into legend—although he emerges from them less a Robin Hood than a kind of blinged-out Tom Sawyer who thinks he's Injun Joe. From local press accounts, volunteered descriptions from his peers, and interviews with local members of the four-thousand-person community, a picture emerges of a precocious, likable kid who invested the free rein that was given him—and the deference paid his schoolteacher parents for their decades of service—into a pathological lifestyle of brazen exploits, compulsive lying, and aspirational violence. In a town that was no bigger than a large urban high school, this became common knowledge very quickly, until finally the U.S. Customs Service could no longer look the other way.

Typical of the stories they still tell are these letters that appeared on the WhoIsWillWright.com Web site after it was launched in late 2005. Borderite, who grew up in Blaine, remembers: "He would regularly come to school with tens of thousands of dollars in his wallet that he would flash around. He paid friends of mine to do his homework, a hundred dollars or more for assignments, and would hand out hundreds to others regularly . . ." Not Sayin' adds: "At the age of fifteen, Will was driving a brand new Mustang GT 5.0 convertible with more toys (gold-plated wire wheels, gold amplifiers, gold hydraulic pumps, etc.) than what he had paid for the car. At the same time, he was also driving a brand new Mitsubishi 3000GT, a lifted Chevy pickup, and a brand new Harley. The drug truck he was caught in was to be used only once and then resold/scrapped." And the ebullient Blaine, Blaine!!!, thrilled to stumble across fellow travelers this far from home, recalls "the rumors and different stories I heard over the years about Willy and the Wrights":

"Will, in his infinite wisdom and cockiness, would pull up to the U.S. border with garbage bags full of weed in the trunk of his 5.0, pretending to be talking on his cell phone with his music blaring, then proceed to roll down his tinted windows, turn down his music, raise up his hydros to get eye level with the border guard, and answer all questions with an air of arrogance before he went right on through . . . He hired a former Canadian Navy Seal diver to swim from the Canadian side underwater with his dope, tie it and maybe some cash to crab pots, and swim back."

And in a letter to the court entered into evidence by Will's own lawyers to argue mitigating circumstances as a plea for leniency, Lee Bouma, a local fisherman, wrote, "For two years, Will Wright was the talk of the community. I was told he was the opening topic at almost every school board meeting; he was the talk almost everywhere I went in town—he was the talk around my house. The entire community knew: the school board, the police, customs and immigration, the chamber of commerce, business people, schoolchildren, ministers, teachers, drug enforcement officers, and our own D.A.R.E. officer . . . I am ashamed and appalled that an entire community, myself included, watched for two years as the drug enforcement agencies and the community did nothing to assist in turning Will's attention away from this criminal activity . . ."

And yet according to the government's sentencing memorandum, U.S. Customs seized cash from him at the border on multiple occasions—$19,000 on December 16, 1994, with which he claimed he was going to buy a truck, and $16,888 on April 13, 1995—as well as two separate vehicles, one of them the brand-new 1995 Mitsubishi, valued at $42,000, and "warned him he would be prosecuted if he continued the criminal activity after he turned eighteen." Six months after his eighteenth birthday, on January 24, 1996, while still a senior in high school, Will was arrested in a Canadian Mountie drug sting operation at the Elephant & Castle restaurant at the Bellis Fair Mall in nearby Bellingham, Washington. He had brought with him five and a half pounds of marijuana to sell to undercover agents, but claimed the kilo of cocaine he had promised them was delayed due to inclement weather. He was also found to be in possession of a stolen 9mm pistol and a fake ID, and bragged to the agents (on tape) that over the last year, he had smuggled one hundred pounds of high-grade BC (British Columbia) weed out of Canada every other day, worth $500,000, the proceeds of which he had buried in his yard. He was charged with conspiracy to launder money and possession with intent to distribute marijuana, later amended to include smuggling, conspiracy to import, and possession with intent to distribute over one hundred kilograms; six others were ultimately charged in conjunction with him. He was also determined to have been involved in a shooting incident in May 1995 during a drug dispute, although it was never resolved who had fired the shots.

Will was denied bail, despite his parents' offer to post their $450,000 home as collateral. In a plea bargain two months later, he agreed to plead guilty to one count of conspiracy with a gun enhancement, and to forfeit $35,000 that was seized, a '92 Chevy pickup, and the '93 Jeep Cherokee he once abandoned in a ditch dividing the two countries while on a drug and money laundering run. The defense sentencing memorandum cited a psychiatric evaluation by Dr. Douglas L. Vaupel from 1990, when Will was twelve, that includes a tentative diagnosis of attention deficit disorder: "Both parents describe marked difficulties with impulsiveness and excess activity. They also note that he has difficulties with distractibility. He is argumentative, oppositional, strong-willed, has trouble with lying, negative, [has] trouble accepting responsibility and [is] resistant to authority. They note these difficulties have been present since he was an infant. They also note that he is naïve, easily misled and is insecure. He does well academically within school and seems to learn quickly. Outside of the home, he seems to want to please people and attempts to be liked. They note that he has difficulty with lying or exaggerating the truth." This and other documents were linked on the WhoIsWillWright.com site. The defense memorandum extrapolates Will's current predicament from this early tendency to exaggerate, connecting the two with a deft understatement: "The defendant and his codefendants are very poor historians."

The document also states unequivocally that, "If this case had gone to trial, the defendant, William Samuel Wright, would have testified that he was induced into illegal drug activity by an adult [who is named]," Will's Canadian supplier, who was never arrested. Darnell claims this was enough to earn Will a dreaded "snitch jacket," identifying him as an informer, which would follow him throughout the prison system and his life beyond.

Will's parents, Bill and Kathy Wright, were both schoolteachers. (For purposes of easy irony, I note that at the time of Will's arrest, Kathy Wright, a high school home economics teacher, was reportedly teaching a class for parents on how to deal with troubled kids.) Bill Wright also wrote a letter to the court requesting leniency, in which he blamed the adult dealer for leading his son astray. However, as was pointed out in the government's sentencing memorandum, issued in response to the defense document, this sentiment might have carried more weight had Bill Wright not been involved in a highly speculative cell phone venture with the adult in question, which the elder Wright termed a "scam" in which he lost money. Bill Wright also filed a claim for $10,000 that had been seized from Will when he was seventeen, saying it had been stolen from the family safe—money that Will admitted in the pretrial hearing had been drug money he was taking to Canada for a buy; Bill Wright subsequently admitted to U.S. Customs he knew where it had come from.

Bill Wright retired as a fifth grade teacher in June 2004, and on Labor Day 2006 was arrested for poaching almost fifty crabs from ten crab pots set up in the waters beyond his beachfront home, for which he was fined $1,260. To be sure, they were his pots and not those of other fisherman, but in a town with limited natural resources from which many are trying to make an honest living, that amounts to the same thing. I don't know how they do it Washington State, but in Rhode Island where I come from, anyone caught poaching lobsters gets a shotgun full of rock salt in his backside. There is no second time.

Among the other letters of community support attached to the defense memo was one from James "Randy" Deming, a local coach and high school teacher and longtime friend of the family, who defended Will as a hyperactive child, "a very bright kid who was hard to be around at times because he asked a million questions and could not get enough attention." He labels Will's claims "the tallest of tales and totally, for lack of a better phrase, BS. We used to tease Will that he was so full of it, his eyes were brown . . . Willy has watched too many movies and likes to play the 'big man' role. So he talks himself up . . . He is a very young person who lives in a world of fantasy and has become a product of the society we live in today."

Randy Deming was the primary subject of a December 15, 2003, profile in the *Seattle Post-Intelligencer* titled "Coaches Who Prey," which presents in graphic detail the charges of child molestation and sexual assault that have trailed him throughout his thirty-year career. Blaine High School valedictorian Kim Staheli Louch recalls avoiding school on gym days, which she traces to the day she was doing stretching exercises and Deming poked his finger in her crotch. "It's not a secret that he was touching girls all the time," she is quoted as saying. Repeated complaints were dismissed by a school board enthralled with Deming's performance as a wrestling coach, which ultimately garnered them a state title. He was reprimanded in 1985 for asking one girl if she had any nude photos of herself, and for massaging another in the boys' locker room. In 1987, he was the subject of a local police investigation for touching a ten-year-old girl near the genitals. In 1990, the year he was named State Coach of the Year, Deming was charged with first-degree child molestation for inappropriately touching another ten-year-old and rubbing her breasts. Charges were dropped in exchange for his voluntary resignation. But after the school district reported the misconduct to a state supervisory office, Deming sued them for violating his confidentiality agreement and settled for $27,500 to drop the lawsuit. He was hired by White Swan High School in Mount Adams, Washington, where he was repeatedly disciplined and ultimately charged with two accounts of fourth-degree assault with sexual motivation for touching two female students. He was acquitted after a three-day jury trial.

As "Anonymous in Blaine" recounts on the Web site: "Randy Deming used to take male students under his wing and confide in them and interact with them on a very juvenile level. He would gossip with his male students and make lewd comments about their fellow female classmates. If one of Randy Deming's female students was overweight, he would comment about 'her fat ass' and encourage his male students to do the same. Never mind the fact that he himself was four-hundred-plus pounds . . . As a result of Randy Deming's twenty-plus years teaching and coaching, he spawned a whole generation of misogynistic, perverted, warped followers/losers from Blaine. Will Wright is obviously a prime example of that. I believe Randy Deming's influence over Will Wright is VERY relevant. Is Randy Deming the only person the Wright family could find to write a letter in defense of Will?"

Will Wright was sentenced to seven and a half years in federal prison plus five years of supervised release. Like Darnell, he spent six years in the finer academies of criminal enterprise, cultivating a career—first at the Federal Correctional Institute in Three Rivers, Texas, halfway between San Antonio and Corpus Christi, then at Taft Correctional Institute in central California, an hour from where Darnell now resides. He was released on September 10, 2002, to a halfway house in Orange County, and his parole finally expired September 9, 2007.

I flew into Seattle and drove due north through Bellingham, a typical postcard image of the Pacific Northwest, which, like most small towns these days if you were to move the camera too far to either side, is locked in an uneasy peace with economic recession and diverted purpose. All the money seems to be in the Indian casinos—literally and figuratively. Besides Will Wright, the area's other exports to Hollywood include Hillary Swank, who grew up in Bellingham, Jim Cavaziel from nearby Mt. Vernon, and Ryan Stiles from Richmond—actors who seem suspiciously Canadian but are not. Blaine is another twenty miles beyond, a picturesque bayside fishing village full of American sons with too much time on their hands, and the town's sole remaining function seems to be so that the rich people across the bay in Semiahmoo have someplace to drive into. Semiahmoo is Blaine's Beverly Hills, boasting waterfront mansions, gated access, and a championship golf course designed by Arnold Palmer for a passel of semiconductor barons, much of the Vancouver Canuck hockey team, and rich Canadians gliding by on dual residency to avoid the 55 percent national tax rate north of the border. This is where Blaine's middle class feels like they should be living, but can't afford it.

My first stop was the *Northern Light*, Blaine's weekly newspaper, to see what my brothers in ink could tell me. I found editor Pat Grubb in modest offices down at the marina. He remembered Will Wright, and knew the family well. "I could never really figure out whether or not the parents knew all about it, or they simply chose to protect their kid all along," says Grubb. "Later on you hear about things where he showed people that he had a gun—*at school*—and he never got turned in. So there was something about him that was charismatic, but he was a bully as well."

That led me to Blaine High School, "Home of the Borderites," where the principal had been the center of controversy as recently as 2005 when he allegedly tipped off a nearby Point Roberts school board member that her sixteen-year-old daughter was going to be arrested the next day for smuggling twenty-five pounds of marijuana across the border on the school bus, at the behest of her live-in boyfriend. The letters to the editor in the *Northern Light* afterward were evenly divided between students, who came to the principal's defense (175 of them signed a statement of support) and their parents, who called for the principal's head on a buffet platter. But it seemed like even this isolated instance might snake all the way back to Will's arrest a decade before, when the principal had to defend himself against charges that he let known drug smuggling continue for years on end while authorities methodically built their case. At the high school, it became clear to me that the administrators weren't big fans of people who showed up unannounced on school property and started asking a lot of pointed questions. After some initial confusion, I was granted an interview by "school officials," which means there were more than one of them, and they didn't want to be identified, citing the constraints of small-town living and the fact that the Wrights had both taught there. Cumulatively, my reluctant hosts remained polite but guarded, no doubt a little shell-shocked still from the blowback of consecutive scandals, but seemed intrigued by my questions. They told me that Will was a decent student but not valedictorian, a decent point guard but never led the state in rushing yards, had not been drafted by the Seattle Mariners, and was not a loner, quiet kid—all parts of his Hollywood bio. "Not at all," said school officials in response to the latter. "If anything, he was loud and obnoxious."

They steered me to Jack Kintner, a sports reporter who also wrote the *Northern Lights* article on Bill Wright's arrest. Kintner agreed to meet me for lunch at a deli on the town's main drag, between two of the town's five stoplights. Jack turned out to be a grizzled U.C. Berkeley veteran with a marked philosophical bent—Lou Grant by way of Walt Whitman—and he structured his local history in long, sweeping arcs, like salmon cresting downstream rapids.

Jack described Blaine as a fishing village built in 1850, augmented over the next fifty years by loggers drawn to the four-hundred-foot coastal redwoods and Douglas firs and miners chasing the British Columbia gold rush. In the twenties, it was a major jumping-off point for whiskey smuggling and rumrunning for the duration of Prohibition, an impulse that may still be loose in its collective blood. He compared the gully that ran through the center of town in his youth to the one in Ray Bradbury's *Dandelion Wine*, obliterated by the Interstate and its promise of accidental riches that would somehow fall off the passing traffic. The "blue period" that sustained Blaine from the fifties on—porno theaters, massage parlors, adult book stores—came to an end in 2003, which led directly to the current high-end real estate bubble, designed for the hordes of Canadians and Californians just waiting to be lured here.

Soon, we were joined by friends of Jack's who had expressed an interest in the subject matter—Vicki Mallahan, a feisty real estate agent and former high school teacher probably in her early forties who specializes in the lucrative foreclosure market up here (and who works next door to Bill Wright, who nominally dabbles in real estate now), and Ross Patersen, who looks to be about Will's age, owns an assisted living facility, flips houses on occasion, and drives a Ferrari. Vicki remembers Will as "very charismatic" and "very good-looking," with a lot of friends. "In my opinion, from being a mom, I would say [he was] the golden child," she says. Ross calls him "a professional BS-er."

I laid out the biography that Will had cultivated, summed up in this paragraph from his promotional material: "Will is Frank Abagnale [*Catch Me If You Can*], Tony Montana [*Scarface*] and Joe Montana [San Francisco 49ers] rolled into one."

"You have to understand that, when this happened, it was pre-9/11," says Ross. "We're a border town, and BC/Vancouver marijuana is the best in the world. And you've got a lot of people growing it, bringing it across the border, and selling it. So pre-9/11, you could walk across the border with it and down the street. It was quick, easy money, but Will was not a drug lord. He wasn't anything like what he was talking about.

"I can tell you also that if he was involved in any kind of thing he was talking about, the HA's were involved—the Hell's Angels. I'm connected with Homeland Security, on both sides. Anything that's happening in BC is associated with the Hell's Angels. The richest chapter is in BC. You won't see them in their jackets unless they're at a funeral or function. They are driving around in their BMWs and Mercedes and hanging out at the fancy restaurants. And they get a cut of everything; they are involved in any kind of trafficking across the border. They are almost trading cocaine and marijuana at the same price. And Will was not involved with them. We're talking about a little side business kind of thing. And we're talking about why they, the Feds, don't care. He didn't have enough to warrant any kind of bigger investigation."

Jack did call Will the best pulling guard who ever came out of Blaine, although probably not college material because of his size, as well as a pretty good pitcher and outfielder—given that at that level, half the team pitches. I got the impression that it was the empirical nature of sports that appealed to Jack, in part because it easily belies the conjurers who pass through it. "Sports is an interesting key to a lot of this, because it ends up being very neutral," he says. "This is what happened and there's records to prove it, so there's a no-bullshit factor. You understand what I'm saying? . . . Sometimes kids build castles in the air—it's all just window dressing to get you to do what they want you to do. He said he was a National Merit Scholar. Well, I was, and he wasn't."

To Will's claim regarding his sophomore class trip to Mexico, that he once traveled abroad on a high school field trip only to secure a distribution deal with an international drug czar, Vicki notes, "That would be difficult in tenth grade," and Ross adds, "You're watched pretty closely." When I asked whether Will would fly on his private jet to one of his five mansions for the weekend, there was laughter all around. (To Will's frequent claim that he was heir to the StarKist Tuna fortune, Pat Grubb had noted that there is a Star King Seafood just down the road, owned by Rev. Sun Myung Moon.)

But all of them were of the opinion that Will was a sociopath. Jack says, "Sociopath is a better word to use than delusional. I don't think he's delusional at all. I think he knows exactly what he's doing. I was a psychiatric social worker for six years when I first got out of grad school, and I used to diagnose people like this. He belongs in a textbook. And when things get ugly with Will, they can get ugly real fast, because he's strong and aggressive."

Asked whether they were surprised by how Will turned out, Vicki says,

"I'm surprised that he has gotten so much credibility with those celebrities that you think are supposed to be so smart."

But what they were really interested in talking about was Bill Wright. I came here for the Will Wright story, but here in Blaine, it was the Bill Wright story—Will was just a small part of it. Like Will, Bill Wright is very charismatic. He drives a twelve-cylinder 600SL Mercedes on a retired schoolteacher's salary, with only minimal sales in his new real estate career, according to Vicki and Ross. In more recent years, local residents report hearing stories of how Will had his friends Leo DiCaprio and Toby Maguire attend his sister's college graduation from Pepperdine University in Malibu (unconfirmed, and considered unlikely by sources who know them both), or how Bill and Will traveled on a private jet to Las Vegas with Paris Hilton to watch the Super Bowl (a story that shows up in the Darnell canon as well). Bill routinely explained his son's freewheeling Hollywood lifestyle by claiming he was a high-stakes poker player.

"There's a rumor that a lot of the stuff that Will has gotten has wound up in Bellingham," says Jack. "There are 'warehouses' there. Paris Hilton's watch is supposed to be in Blaine. So the local visitor bureau wants to put up a sign that says, 'Come see Paris Hilton's Watch.' Every little small town has something to brag about."

And then there's Bob Bailey.

Bailey is the chairman and CEO of PMC-Sierra, a billion-dollar semiconductor company currently based in Burnaby, British Columbia, with design centers in Northern California, Israel, India, and China. He was named one of the top ten CEOs of 2000 by *Investor's Daily*. Vicki and Ross, who are steeped in such details, elaborately describe his 14,000-square-foot mansion on a gated sixty-acre estate, one of the plums of Semiahmoo's privileged redoubt. According to their assembled reconnaissance, Bailey and his wife, Lisa, and Bill and Kathy Wright have become inseparable: the couples travel together frequently, with Bailey picking up the tab, or spend time on his sixty-five-foot yacht. He is allegedly the prime benefactor of the numerous golf tournaments Bill Wright hosts.

All were quick to point out that both Wrights had been exemplary teachers and were widely missed when they retired. "If you had a problem, they would bend over backwards to help you," says Vicki. "A heart of gold and then some. That being said, I also believe wholeheartedly: if you cross Bill, then you'll be sorry."

We took a drive over to Semiahmoo to see how the other half lives. Vicki accessed the gated community with her real estate agent's code and drove me past the Bailey place and the Semiahmoo Resort, built on the site of what was once the world's largest salmon cannery, where Barbara Walters hosted her daughter's wedding. On our drive, Vicki mentioned that a lawyer had been calling her from L.A. looking for investment opportunities.

"It wouldn't be Ron Richards, would it?" I ask.

"Why yes," she says, startled. Will's lawyer reportedly called her every two weeks looking for waterfront foreclosure properties he could pick up. According to Vicki, he was looking to spend between $2 and $3 million, and had the cash ready to go. Once I returned to Los Angeles, Vicki checked in with me regularly. She reported that she placed a courtesy call to Richards and sent a one-line e-mail saying she might have found him something; two hours later, she got a call from Bill Wright, whom she hadn't spoken to in six months, saying his son had money to invest. They settled on a $1.3 million property in a gated community that was coming up at auction.

"Ross and I have a corporation for buying foreclosures," Vicki explains. "Bill put me together with Ron. Our deal was that I'd put the deal together and get the finder's [fee]. I'd be the one bidding at the auction. Then Bill would list it on the MLS [Multiple Listing Services, the standard real estate agent's Web site] when it came time to flip the property, and he would get a percentage negotiated between him, Will, and Ron—usually two to three percent . . . [Ron] may have wanted to run it through our corporation, but I'm guessing he'd want his name on it. He has implied over and over again that he has unlimited funds."

I dutifully reported this all to Koman, my LAPD connection, who told me he would forward everything I told him directly to the FBI. Then one day the line went cold. Vicki wouldn't return my calls or e-mails. Blaine was on lockdown. I eventually learned that a month after I spoke to them, Ross and Vicki had been charged with securities fraud. Ross's company CANUSA Capital, with Vicki as his principal salesperson, was charged with not being registered to conduct the sale of securities in the state of Washington. They allegedly raised money from multiple investors in Canada, in one instance $200,000, to purchase foreclosure properties (with a return of between 40 and 80 percent) and businesses (with a return of 18 percent per quarter) without doing either. The investments were to be secured by Heritage House, Ross's assisted living facility in nearby Ferndale, which he neglected to mention was itself under investigation for the offer and sale of unregistered securities, and had recently entered Chapter 11 bankruptcy. According to the summary order to cease and desist, after returning $150,000, Ross told his largest investor the remaining $50,000 would not be available because "the money was lost in a 'get-rich-quick scheme' involving an investment in bull semen." Ross and Vicki were fined $15,000 and $5,000, respectively.

After I got back, I rang up Lee Bouma, the fisherman whose letter to the judge at Will's sentencing first confirmed that Will's activities were widely known. Nothing he had seen in a decade of watching the Wright family seems to have changed his mind. As a commercial fisherman for forty years who now has to make ends meet driving the local school bus, he told me how he felt about Bill Wright's crabbing. "Basically people were watching him, wondering when he'd get caught," he says. "And they still are watching him, trying to live life like a millionaire, traveling all over the place." On Will, he says, "He was a good kid, a talented kid, and a good athlete. He was misdirected, and it bothered a lot of people that the Feds [didn't intervene] while he was still a kid. Maybe he wouldn't have turned the way he did—instead of going to prison and learning how not to get caught next time. I saw Willy maybe three years ago over Christmas. He was Willy Wright with the big story, talking about how much money there was to be had in Hollywood."

Here's Darnell on Will:

"I felt sorry for Will. He had so much potential. He had lost some good years, like I did, so I felt for the guy, and he was bringing something to the table, so I took him in to get paid. I knew Will was acting out all the dreams he'd had all the years he was locked down . . . [But] if you read the psychological profile that was on that Web site, you would've seen what the doctor said about his obsessive-compulsive disorder. His need to lie to fit in with friends."

7

BACK IN THE WORLD

Darnell walked out of prison in February 1999 at the age of twenty-two, having spent the past six years in juvenile detention—children's prison—effectively grounded by the state. He had some money left on his books and some TWA stock from his time in Youth Authority, he says, as well as the promise of hundreds of thousands of dollars on the outside owed him in hush money. Of course, Alex Vaysfeld and other would-be confidants remember times when he seemed willing to do almost anything for ready cash, and Shelly thought the bulk of his resources were on loan—an elaborate uniform provided him by the people whose company he kept and whose business he handled. But it's Darnell's story, so let's let him tell it. Even more important, at least as far as controlling his own narrative goes, was the reputation that now effortlessly preceded him. "When you've taken the rap for a major gangster and never said a word, you've got a lot of currency in respect waiting for you," says Darnell in one of his many reflective moments, the kind that starts from the movie poster and works backward. And when you've capped two civilians in a misbegotten firefight and been to the Big House to prove it, the details of which only become more enflamed the less they're talked about in open daylight, then people tend to get out of your way.

Staying in a halfway house in downtown Los Angeles as a condition of his parole, Darnell looked up Rick Salomon at the gym where he'd left him. They had stayed in touch throughout the long season of Darnell's stunted adolescence—Rick's effusive details of night-crawling and his celebrated conquests providing fodder for Darnell's fevered teenage dreams, not to mention a mental architecture for the world he would find waiting for him on the outside.

"Rick kept in contact," claims Darnell. "Money, photos. I'd call periodically. He'd keep me abreast of all the crazy parties. I'd go back to my room and make a fee-fee and have my own party." (A fee-fee, or fee-fee bag, is a sock or rolled-up towel fashioned with duct tape and filled with petroleum jelly, used as what in any other context might be referred to as a marital aid. This is the kind of thing you learn in my line of work.) Hooking up with Rick, looking to make up for lost time, Darnell hit the ground running, racking up a six-month party in the process. Although he avoided drugs and alcohol, he was not immune to other temptations of the nightlife, burned into the retina of his mind's eye by all those long-distance phone calls and exotic tales from the life he should have been living. (Through his attorney, Rick claims that he "has never had any affiliation with Mr. Riley.")

The son of a Warner Bros. film finance executive, and the uncle of actress LeeLee Sobieski, Rick had a privileged upbringing in Wayside, New Jersey, and a grandfathered access to Hollywood's second-generation film colony. His friends Leonardo DiCaprio and Tobey Maguire—kid actors at best when Darnell went into prison—were now, thanks to *Titanic* and *The Ice Storm*, full-fledged movie stars, and the undisputed lords of the Hollywood club scene, a fledgling subculture that just then seemed to have coalesced out of no better inspiration than to try and catch a fleeting glimpse of the pair of them, out in their element. Soon enough, the imperious façades and art-directed interiors of clubland would spread east from the Sunset Strip, jump the firebreak from Crescent Heights to LaBrea, and continue across Hollywood Boulevard to Vine and south down La Cienega like a walled city or a giant jewel-encrusted cross: serving the rich, cultivating the famous, and ultimately settling on the pretenders to both.

But along with the clubs—moral gymnasiums where working Hollywood could go and play—there was a whole subterranean support system to keep its denizens happy and distracted: gambling, recreational drugs, the endless waves of women, the prizefights on the weekend (with their own inherent criminal element), sudden available money, and the brokers and facilitators who made sure that each of these worlds fit into all the others, smoothly and without friction. If Hollywood, the entertainment-industrial complex, is a firmament—more stars than there are in heaven, as MGM used to brag—then this mirror world existed underneath it, matching it at every point, but obscured from our gaze by a shield of lawyers and shell corporations and cash transactions.

We know it exists all around us, because we see the fallout constantly: measurable excess, too much too soon, its marquee casualties the actors whose last close-up is on the tiled bathroom floor of their bungalow or dead outside the Viper Room, or the starlets who depart the lives assigned them in flights of manic glory. And yet, despite more reporters working this beat than any other, possibly ever; despite more man-hours poured into chronicling the marginalia and unguarded moments of celebrities, all of them deer in headlights, as if unguarded moments were even possible anymore with a dozen paparazzi assigned to Britney Spears and her every casual gesture; despite the attention paid to its outward face, we never see the inner workings of that other world. The one that allows celebrities a measure of escape in their so-called natural habitat. This island paradise is routinely depicted in all its tropical glory, bathed in ravishing colors and preternatural light, and yet no one ever sees the nine-tenths below the ocean's surface.

This was the world Darnell walked into with nothing but his revved-up ambitions and a dream deferred. His six years in the animal factory of the California penal authority, junior division, had made him a practiced observer of closed systems and a necessary judge of character. And he quickly set about making himself indispensable.

Darnell first made his bones about a week in, at a typical after-hours party at the Argyle on Sunset. "When I was still in the halfway house," he says, "I would sign out for work and hook up with Rick. This was before I got my apartment. Probably at the end of the first week of hanging tight every day, crazy debauchery, meeting random Playboy models, trust-fund brats, and wannabe tough guys, we were at the Argyle Hotel [now the Sunset Towers], the old Art Nouveau–style hotel on Sunset. [I think it's Art Deco, but no matter.] It was an after-party, about three in the morning. Rick had a couple of players that gambled with him, and one prick who owed another buddy some of his cash from bets he lost. The guy had the cash, and he knew these characters were just puffing up their chests, acting out the parts of the gangsters they wanted to be. No one stepped to the guy. I had no obligation to do anything, but it was the principle that got me involved. They had a poker game going. The wannabe was a character that goes by Mikey. He positions himself as Mob royalty of some kind. Whatever. But he owed Justin Murdock [heir to the Dole fortune]. Rick was talking to Mikey, trying to set up a payment, but the guy had been owing him for months and was smearing all of their faces in his shit. He puffed his chest up one too many times, and without an introduction, I asked Mikey to come walk with me into the bedroom area of the suite. I put it on the line and asked him how much money he had on him. He owed Justin about fifteen thousand. He had at least $5K on him, and I told him, as a goodwill gesture, to just give Justin something so he could see he wasn't getting fucked. With Justin, it ain't about the money, he got that; it's the way this creep was fucking him around.

"He positioned himself to snake a punch in, and I unleashed a quick combo on him, went into his pockets and got the cash and gave it to Justin, and then tossed the guy out. As you can imagine, the room was in Tupac-movie mode now, talking all the hype about how they were going to do this to him, and how they would call their boys to get with the guy. Of course, the guy owed almost everyone in the room, so all this posturing was for dramatic effect. Justin tried to give me some cash, but I refused. I didn't have a hundred dollars to my name; I could barely rub two Lincolns together. Rick was paying for everything [clothes, food, hotel]. I hadn't been taken care of by Ocean or Bolo yet, so the cash would've helped. But I didn't take anything from Justin, just so he knew that I wasn't some hired hand. This was one friend helping another. I guess the best explanation for the way I viewed my take-charge approach with Justin's bully and Hollywood as a whole was that if I stirred up their status quo just enough and stayed under the radar, then I could eventually get to the point where I was comfortable enough cash-wise to do my own [legit] projects. Which is a point I was at several times throughout my six-year run at Hollywood. I guess that's why I'm not concerned with who accepts me back, or under what terms. Criminal worlds, or just the Hollywood world (legit characters or just the fly-by-night types), when you go with your own agenda or plan, all the bull don't matter."

Whether he knew it or not, this was the life Darnell had been trained for. A whole stratum of society with nothing but money and self-regard, who fancied themselves the heroes of the hip-hop operas they jacked into every morning, steering their Escalades and Porsches to the Beverly Hills boîtes and breakfast nooks where they gathered in self-possessed herds, buffing up their imagined exploits from the night before to recite to each

other with studied nonchalance. Awwww shit. Yeah, boyeeeee. And striding into their midst—quiet, contained, even deferential—was a real criminal, one with an outsize sense of purpose, who eventually fancied himself
their incidental conscience, sent here to introduce the wholly foreign notion of consequence into their sheltered lives, much as Cortez introduced
forged steel and horses to the Aztecs.

Through doing gambling collections, he had the use of a Porsche and a
Ferrari 575M Maranello until it was stolen in 2001 (he briefly dated the
female cop assigned to investigate the incident). He was good with his fists.
He was a tireless worker, a good study with a mind for details. He had a
first-hand familiarity with what he still refers to as "the real-life *Sopranos*"
back in New York. And he was fearless.

Another old friend from the boxing gyms whom Darnell looked up was
Mickey Rourke, who had the incidental virtue of being a gateway to fashion models. Mickey was one of the first people to whom Darnell showed
the Joe Francis tape, at his bungalow near the Chateau Marmont where
Mickey lived alone with his dogs, and *The Pope of the Sunset Strip* contains
a long set piece from December 2004 where Mickey and Darnell meet two
girls at Club Prey (now Area) on La Cienega and take them to a hotel in
West Hollywood. ("Mick stops in mid-sentence and turns to the Asian
chick, and without missing a beat, he says, 'So you wanna fuck or something?' The girls' eyes light up like candles and lock themselves on Mick's.
All three of their heads nod affirmatively in unison. Mick replies, 'You
gonna fuck Darnell, too?' Again the bobblehead dolls nod in agreement,
without them ever looking over to see who Darnell was.")

Mickey wouldn't talk, but I did talk to a friend of his, a guy who goes
by the name of One-Eyed Ray. Ray has what he calls "a lot of history"—
he grew up in the old neighborhoods in Brooklyn where his father was a
bodyguard to Anthony Scotto of Murder, Incorporated, and his best friends
were Crazy Joe Gallo, actor Ray Sharkey, and John Gotti's future bodyguard. One of my only rules going into this project was that it's not a Mafia
book, meaning that when illicit activity washes up on the shores of Mafia
enterprise, I wouldn't try to follow it any further. There's a big book waiting to be written about the history of the Mob in Hollywood (Gus Russo's
Supermob is a good place to start), but this isn't it. So when I talk to guys
like One-Eyed Ray, I try not to crowd them. But Mickey still garnered respect in certain circles for attending the Gotti trial, and Darnell claims
Mickey first brought him to Ray's attention by saying, "I wouldn't want

him after me." So I found Ray and asked him his impression of Darnell, personally and professionally.

"He was a standup guy," says Ray. "A pretty tough guy. He will do whatever the fuck he has to do. He's a pretty crazy motherfucker. He don't back up. Whatever he's got on his mind, he'll do. He's a gangster—you never know what move he's going to pull. We're from the same school. He's not going to do anything to me. Anyone else, I don't think he gives a fuck. You got to be careful with him."

Darnell tells of attending the Oscar De La Hoya-Fernando Vargas fight in Las Vegas in September 2002, and Rick trying to get Ray to come by his hotel suite to meet Leonardo DiCaprio. "I was invited; I never went," says Ray of the entreaties from Hollywood's fast pack. "They wanted me to go up to [Tobey] Maguire's for a goof. He had a poker game up there. But I never went."

Darnell began to do collections for people—chasing down nightclub scofflaws who had run out on their tab, or making withdrawals from often reluctant individuals and depositing them with other, often grateful individuals, then harvesting a transport fee. Alex Vaysfeld, the Russian bail bondsman, calls him one of the best bounty hunter's he's ever seen. And actor Joe Campana, an acquaintance from the club scene, states unequivocally, "There was one thing Darnell was known for in Hollywood: collecting debts."

"I was never a skip tracer for Alex," says Darnell, somewhat defensively. "I've put in work for Alex and his boys on a lot of things, and a lot of it required me to track characters down. I'm resourceful, like with deadbeats running out on gambling debts, so I gotta get mine and I'm on the prowl. But the bonds that I tracked for Alex were connected to his Russian boys back home and it crossed Alex's desk. For example, his boys brought over a dentist who was legit in Russia, but once he got here he needed to be recertified and take courses to be able to practice in the U.S. They brought him over, got him legal, set him up in a practice, and he worked for them. It was all an insurance thing for them. So they'd send 'clients' through and rack up fake charges. They did the same with chiropractors, and everyone played ball—except the dentist. He got big-headed. He had a nice condo in Brentwood. He and his wife had nice sports cars, and he decided he wanted to go out on his own. Fuck the boys. So I got a call."

He also was summoned to Russia by Alex's contacts there who asked

him to track down the owner of an eBay-style auction site to collect a sub-
stantial debt.

"When I returned to L.A., the guy had cut town," says Darnell. "He
heard that I was summoned to Russia, and he knew what that meant.
Granted, I'm not Russian. I'm not Italian, but I've done right by all, and I
produce results. I found the guy holed up in Vail. He was with his new girl.
I believe he's married to her now. She is a former Playmate. But he knew
what time it was. I got my ways."

Darnell describes his skill set as follows: "I was the man that the heavy
hitters would call in to clean up a messy situation. In the vernacular of
Hollywood, I'm what some call an expediter or fixer. I was a bachelor of
the blacker arts: bribery, blackmail, beat-downs, criminal threats, terrorist
threats, extortion, mutilation, and good old-fashioned frame-ups."

He tells a long story bubbling out of the Garden of Eden, the sprawling
nightclub at the southeast corner of Hollywood and La Brea, where he got
a call from Timmy Iannello, who worked there. "P. Diddy" "Puffy" Combs
had skated on a hefty tab—well past the one-table, two-bottle limit most
clubs agree to comp the name celebrity in exchange for license to plant a
flattering quote in the right columns. The next morning, Darnell put out an
"all points bulletin" and received word from the concierge at the Four Seasons that Combs and mini-entourage were headed to lunch at the Ivy. Parking up the street ("never at valet—this is in case I need to make a quick
getaway"), he alerted management as a professional courtesy and approached the table:

"He had two dudes with him and two hot chicks. One of these dudes
had to be the bodyguard. Well, now I know who to punch first if shit goes
bad. I didn't pay too much attention to the chicks. I figured I'm about to
put this prick on the spot, so talking to his girls would be a serious 'fuck
you, punk.' I might as well just bend him over and wax him right on Rob-
ertson Boulevard for all the world to see in this week's *Enquirer*.

"P. Diddy recognized my face, but stumbled with my name. He was
holding his hands out like he was the king holding court on his throne,
overlooking all the peasants. So I knew how to fuck with his vibe. Don't
give a fuck. I leaned in close like I was going to be discreet and purposely
spoke loud enough for others to hear. I let Sean know that he left the Garden of Eden without covering his tab. To save face, he acted like he didn't
know. 'Oh, okay. I'll send my boy over to take care of that tomorrow,' he
said. Yeah, right.

"I let P. Diddy know that we could just straighten out the unpaid debt by having my people at the Ivy run his card and send the cash over to us at the Garden of Eden. Diddy's mouth was stuck in the awe position. Not wanting to be put on the spot any further, he tried to blow off the incident as no big deal, a simple mistake. The kicker was that I informed him he forgot to tip the waitress and we had to add a ten percent gratuity to the bill. At this point, Puffy wanted to be spared any further embarrassment, and he sheepishly coughed up the card."

And yet, Darnell insists most of his strong-arm work was done as favors to friends or in situations where he retained equity, as in the case of gambling debts, where he had a stake in the outcome. By his own accounting, Darnell was involved in a lot of day-to-day enterprises: sportsbook betting, drug running and conflict resolution with drug entities, securing investments in nightclubs, trafficking in illicit artifacts, working the day job at the bank, working in his off-hours as a boxing trainer and manager, donating his time to charitable causes, trying to carve out a film career, living the high life, collecting the residual spoils of his chosen professions (often profligate beauties with a taste for danger), and generally managing the meticulous demands of life as a working criminal. Yet one of the few things that seems to ruffle him—that gets his Irish up, even if his surname was purchased dockside in the port of London—is this stealth image of him, carefully cultivated to preserve his anonymity, as a figure perpetually in the background, an extra in his own story, a necessary fiction now elevated to biography. For the life he says he's lived, the hardest part seems to have been that he couldn't tell anybody about it.

"No one person can verify everything in my life," says Darnell. "No one person can verify a quarter of the shit in my life. I made it into an art form to keep my respective lives compartmentalized, to maintain distance between the worlds I traveled into and out of. It was necessary. My life and all the people in it were separate by design. I needed it that way for my comfort. As an adult, I rubbed elbows with the Gettys at the Malibu museum, had season tickets to the Geffen Theater, and donated to charities. I moved with a free pass in all circles. People viewed me as a businessman. Yeah, I've busted up some heads, but I was always the unknown guy. I did no advertising; those that fucked up expected something.

"I once had a job that put me in a familiar situation. Picture this: guy tied up, before he has been told what this is all about, he squints and asks, 'Hey, are you an actor?' My answer, like always: 'Naw, but I'm here on behalf of one. You've got some things she needs back.'

"I remember coming out of a club with Mickey Rourke when [E.L.] Woody, the chain-smoking paparazzi camera guy, slides up to Mickey [Rourke] wanting some photos. Mickey, being the accommodating type, busts a couple of headshot poses and hugs me into the frame, telling Woody and the other lightbulb holders that I was his roommate in prison. This got a laugh out of the paparazzi, who started asking my name and what I do. Woody says, 'I know this guy, he's with Paris a lot.' As he snaps more photos, I wiggled my way out of the bullshit and let Mickey have his moment alone. That wasn't my forum. I have a knack for productions that don't include interviews and red carpets."

How much and whether those braids of narrative connect to the tapestry of consensus reality is the subject of this book—as well as Darnell's résumé, his jacket, his CV and legacy, and quite possibly his art form. Balancing it all—while I was mucking through the refuse of conspicuous consumption and door-knocking ingrates and sponging up the color coming off my dubious sources in buckets—is the fact that crimes were committed. People suffered. "Ma'fuckas" got served. Police were alerted and investigations are underfoot. Work backward, and the two would hopefully meet somewhere in the middle.

For his part, Darnell didn't ask me to take it on faith that he was a Hollywood insider. He says he had photos—hundreds of them: of Paris, in white cotton panties and wife beater, calling down for room service at the Beverly Wilshire Hotel, "*Pretty Woman*–style"; with Corey Haim; on the road with *The Simple Life*; of "Paris before she was Paris." Photos of Fergie of the Black-Eyed Peas, Naomi Campbell in the clubs, Tara Reid "before Paris turned on Tara," Playmates Nicole Lenz with Bijou Phillips and Casey Johnson or Summer Altice with Mickey Rourke. Travel photos from Japan, Germany, Russia, Hawaii (of Shannen Doherty, Rick's ex); with Will at the start of the Bull Run Rally overland road race in Las Vegas, where Paris was the flag girl, and with "the porn chicks that we flew to Miami when the race ended"; or at Joe Francis's 2003 Halloween party—three months before they supposedly met, which he calls "exculpatory evidence."

"The photos will speak volumes," says Darnell.

Unfortunately, they are still in police custody: Item #66 on the Property Report shows ninety-seven miscellaneous photos that were never returned (police initially speculated they came from the Paris and Nicky Hilton burglary), and Items #40–48 are eight Sony Magicgate (and one Lexar) memory sticks that were either returned empty or else transferred to CD, with many of the images deleted, according to their putative owner.

"Koman says, 'Why do you have so many photos of [Paris]?' " says Darnell. "Well, you only took the photos of her when you raided my house. There are a million other photos of models and whoever else that you didn't take. You only took what you wanted to build your case." Unfortunately—again—Darnell claims the "hundreds of photos of models, actresses, and trust-fund kids that they didn't take" are, he says, in the possession of his ex-girlfriend.

I went to see Alex Vaysfeld, the Russian bail bondsman, again at his Spartan offices off Santa Monica Boulevard in the heart of West Hollywood's Russian expatriate neighborhood, centering on Santa Monica and Fairfax. The extremely minimalist décor of the Union Bail Bonds walk-in storefront had been recently augmented with a shattered front window and a single bullet hole right above where Alex, a local fixture, sat with his back always to the wall. Alex is maybe five feet five tops, muscular and mean-looking, a junkyard dog without the safety chain, and the cross-stitched scarring on his knuckles makes it look like maybe he once got Love and Hate tattooed on some shore leave bender, and then Xed them out the next morning with a pocket knife. This time, I came bearing gifts—Russian sugar cookies from the Stolichnaya Bakery three blocks away. When he buzzed me in, Alex was still on the phone.

"If they bring in the twenty grand . . . If they bring in the money to me, I'm shooting straight. Remember who we're dealing with—they're fucking gypsies. They were calling me until two in the morning, asking me what I guaranteed. I don't guarantee shit . . . Maybe she murdered somebody in the process . . ."

He hangs up and says, "I have to deal with this fucking shit. It's not about the money. There was a gunfight here last night." He points at the bullet hole in the wall above his head. I offer him the cookies.

"What's this?" he asks, clearly still pissed off about something.

"You won't let me take you to Dan Tana's for a steak, so I bought you something from the old country," I tell him.

"What is it that you're trying to do?" he asks me.

"I'm trying to write this fucking book, Alex," I say.

"One thing that I didn't like, is that you put out . . . I told you not to put it out there, but you did. That fucking twelve-year-old shit."

"I didn't put that into my story, just like you told me not to," I say. True enough, technically.

"It's all over the Internet, and I did that fucking interview with you," says Alex. "We can talk about anything else, but that shit is a direct implication of child pornography. And, if you know the law . . . Look: I'll go to bat for Darnell; Darnell is my boy. But my problem is, I don't want to be fucking mixed up and have fucking detectives calling me. Fucking Feds calling me. Those fuckers are calling me and asking me to get into details and how it happened and all that shit."

"I said you were an investor in Night Flight—"

"I'm a *silent* investor in Night Flight," he says. "And the investigators will come right after me so don't put that out there. I manage fighters. I've got future champions. I own five businesses. My guy is fighting on the card with Mayweather . . . It doesn't matter. It doesn't matter."

I point out that it's already out there, and ask him if I can at least use it in the book. "Look—I've got to talk to Darnell," says Alex. "I'm not sure if it's the best thing for him. But I can tell you right now, there were like seven girls there. They had Viagra and there was all kinds of fucking. And they had a camera with them. But I'm not sure I want to talk about that. He could have gotten arrested, and that would have been the end of it. The end of him."

I ask him his impression of Will Wright.

"My first impression was, I wanted to slap him around," says Alex. "He was just a fucking wannabe. I mean, without Darnell, he'd be fucking *nothing*."

He confirms that Darnell was in Moscow at the same time as Joe Francis. "Here's the thing," he says. "I'm a known guy there. At the government level. Not just street thugs. In fact, I don't know any street thugs these days. People know me, and they want to get with me. And Darnell could go into a foreign country and get things done. No language skills—nothing. He could go pick up a Russian girl with no language in common at all, and go and spend the night with her. I was like, 'How the fuck did you do that?'

"You can call him a criminal, a con, or you can call him fucking Robin Hood. It doesn't fucking matter. He was doing something that he thought was right, and making money. And now he's doing his time. People are asking me every day how Darnell is. Pauly Shore, everyone. And the one thing they are asking me is, 'Hey, when is he getting out?' I tell them, 'Look—he's well off, he's got money. You're not going to employ his services anymore.' I know Darnell better than anybody. And if Darnell is one thing, he's not stupid. He's a very bright kid, I'm telling you right now. He'll come out, he'll go back on top and he'll be very rich one day. And very

socially acceptable. And every single motherfucker that didn't want anything to do with him will want to have him at the dinner table and hang
out. He's going to have a business waiting for him, a car. He's not going to
come out wondering who to call.

"He should stay with me. Stay with me, and then go straight to
the top."

8

FIGHT CLUB

S et adrift in a new world, one of Darnell's few familiar touchstones was the boxing gyms of his youth. After returning briefly to Broadway Gym, he followed Rick to World Boxing Gym on La Brea, where he was training with a barrel-chested former light middleweight named Jerry "the Jewish Bomber" Rosenberg, a menacing *shtarker* with some hip-hop flava and a weak spot for mutts and strays. Jerry is bathed in tattoos and still manages the occasional mohawk from his thinning, bleached blond hair; as Darnell describes him, "he loves Tupac, he rolls with Masta P and the No Limit Posse, he spars with Tyson for fun—he's a daredevil, no fear, and a straight fool." He was also the head trainer for "Cool" Vince Phillips, who at that point held the WBA welterweight title. Jerry and Darnell immediately hit it off—a mutual recognition of criminal mischief would have been likely—and Darnell signed on as a conditioning coach on the Vince Phillips team.

For the sixty-seven amateur fights he claims, Darnell never seemed to harbor much hope of a professional boxing career. He fought steadily from the age of twelve on—Blue and Gold tournaments, Police Athletic League, open tourneys from various branches of the armed services, Golden Gloves, as well as all during his time in the joint. At an adult fighting weight of 165, a middleweight or super middleweight, he would fight anybody— "I put him up against all kinds of animals; he wasn't scared to fight no one," says Jerry—and as a trainer, he claims to have sparred with Vince Phillips, "Sugar" Shane Moseley, Oscar De La Hoya, Floyd Mayweather,

Vernon Forrest, and other name fighters. At one point, he apparently harbored aspirations of making the Olympic team—or at least the U.S. National team, which functions as an Olympic farm team—but that seems to have gone down to pragmatism and the long view. From the one fight I've seen on tape, a split decision in three rounds from just before Easter 2004, I'd say he got robbed. Darnell fights like I imagine he does everything: he leads with his chin, he can take a punch, and he never backs down. But the part that impressed me the most was that he was a gracious loser. He took off two days later for Europe and never looked back.

Chris Reilly is a pro fighter and kickboxer who opened Bomb Squad Gym in 2002 at Santa Monica and Gardner in West Hollywood as a place where his old friends Rick Salomon, Jerry Rosenberg, Vince Phillips, Balthazar Getty, Scottie Caan, and Darnell (with occasional appearances by Eric Dane, Heavy D, and assorted actors and musicians) could train and connect. He currently runs Legends Gym on Santa Monica Boulevard and primarily trains MMA (mixed-martial-arts) fighters. He saw three of Darnell's Golden Gloves matches.

"Darnell is the kind of guy that in my opinion could have been or done anything he set his mind to," says Reilly (no relation—his joke, not mine). "Darnell was, just as you've heard, articulate, likable, I think innately intelligent. But was he going to become a world-class boxer? No.

"It's a fascinating story, there's no doubt about that, especially because Darnell is such a fascinating individual. He in so many ways belies the stereotypes that people think of, that people of his background have who have come through some of the stuff that he's come through. That makes it fascinating. [But] there's always a Darnell around, you know? It just very rarely becomes national news."

Reilly remembers Darnell as a tireless trainer around the gym, knowledgeable, always working with young amateurs, a sentiment echoed by others. Cliff Canter, a former record executive and now a professional poker player, remembers Darnell from Bomb Squad and Tru, the gym that Jerry opened in 2003 on La Brea and later Highland. "He was the most charming, personable, nicest young man," says Canter. "Always helping boxers out. Came across well spoken. Knew his way around the ring. I heard he had sociopathic tendencies, so I kept our relationship confined to the gym. But anybody that met him was just drawn in. He was just the nicest guy." But he does volunteer his impressions of Will Wright. "I don't know much about him, but everything I've heard was that he is evil and to be avoided like the plague," he says.

Outside of Vince Phillips, Rick was the only one of the Bomb Squad crew trying to fight professionally. Darnell claims that in cahoots with Jerry Rosenberg, they planned to pay deadbeat fighters two grand apiece to take a dive against Rick—in a kind of pump-and-dump scheme using human cargo. Darnell's plan (and without Rick's knowledge) was to get him to 15–0 so he was undefeated, then get him a real fight with a payday, even if it meant getting his ass handed to him. As a final blowout, they would stage an automobile accident and claim professional injuries for the insurance payout. "Rick wanted the recognition of being a bad-boy boxer," says Darnell. "The only thing is, Rick can't really fight. He uses banging a broad as a way to drop weight and get some cardio training. On the other hand, he's white, and boxing is always looking for the next great white hope—or hype. We would have had him on the Las Vegas odds charts, flooded the bets to move the lines in his favor if he was the underdog. We had the white guy. We were almost home free." Darnell says the plan finally fell apart when Rick couldn't make his weight limits and didn't keep up with his training.

Darnell also claims he owned a piece of Vince Phillips and later briefly managed two fighters—Javier Virgen, who was taken over by De La Hoya's Golden Boy Productions, and Desir Alexis. As an assistant trainer, he worked with Phillips during the Nick Acevedo fight at the Paris Paris in Las Vegas on March 29, 2002 (won in ten rounds), and the Sharmba Mitchell fight seven months later in Oklahoma City, November 9, 2002 (lost by decision, although "Sharmba's face and bleeding kidney told a whole 'nother story"). It was in that capacity that he met Cassius Green— "the Captain"—a legendary trainer and Muhammad Ali's cut man, who now works with Ali's daughter Laila among many others.

"I was meeting up with Vince Phillips as he was getting ready for a fight with Sharmba Mitchell," recalls Darnell. "I had just quarterbacked a shipment that touched down in New York. I took care of everything and made the appropriate transfers, then I caught a flight to Las Vegas where Vince was training for the fight. He moved the camp to Las Vegas for the last three weeks before the fight because Cassius Green had taken over as the head trainer, and he had his training camp going with 'Sugar' Shane Moseley, who [also] had a fight coming up. So I get off my flight. I had just transferred, in about twenty different ways, nearly two million in drug money, and I had about thirty thousand on me and another hundred thousand in cashier's checks. I only had carry-on bags, so I caught a taxi to the gym everyone works out at, owned by Laila Ali and her husband Johnny McClain [now ex-husband, but still her manager]. The Mayweathers [Floyd and his uncle-trainer and former fighter Roger] work out at that gym. Tyson does also.

"I had just stepped out of the taxi, and I see Cassius in his 1970s serial killer van (that has about three hundred miles on it) putting on his Murder One gloves, and he is clearly mad. He tells me as I'm paying the taxi, 'Watch my back, I gotta take care of a ma'fucka.' I told the taxi to wait for me and handed him a twenty. Cassius walked back into the gym and began to unload on this dude. Cassius is close to seventy years old. This dude was mid-to-late thirties. I can't remember his name, but he's a hustler and shyster who fucked over Cassius seven years before, and Cassius had just caught up with him for the first time. The guy deals in credit cards and merchandise, and has been shaking and dodging plenty of people. He probably forgot, or thought Cassius wasn't tripping. Everyone knows Cassius has money. He's very well off. He won't be getting his hands dirty. Bullshit. Cassius is an old-school brawler. He walks in and floors the guy. The whole gym froze. He breaks the guy's nose—saw that I got his back, so I go with him in his serial killer van and he takes off to his condo in Las Vegas. Vince Phillips takes off with us. Laila is pissed because the dude called the cops.

"I had to fly back to L.A., but I come back out to Las Vegas two days later to train with Vince, and then the last week before the fight, we fly to Oklahoma. There is a warrant out for Cassius. He later turned himself in. Vince fought on Saturday night, and Cassius was in Las Vegas for one of his other fighters fighting Friday night. So he worked it out with the cops that he would turn himself in once he returned from Vince's fight. He gets ready for his preliminary hearing months later (it's now July 2003) and I went to testify on Cassius's behalf that the guy made a move at Cassius and swung at him first. The guy didn't show up to court, so the charges were thrown out."

It was also while inside the Vince Phillips camp that Darnell says he had the brainstorm that briefly took the boxing world by storm: stenciling the names of advertisers as temporary tattoos on the backs of fighters. Darnell claims it was a joint idea between him and Rick, piggybacking off Rick's already established working relationships with the online sportsbook betting companies GoldenPalace.com and SBG.com.

"I hadn't seen anyone do the ads on the backs before 2000," says Darnell.

"I hooked it up with a couple of fights on ESPN through Rick [for] ads with Golden Palace and SBG. I did Carné Jones and Antonio Margarito first, and then we got others catching on. Bones Adams was Rick's connect, and that was a big ruckus when he had a tag on his back on ESPN in 2002. I thought it up with Rick as a way to bring in cash. A collaboration of sorts. We always had boxers wearing hats/jackets with the sites' names, so we took it a step further—just, you know, 'There's got to be more revenue.' I've got the whole fight world down pat, so I would be a fool not to take some of this. Any fighter that you need, I got. So that was my thing with Golden Palace. The back shots were fifty grand a pop. Pocket thirty, give the fighter twenty."

This reached its culmination with the Vince Phillips-Sharmba Mitchell fight in Oklahoma City in November 2002—a fight that was broadcast on Showtime. "The boxing commissioner thought Vince Phillips was going to have one and they tried to shut him down, but there was nothing in their laws or his contract that would have limited him from having advertising on him," says Darnell. "So I immediately hooked up one on Vince and we made some extra cash. SBG.com—Sports Bet Global—was the tattoo on Vince. You'll see me in his corner [on the Showtime tape] and listed as Chief Second. Look at his March 2002 fight at the Paris Paris on ESPN's *Friday Night Fights*, you'll see how I hooked up Vince's competitor [Nick Acevedo], because they threatened to withhold Vince's purse. So I still made cash off his competitor. And we won the fight."

"Anything's possible," says (Chris) Reilly. "I think he was around the Vince Phillips camp at the time that stuff was new. And Vince was one of the first guys to really do that."

Various boxing authorities trace the phenomenon to September 2001, when the agent for Bernard Hopkins, Joe Lear, approached GoldenPalace .com offering name placement on his fighter's trunks for his upcoming bout with Felix Trinidad, and the company jokingly countered with an offer for his back instead. Hopkins was paid $100,000 for the temporary tattoo (even though it completely melted off of him by the third round), which he promptly bet on himself at 3-1 odds, tripling his money when he scored an upset. Lear quickly formed a company called Big Boxing to capitalize on the phenomenon. The Nevada Athletic Commission soon issued an injunction against the henna-based human billboards, beginning with Bones Adams in his rematch against Paulie Ayala, scheduled for February 23, 2002, at Mandalay Bay in Las Vegas. They claimed the ink from the tattoos could get in a fighter's eyes, they were a potential distraction to the ref or judges, or they were simply tacky or demeaning in a sport that routinely leaves its participants in penury, working as casino greeters, or permanently brain damaged. Every reason, in fact, except the most obvious one: that some sharpie had figured out a revenue stream not already carved up in a back room somewhere. In truth, fighters' backs are practically the only free space at a big-money boxing match not adorned with some sort of corporate sponsorship—there is signage in the center of the ring, at the corners of the ring, and on the ringposts; the ring girls; placards placed below the ropes; banners in the back of the hall; and logos on the fighters' robes, trunks, and gloves. The NASCARization of professional boxing started long before the fighters tried to break off a piece. Golden Palace filed suit, and Lear was there with Bones Adams when the Nevada State Supreme Court reversed the commission's decision on free speech grounds, allowing Adams an additional $50,000 payday for wearing the Golden Palace logo in a fight that was broadcast on HBO, and which he won.

I contacted Darnell to get his read on what I'd learned. Once again, all the pieces were there, but they had been slightly rearranged since the last photo I had. But the thing that set him off was Chris Reilly's assertion that he only had three Golden Gloves fights, far from the sixty-seven amateur bouts he laid claim to. He was counting everything, not just those fights certified by some sanctioning authority. But it moved some piece of mental furniture, one that had been pushed up against a wall, and dislodged the following story, which he told rapidly, with a wounded kind of rancor. I present it more or less in its entirety:

"In your article, you reported how I had a slip and fall at Stevie Wonder's mansion before I was arrested. You had it half right. But, you ever wonder why I was even at one of Stevie Wonder's homes? Well, I'll give you the history to it. Now, had you not already known that I was suing him for an accident at his home, you would not believe my story, or the fact that I was suing. You found that out on your own. Shelly knew nothing about it. Frankie knew nothing about it. Timmy didn't, or Will. Do you see my compartmentalized work here? Okay, the backstory.

"In Panama and a couple of Caribbean islands, a lot of gamblers and underworld characters and above-board corporate guys who stash away cash that they've stolen like to hide shit in boutique banks' safe deposit boxes. These are spots that are off the radar. If any government inquired, they'd run into a dead end. Real discreet. No name on the building. You can't walk in off the street and open an account. You gotta be in that world, and it's referral only. Here is where Stevie Wonder's world and mine crossed. He has a son, Mumtaz, from a former marriage. Mumtaz gambled with me. He also has a cousin Damian who has been with Stevie since childhood.

"A collection of Patek Phillipe antique watches I had went missing from a box. They were valued at over a million dollars. I had all the papers. The watches were from the early twenties. These were investments. History and art. Shit you leave your kids when you die. I found out Damian bought them, or came into possession of them.

"So I hit Damian up about getting my shit back to me. At that time, Mumtaz owed me some cash, so all of it had me hot. My boy Jerry [Rosenberg] used to live at the house of Stevie's ex-wife (Mumtaz's mom) and he was in the middle of buying a new house, so he and my other boy Doc lived in the guest house. The actual owner of the house is still Stevie Wonder, but the ex-wife had it to do whatever she wanted with for years. She threw big parties there, and rents out two rooms to music producers visiting L.A. In the basement, she has a full recording studio and theater. So she has all of the top house empty. Old photos of Stevie and Mumtaz and his daughter Iesha, the one that inspired his song "Isn't She Lovely"—a lot of history. So I devised a plan. The creative me.

"In the guest house, the shower wiring is fucked up, and you can get a jolt if your foot touches the metal drain. So I had Doc and Jerry in on it. I did research on the home and found out that Stevie owned the house outright. He probably didn't know that the house was still in his name. So I took one for the team. I faked like we were on a training run, and when I came back I jumped into the shower and got shocked, and I fell, hitting my head in the shower, blacking me out. Of course, it didn't happen, but we called the ambulance, and once we heard the sirens, Doc got the hammer—the thick, solid wooden end. He had me brace myself and he clocked me with the handle. Fuck, it hurt! Pain. Stars. Spinning dolphins. The ambulance was close. I had a big lump on my head. We threw water on me to make it seem like I was in the shower. I put a towel over me, but was still naked. Doc told them that he pulled me out of the shower, and I was unconscious. It looked real. I got transported to the hospital. Frankie [Liles] rushed to get me, not knowing that it was all bullshit, and he never found out either. Once again, not everyone in my life knows my business. So, I got all the medical treatment—EKG hookups, CAT scans, X-rays—the works.

"The next day, I contacted a lawyer. When I was on the phone with him, he was going through the motions of a Q and A for a slip and fall case. Then I told him that I believed the owner doesn't have insurance on the house. It's a three- to four-million-dollar mansion in Los Feliz. He said, 'Do you know who owns it?' I said, 'Yeah—it's Steveland Morris, but you probably know him as Stevie Wonder.' He shot up to attention hearing Stevie's name. He was juiced. I went to therapy and played the part, and then got a call from Stevie's people. Met up with them a couple of times. Had dinner. They offered to have a limo pick me up. I declined the limo and just met them at the restaurant. At dinner I was asked what it would take to make all of this go away. I didn't answer, and ended the meeting. I didn't know if I was being taped. I later told them the price, and also that I wanted my watches back. I got my watches first, and then I was arrested on March 28, 2005, for this shit. When I was in L.A. County, we settled the rest. The main thing was that I got my watches back, and they're safe right now. The figure was nominal, just to pay off my guys. The medical bills got paid. All's fair. I'm in L.A. County.

"So do you see how if you didn't know about the accident already, how unbelievable or spectacular it would sound? But that's it right there. The shit that I did on any given day was nothing to me. It was effortless. But when you're not involved, you wouldn't understand me taking a shot to the head with a hammer. Outsiders couldn't believe it. Insiders are in awe at how far I'll go to get the job done, but it's all another day at the office for me. Crime as a profession is a concept some may not fully understand. You see the tough guys being portrayed on screen, but I see all the flaws in the crime story. I see all the real shit as well. If you think I'm embellishing about having had boxing matches as an amateur, then you should just stop your project right now. If you think I'm pulling your dick on stupid shit like that, then I'm anticipating you're going to make me out a lying prick in your book. Shit like taking a hammer to the head was nothing to me. It had to be done. The Joe Francis job was effortless, but when you look at all the obstacles, you wonder how one person could have done all that. All the reasoning into 'why' aside—it was work."

Shelly could confirm the broad outlines of the story. "I learned about this after Darnell was locked up," Shelly says. "Doc was my contractor/tenant for my rental property and he told me the story. He wanted me to pursue the claim—obviously I didn't. Doc is no longer living in L.A. He was a liability to me, so he had to go. He did tell me the story about the hammer, though. And Jerry is a straight criminal; I don't believe anything that comes out of his mouth." Doc and Jerry were also the pair who repo'd Darnell's Chevy Nova after he was arrested.

When I contacted Steveland, Stevie Wonder's company, I was told they could neither confirm nor deny my allegations. The subtext I took from that, since why not deny it if it's false, was that this matter had already been resolved. I contacted Mumtaz through his MySpace page and got a call back from a Mr. Goins purporting to speak for him, who I promptly never heard from again. I left a message on Mumtaz's mother's phone— Melody McCully, *not* Stevie Wonder's ex-wife—and got no response. I even found Damian—or at least the hotel where he's presumably living. When I rang through to his room, somehow I was transferred into his voicemail, where I could access his messages: something about a mix-up with mail-order hair care products. Just to be safe, I drove up by the house, a Spanish Colonial villa in the foothills district north of Los Feliz in the shadow of the Griffith Park Observatory.

This is Wayne Manor after the fall: garbage in the driveway, cracks in the façade, lawn care or landscapers summoned perhaps never. A gas bill on the welcome mat confirmed I had the right place, although the doorbell seemed disabled. I called out and was greeted from an upstairs window by a young woman who rented the main house with her boyfriend and was leaving at the end of the month. Intrigued by my story, she gave me a brief tour: There was an enormous grand ballroom without a stick of furniture in it, only a black grand piano beneath a mist of plaster dust from the crumbling ceiling above; a kidney-shaped pool coagulated with algae; beyond it the guesthouse, the original scene of the crime, where the wiring looks faulty to this day. Through ground-floor windows, a recording studio looked like it recently had been flooded; amp shells were strewn about and a keyboard upended. Upstairs in the main house lived a woman who stalked the grounds casting spells and kicking the couple's car, and the lower wing was occupied by a porno director who used it for weekend film shoots. "We can't take the creepy vibe anymore," the woman tells me. "The people coming through here are not good." The only thing missing was an orangutan's funeral.

I decided it was time to go see Jerry Rosenberg, so I made an appointment at the gym where he kept hours: Fortune Gym on Sunset between La Brea and Fairfax, behind a liquor store. Jerry had his own gym for a while—Tru on La Brea, circa 2003, and then at Sunset and Highland a year later—but that's apparently long gone. Those who frequented it tell me the vibe was straight-up gangster. They also tell of Mike "the Bounty" Hunter, a heavyweight prospect from the mid-nineties who was a trainer there. He had once done a seven-year bid in a Maryland prison for armed robbery, and died in early 2006 in a bizarre incident on top of the St. Moritz Hotel on Sunset, an aging SRO hotel that once housed Raji's, a club and drug den from the heyday of eighties metal. Hunter was on the roof allegedly buying crack in an undercover LAPD sting operation and pointed a toy pistol at the arresting officers, hastening his demise.

Another story I heard was that Jerry had been banned from the popular trainer Freddie Roach's Wild Card Gym at Santa Monica and Vine for over ten years—which Roach himself confirmed was because he stole $15,000. Speaking with a slight slur from the Parkinson's he suffers from injuries sustained in the ring during his journeyman boxing career, Roach found plausible Darnell's role as a middleman on the back tattoos, since Golden Palace would reportedly always go through the trainers. He even took a couple of drives up to the Stevie Wonder–owned mansion with Jerry before their falling out. He thought Jerry was McCully's bodyguard. Where he drew the line was on Darnell's stories to get a fighter to take a dive. "That's only in the movies," says Freddie. "It don't happen in Vegas, or anywhere in professional boxing, for that matter."

As I entered Fortune Gym through a back alley, a short-leashed pit bull was sunning himself near the entrance. The Aussie tank behind the counter, the eponymous Justin Fortune, just laughed when I told him I was a crime writer and ushered me through a maze of state-of-the-art workout equipment to my obvious source. Jerry was ringside, encouraging his latest prospect, Buddy Tyson, an undefeated (10–0) junior welterweight who was taking on all comers. However Darnell described Jerry, it didn't begin to do him justice: five feet six, forty-eight years old, jailhouse tattoos from head to toe, including "Whiteboy" on one arm, "Outlaw"—the name of Mickey Rourke's gym—on the other, and tribal bands on both. (Jerry lived with Rourke at his place in the hills for a year and a half.) He also had his initials tattooed on the backs of his calves from knee to ankle, just in case his opponents forgot who just put them on the canvas, or he needed to be identified at the morgue. He sported a shaved head, a nose ring, double-hoop sterling silver earrings, and a fearsome solid-gold grill, and he looked like Phil Collins just entering his Ol' Dirty Bastard phase. His eyes are the kind of milky blue you can't read, but you feel certain that he has little to hide. Clean and sober for seventeen years, Jerry says, "It kept me out of the joint."

We stepped outside, as an adorably sweaty blond in body-accentuating black tights and a gray T-shirt bounded up the stairs. Turns out it's Reese Witherspoon, who greeted Jerry warmly.

"You should put her in your book," he tells me.

"She don't want to be in my book," I say, remembering back perhaps a decade ago to what was probably my worst celebrity interview ever. She gave a kind of fizzy, confused smile that still lingered after she had scurried inside.

I told him that Darnell had been fairly candid about some of his exploits, including some that involved Jerry. He says, "I don't give a fuck. Whatever," and then laughs and adds, "Did Darnell tell you about the bank we robbed?" I can't tell if he's kidding.

Jerry has been to prison twice—in 1979, when he was nineteen (he doesn't specify for what) and later for sixty-four counts of residential burglary and two armed bank robberies, for which he received a scant seventeen months, spent in drug diversion at Wayside. (Jerry comes from a prominent family.) His lawyer was Robert Shapiro of O. J. Simpson fame.

He calls himself Darnell's best friend. "All these people you're talking about, I introduced to him," he says. "Every one of them. The Russian motherfucker—all of them. He lived with me for about a year and a half [at his ranch in Valverde in Orange County]. You can't tell a crazy motherfucker like him anything when he's doing what he's doing. But boxing really helped Darnell a lot. He'd probably be in more trouble without that."

He says that Shelly hates him because he bounced a check that she cashed for him one time. (He neglects to tell me it was for $4,000.) I ask him if his tattoos—specifically "Whiteboy"—indicate a gang affiliation in prison.

"No, that's another thing," says Jerry. "I hung out with niggers all my life. Even in there. Wherever. People that know me say, 'Jerry—he thinks he's a nigger. He tries to be black.' But I don't try to do none of that shit. Why would I want to be a nigger? How stupid is that? I already got four strikes. I don't try and be nothing that I ain't. I will tell you right off the bat what I think—and I'll tell you right to your face."

I got about halfway through the Stevie Wonder story before he asks, "He's saying that didn't happen—that he didn't get shocked?" then admits the whole thing. I asked him how Doc was doing, and he says he was in an accident and lost an eye and a leg. He promises to put me in touch. He also mentions that he met Will Wright through Mickey Rourke.

"He loved that motherfucker," says Jerry.

"Who—Darnell?"

"No, that Will Wright motherfucker," says Jerry. "I guess he thought he was some kind of shit. When I first met him, we went and ate lunch on Sunset. Mickey was there, and Darnell. Mickey said, 'This dude's a bad-ass—he just got out of the penitentiary' and this and that, and I said, 'Mickey, that shit don't impress me.' And we weren't in there five minutes and the dude starts talking about how he had a van full of money and all that shit, and I got up and said, 'This lying motherfucker couldn't carry my jockstrap in the penitentiary.' They were like, 'What's wrong with you?' and then he stood up and said, 'Hey man, you don't know me!' And I said, "Man, I know one thing—you're a punk motherfucker.' That's why I went to the joint a couple of times—because of motherfucking snitches.' He's a snitch—there ain't no question about that."

I tell him that I've heard that a lot, from Alex on down.

"Anyone could see that," says Jerry. "I wouldn't even waste the paper to put him in the book. He don't even deserve that much credit."

We talked for an hour or so, and then I asked him if he thought Darnell had a shot at any kind of redemption when he got out. Jerry laughed and said, "I don't know—I couldn't say."

"Well, obviously you got out and cleaned up," I say. "Something must have fundamentally changed in you. How come you're not still a criminal?"

"I *am* a criminal," Jerry says softly. "I just use my head a little bit more. Darnell will tell you, I'm a real motherfucker. Believe that shit. Believe it. But I'm not going back to the penitentiary."

The next day I contacted Doc Holiday, Jerry having alerted him that I would be calling. I wasn't two minutes into the phone call before he started trying to shake me down for money—even though I specifically told Jerry that I couldn't pay him. I called Jerry, and he said he'd intervene. He called me back an hour later and said he'd spoken to Doc. "We talked about it," said Jerry, "and I've really given you the best parts of your book. You need to break me off about five thousand dollars," which Jerry would then share with Doc. I told him we had discussed this beforehand, and he had nothing coming.

Later, when I ran down my interview, Darnell says, "Jerry will sell a million-dollar plot out for a thousand-dollar payoff. He's a cool buddy, but a lowlife, as you've come to see. If he asks me for fifty dollars, I don't expect it back, I just give him the fifty. People always ask me how I can hang with him after all the shit he's done to people. Jerry knows how much shit he can get away with [around] me, and he doesn't cross the line."

When I ask him about the bank job, he says, "I forgot about that. I was included in so much that I've forgotten more than I've told you."

9

SCUM

Darnell is like my own private TiVo. Prisoners don't have access to the Internet because—well, because they're criminals—but he apparently sets his clock by *TMZ, E! News, Entertainment Tonight,* and whatever other outposts of celebrity dish are available to him on the fifteen-inch portable TV he listens to on headphones in his cell. He was the first one to tell me that Pamela Anderson was dating Rick Salomon, having seen her televised confession on *The Ellen DeGeneres Show* of how a mysterious Vegas figure had appeared to rescue her and covered a quarter-million-dollar gambling debt in exchange for a single night of bliss.

The couple's dating trajectory since then has been a roller-coaster ride—a whirlwind courtship (September 2007), marriage (October 6), separation (December 13), reconciliation (December 17), annulment (March 24, 2008), counter-annulment (same), and rumored pregnancy. It also managed to compress an entire life cycle into the standard time frame of a single-season reality series—which is a coincidence, in that they were rumored to be negotiating just that for the E! Channel as late as December. (Anderson subsequently pursued the E! series alone.) And in fact, what could be a more media-perfect union than the progenitors of the two most popular sex tapes ever—the Ur-tapes of celebrity coupling—themselves conjoined in an unholy matrimony of marquee intimacy? It's almost as if their lives were mere advertisements for the coming show launch. But the truth is arguably even stranger, according to an inside mole I managed to get a line to. Anderson's and Salomon's extended families were reportedly planning a vacation together in Aspen, and the pair sold the story to the tabloids, setting up a mutual bank account with the proceeds. When an argument erupted between the families, she accused his family of snubbing hers—"Love me, love my family"—and the rift never healed. Complicating this was the fact that the couple had invested equally in a painting that Rick got for half its $700,000 asking price. When they split, Pam reportedly kept the painting. The claims of fraud, cited on both petitions of annulment, stem from that.

We also learned that during their six-month epic romance, Pam called Rick by the endearment "Scum." Darnell reports that this was a nickname Rick cultivated after the whole *1 Night in Paris* ordeal. But an inside source close to all parties claims the nickname predates the Paris tape altogether. "Rick wanted to be called 'Scum' long before the tape," says the source. "He thought it was funny, and adopted that nickname long before. What can you really say about someone who responds to the name Scum as if it's a good thing?"

Anderson initially identified Rick as a professional poker player, an occupation widely attributed to him in the media, and the same livelihood Bill Wright ascribed to his son when talking to the townfolk of Blaine. It's a literary construct—colorful, rakish, devil-may-care—a lifestyle choice that's at once daring and victimless. Prior to his sex tape windfall, he also started Beverly Hills Pimps & Hos—a clothing line featuring "tight-fitting tanks, velour 'honey suits' and trucker hats," according to partner Zack Bautzer in *Entertainment Weekly*. (The third partner is Seth Binzer, aka Shifty Shellshock of the rap-metal band Crazy Town, which also featured Adam Goldstein, aka DJ AM, Nicole Richie's erstwhile boyfriend who shows up in multiple episodes of *The Simple Life*.) The company is also an occasional party promoter and, according to its Web site, a lifestyle choice, even if the storefront address listed on the Web site is actually a modest residential neighborhood in Hollywood (or like they say out here, "Beverly Hills adjacent"). And having been married to E. G. Daily, Shannen Doherty, and Pamela Anderson and linked with (according to Darnell) Drew Barrymore, Kirsten Dunst, *Playboy* Playmate Nicole Lenz, and porn stars Jenna Jameson, Bella Donna, and Kobi Ty—not to mention having turned out a bona fide heiress and gotten real paid—Rick may well be seen as the ultimate Beverly Hills Pimp. You have to look no further than the sex tape itself to see a man in search of an identity, from blond buzz to jet-black sidewalls with ape-hanger sideburns six months later, blown by the winds of fashion (literally).

"Rick Salomon, the boy with the grimy life," says Darnell. "The guy sticks his dick in gold mines all the time. He is the accidental pimp. He's got luck.

"I'll take you on a quick journey. It's funny that Nicole [Richie] is pregnant right now, and when I've seen her on some of the gossip shows, they ask her when Paris is going to start a family. That's some of the drama behind Rick releasing the *1 Night in Paris* sex video. He'd been banging her for years, off and on, but when he married Shannen Doherty in 2002, he had to ease up on the booty calls with Paris, and Shannen wasn't going for all the shit he was perfecting around the world either. He'd tried to clean up his act, but a cheetah never loses its spots. Never.

"In July 2002, an ex-champ I managed named 'Cool' Vince Phillips had a fight in Las Vegas, which aired on ESPN2 from the Paris Paris, and Rick was using the fight as an excuse to get away from Shannen, under the guise that it was a boys' weekend. Shannen trusted me completely, plus Balthazar Getty (now on ABC's *Brothers and Sisters*) and Eric Dane (McSteamy on *Grey's Anatomy*) were with us, and she knew Eric was dating her coworker Alyssa Milano (they had the show *Charmed* going at the time) and Balt is happily married with children. So I'm doing all the press junket bull for the fight. I got Golden Palace to put the temporary tattoo on our opponent's [Nick Acevedo's] back. (I didn't set it up with Vince because ESPN was threatening to withhold his bonus check if we came out with the tattoo, and they had the gaming commissioner check us ahead of time.) Shannen is blowing my phone up making sure I had babysitting duties with Rick. I reassured her, then checked the lines at the Hard Rock, Bellagio, MGM and went and prepped to break the bank: ten dimes on Vince to win and ten dimes on the over (the over was nine rounds) at each casino. I'm dodging all the boxing and gaming commissioners, who are trying to get us to commit to not cutting any side deals beyond what the network has agreed to.

"So before the fight, Paris comes into town with Nicole Lenz. She just wanted him to show some love. Of course, he couldn't. All he was tripping on was how Shannen was going to kill him. But it gets deeper. I had gotten tickets for Paris and her crew for the fight, and then while Rick was having a light lunch with Vince and our boxing crew, he gets a call from Shannen and she's in town for the fight also. We were in a suite at Bally's having soup (out of respect for Vince not being able to eat any big meals), and Rick turns white knowing he just fucked up. Rick put [Eric] "Stiff" Dane and

Balt on Shannen, and I was going to help out as much as I could with Paris and Nicole [Richie]. We got Shannen tickets farther back and on the opposite side, hoping that the lights and all the action would keep her attention away from Paris (her rival at the time). It all worked out, but we had a fuck-fest set up for after the fight. We kick ass in the fight and Dane leaves us and goes back to the room he and Balt had at the Bellagio. Balt was left with Shannen. I had Paris and the girls on my hands, and I had other friends in town also. Shelly was there with friends, and she can attest to how rude I was—I didn't even entertain them afterwards.

"Then Rick disappears. Balt's got Shannen, I've got Paris, and now I'm running them around with me while I go collect all my chips from the Bellagio, MGM, and Hard Rock and drop it all off in my safe deposit box at the MGM. Still no Rick. Shannen is calling me like crazy, and I got a crying, bitchy Paris in the other ear. After I dropped Paris off at her room at the Hard Rock, I finally heard from Rick—he was back at our room at the Bellagio with all the escorts. He and Stiff Dane had left Balt and me with all the drama. Balt got Shannen back to her room at the Hard Rock. Rick just said fuck it and turned his phone off. I get to the Bellagio and the girls were just warming up. Vince and the rest of the crew showed up. I had already taken care of the girls, so it was all fun for everyone. Rick felt like if the shit was going to blow up in his face, then so be it. Shannen and her girls entertained themselves some kind of way, while Paris was staying at the same hotel. Rick had told me about how he had filmed Paris fucking— that was the first night-vision version—and he was amped about how she was about to blow up: her name was going to be everywhere soon. Oh yeah, we just had to wait.

"We partied hard. A quick rundown of my monthly expenses: twenty-five hundred for my place in L.A.; three thousand for half a loft in New York. I didn't have to pay for the Range Rover I had in 2002, the Ferrari (two different kinds) I drove in 2001 and 2003, the Mercedes I had in 2004–5 (until my arrest), or the Escalade, because we had several dickheads who lost big cash gambling and would put the cars on their company credit, and we would drive them until we got tired of them. They paid the monthly notes; it was our car. Fair exchange. Rick had the same Ferrari I had, and an Escalade. It isn't until 2002 when Shannen bought him the sports Benz that he had a car in his name. He didn't have another car until 2005 when he bought the S500 Benz like the 2004 one I had.

"I flew back and forth to New York weekly. I was in Europe at least once a month—if only for a couple of days visiting Rick's brother in Prague. My monthly travel bill was upwards of fifty thousand. The daily club/dinner bill was two to four thousand for dinner and the same for the club, and partying was part of the gig. You gotta pay the cost to be the boss. We paid Flexjet or NetJets a quarter million for twenty-five hours of air time, but we would go through that in two or three trips. But the club-dinner-lunch bills were what ate up big money. Clothes? Forget about it. Stupid gifts like a two-thousand-dollar Chrome Hearts robe or five-hundred-dollar beanie hat. We lived at Chrome Hearts; a lot of my furniture was custom made from them. And we spent millions on nothing: hotel bills; hookers and mistresses. I guess they're one and the same, but Rick was much more wild than me. I'm much more fiscally conservative, and I didn't owe child support or have a coke habit. I was handling everything because he couldn't cope. I mean, we'd have a conversation, and he'd say, 'Take the battery out of your cell phone before I talk to you.' He was out of it. 'Aliens in space can hear us'—you know? I remembered what he said about taping Paris. But in late 2002, Rick fucked up." Darnell recounts a story about Rick getting in over his head and owing a lot of money. "So the rest of 2002 and 2003 was spent paying it back."

"Mind you, this is all at the same time that Rick was dealing with this Shannen Doherty-Paris Hilton bullshit around town, and I'm out hustling. Rick had no clue how much I did for him . . . This is what led Rick to finally getting the balls to release the video. Paris was a part of it all the way. That is, once I convinced her that it wouldn't appear like she was a part of it, but of course she would get paid." During Darnell's time on the inside, Rick had gotten married—to E. G. Daily, the actress who starred as Dottie in *Pee-wee's Big Adventure* ("You don't want to get mixed up with a guy like me. I'm a loner, Dottie. A rebel"). ("Ah, that's Rick," says Darnell, "the New Millennium Pee-wee Herman.") Daily briefly had a successful recording career in the mid-eighties—her song "Here It Goes Again" from the 1999 release *Tearing Down the Walls* is reportedly about Rick's substance abuse ("I press my mouth onto your chest / Look up into your eyes / Hoping you'll be there"), and many of the public events in her life are chronicled in her "one-woman autobiographical musical," *Listen Closely*. In the nineties, she found steady work voicing animated or personified characters like Tommy Pickles in the *Rugrats* series, Buttercup in *The Powerpuff Girls*, and Babe, the Gallant Pig in *Babe: Pig in the City*. The couple have two daughters, and according to her, Rick was a devoted and attentive father when he was not consumed by the tidal swell of a debilitating drug habit that would send him off on extended benders. They divorced in 2000—not as a consequence of the infamous Paris sex video (a version of which was in limited circulation a year later) or even Rick's recurring relationship with Paris, but rather, according to Daily, his precarious struggle with sobriety.

"I wanted to get out of my marriage because Rick has a substance abuse issue, and he does really well with it sometimes," says Daily. "Rick is the most amazing drug-addicted person, where he can literally be sober for a year at a time, but then he has these slips. And I've watched him in the worst stages, because he always comes to my house when he wants to clean up. He has to clean up around my children, but he always comes. Our home is his home, and he feels the most safe and secure and calm. And he comes because there's no judgment about him, and no beating him down about it. It's a bad addiction. But he really loves his babies, and I think they are the one thing he's most proud of in his life.

"Rick and I are really close, and get along pretty incredibly for a divorced couple: we travel, we go on trips together, and it's a pretty amicable thing. Rick is super charismatic. There are always people that want to be around him—he's just a super fun guy, and chicks like him. When you look at the track record of women he's been with, it's endless high-end women. As far as Paris goes, they were definitely connected. They were friends for a long time, and I think towards the end of our marriage—the way Paris would look at me—and I'm a woman, so I know these things—she'd look at me like, 'That's the wife.' Okay, I know what's going on. But Rick did not date Paris to get ahead. I think that she was just a symptom of his addiction. Paris has been in clubs and partying like that since she was way young. I would lock my children in their rooms before I would let them go hang out at Hollywood parties. So Paris was partying, and people that party want to party with partiers, and I'm not a partier like that. I mean, we actually talked about it. I know that she really loved him, and he loved her, and it was real—not, 'Oh, we're going to get together and make a porn tape,' because I don't think that was what they were actually doing." (Daily doesn't recognize Darnell's name.)

Darnell still holds a grudge against Rick for failing to post bail when he was arrested for marijuana trafficking in Laramie, Wyoming, in early 2003. "Rick's no gangster," says Darnell. "Rick was great at making connections, but he was too much of a pussy to deal with them face-to-face.

When he heard I got touched, he took off for Thailand. I couldn't reach him or anyone that could get to him. He didn't want to take my call and face me. When he finally came back in town, some buddies of mine ran into him and jammed him up and he ran some drag about taking care of my bail, but by that time I already had the no-bond hold out of Wyoming, so I couldn't get bail.

"I had a desperate crackhead friend who had the world on his back and he didn't have control of his life," says Darnell to sum up the moment right before the perfect storm of the Paris Hilton sex tape. "I kept the prick alive, and this is how I got repaid. Now can you see why I have anger toward Rick, after I helped save his life?"

Jack Ninio, a professional gambler and one-time sportsbook impresario in Costa Rica, who is also Heather's husband and one of Rick's oldest and closest friends, says, "People are too forgiving, you know? And I'm one of them. You can print this: for some of the things Scum did to me back in the day, I should never talk to him again, but I love the guy. I don't know why."

About all the people who he feels betrayed him, Darnell says, "They all know that they got to see me now. It ain't tomorrow or next year, but it ain't long, and then they got to stand up to how they treated me. I ain't out for blood. I don't want to see any of them. I know once I'm out and everyone knows—all types of characters will call me out of the blue asking when they could take me to lunch, or 'let's go sailing.' A couple of characters will move back out of the country."

THE MOST RECKLESS GIRL I EVER MET

Wars, nations, presidents, and popes may come and go, but the one constant that anyone seemed to care about for most of the decade was Paris Hilton, the poor little rich girl with a name out of Greek tragedy—born of unspeakable privilege, flaunting her feral charms, flouting the laws of God and man alike, and blessed with both the callowness of youth and the callousness of impunity. For reasons that still mystify, even as her moment in the sun finally draws into merciful eclipse, Paris Hilton became the critical pivot in this as well as all stories—the celestial body around which all planets seem to revolve, and to which all her subjects, royal and commoner alike, are connected by no more than six degrees. She is the You Are Here sign in the universal shopping mall that is postcapitalism, the embodiment of what Darnell calls "dizzying, narcissistic wealth, and its corruption that predated her."

She is the doorstop at the end of the long century of mediated fame: from Marilyn, whose effortless sex appeal was as streamlined and aerodynamic as the Cadillac Coupe de Ville, whom the camera loved so desperately that its handmaidens would tolerate any unspeakable behavior to keep her before it; to Madonna, an irresistible force who bludgeoned her way into fame through tireless effort and burning will, yoked to an outsized sexual persona at once brazen and pure burlesque. Who was briefly succeeded by Courtney Love, rank ambition enflamed to pathological proportions, who gave way to Britney Spears and Lindsay Lohan, creatures cloned in a lab somewhere and incorporating the seeds of their own destruction—up-sold as garish fad or guilty pleasure, down-sold as *schaden-freude* for the masses, their prefabricated rise and fall marketed to identical effect. Each brandished a more virulent sexuality: hyperbolic, vulgar, burrowing deeper and deeper into taboo as the surest path to notoriety.

And then there's Paris, who strays beyond those gates, out into a post-apocalyptic landscape where fame carries none of the imagined perquisites, only a hunger sated momentarily by the flesh of her rivals. She is *American Gladiator* meets *American Idol*—the perfect star to preside over the eclipse of stardom itself. As fame has grown ever more corrosive, its victims are inevitably someone else's investment—singers, actors, cultivated talent. And Paris is saddled with none of it. She is a catchphrase. Having appeared in over twenty films and sixty episodes of television, she shows not the slightest aptitude for acting. She is the first reality superstar. Her one acknowledged accomplishment, *The Simple Life*, professionally humiliated her and made her into a standing joke, a symbol of inbred money and louche entitlement, a class division bordering on speciation, all with her willing complicity. And having no particular talents, she can be replicated at will by the cynical Hollywood machinery that produced her, her exit hastened by the venues that once prolonged her and are now turning on her, who will ultimately consume all of her—hooves, horns, and hide—until there's nothing left. She is the perfect pop artifact. Her cultural role is that of pure spectacle. Her only job is to be eaten by lions.

The world that Paris Hilton inhabits isn't even Hollywood, no matter if the name sticks like a noxious cloud to the club life for which she has become a media billboard and roving ambassador (paid per appearance): its own private Angelyne, doomed to travel endlessly from one end of Hollywood Boulevard to the other for all eternity. With the exception of Leo and Tobey, Ashton and the Wahlberg entourage, the real Hollywood is usually home in bed, in anticipation of its 6 a.m. call time. If anything, this is Sub-Hollywood, a special circle of hell populated by cautionary tales in training, opportunists who fall prey to bigger opportunists, shark-eyed waifs, usurpers, bloodless parasites subsisting on cocaine dreams, Old Money gone rancid, curdled youth, lemmings drawn to sound and light. Whatever Elizabeth Taylor became at the end of her life (presuming she doesn't live forever)— a mythological creature that outlived the movies, the premieres, a flotilla of husbands, and everyone she's ever known to cling infantlike to the morphine drip of fame, with people like me parked at her curb, punching a clock on celebrity death watch—these people were born into. It's their starting point. They are denizens of the perpetual night.

I ran into Paris while I was writing this book. She was a presenter at the Scream Awards, the horror-fantasy-science fiction prizes sponsored by Spike TV that were presented at the Greek Theater. When she took the stage to show a clip from her upcoming horror remake *House of Wax*, she was met with an insistent chorus of boos. After the clip ended, someone in the upper tier yelled out, "Fuck you, bitch!" and the place erupted in laughter. Later, at the after-party at the Hollywood Roosevelt Hotel, she made an entrance surrounded by half a dozen younger girls, stood up on a table so she could survey the room (and bask in its attention), and then launched herself into the crowd—whirling every which way, desperately looking for someone she knew or at least who would talk to her, as a kind of a life preserver. *And no one paid any attention to her.* She was close enough to touch at one point, her smile stretched into waxen hysteria, and when she reached for her phone and seemed to pretend to take a call, it rendered her suddenly tiny and pathetic. It seemed like an awful way to live. She and her friends left soon afterward.

But as Darnell points out, and he was ostensibly there, it was Paris who created the paparazzi. Or at least the digital, point-and-shoot gangs who hang out in front of the Ivy, chase down SUVs fleeing nightclubs, and think that F-stop is a porno term. It was the Paris Hilton sex tape release timed to the *Simple Life* premiere in the last half of 2003 that stoked the proliferation of photo agencies and gossip Web sites, created a feeding frenzy outside Hollywood nightclubs, and made anyone think they could sell a random frame of video for $20,000. These people are the new day traders or real estate speculators.

"I can remember in late 2002 we came out of Dublin's on Sunset, when it was still a place to be," says Darnell. "Paris Hilton and Nicole Lenz, Rick, me, and others. We caught a game on the telly, and there were about three paparazzi outside waiting for Shaq to come out. He wasn't even in there. But one of the photographers said, 'Who's that girl?'—he was talking about Paris—and [photographer E. L.] Woody said, 'Oh, that's Paris Hilton, she's a rich chick.' Woody knew Paris, but no one else knew Paris or Nicky. They dressed trampy, with crazy colors and dirty, greasy-looking hair weaves and were still looking for their in. Only fashion or Hollywood insiders knew that shit was on the horizon."

As noted, Darnell first met Paris and her more demure younger sister when he was two weeks out of prison, at Rick's hotel room. Paris had just turned eighteen. Rick had prefaced their arrival with a copy of "the Gold Dust Twins' " first appearance in *Maxim,* and he seemed excited at the commercial prospect. "He told me that their names had just started making the rounds in *US Weekly* and the Page Six gossip columns," says Darnell. "Rick said the media was jumping on the socialite bandwagon, but insiders around town knew it was all just hype." When they finally showed up at the hotel, Paris was barely ambulatory and virtually unrecognizable from her *Maxim* spread, and Nicky was "as reserved as she always is."

The next time he saw Paris was in New York that fall. Darnell divided his time and rented half a loft there from an Austrian model named Simone, and he frequently spotted Paris out at the clubs, where she had been a fixture since she was fifteen, always wearing her signature roller skates, in a kind of disco day care while her parents went about their own business. On one such outing, Darnell led her onto the dance floor and then joined her table, which included Nicole Richie, the future Ethel to her Lucy. "I heard that you were fucking Rachel Hunter," Paris told him. "I heard you were like some Mafia guy. What do you do?" Darnell told her what he told everybody: "I invest money for people. I run a cleaning service." That night, the three of them stayed up playing arcade Pac-Man in his loft and watched the sun rise. The next day, he and Paris met for lunch at the Bull & Bear inside the Waldorf Astoria on Park Avenue, part of the Hilton chain where Paris could stay for free due to her family connection. Paris spent most of the time asking if Rick had a steady girl back in L.A. Soon after, Darnell caught a cab to LaGuardia.

A year later, he ran into Paris and Nicole (Richie, as opposed to Paris's sister, who is known as Nicky, and whose given name is Nicholai) driving Rick's Escalade, dropping him off at Hollywood Gym. Darnell invited them out and they climbed into his Range Rover (another collateral perk of the gambling business) and went to lunch. There they crank-called their friend Chuck Pacheco—Nicole playing a nurse from the free clinic informing the club promoter that he may have been exposed to a strain of herpes that could mutate into a flesh-eating virus. (Chuck reportedly called them back within ten minutes and told them to grow up.) That afternoon, after they dropped Paris off, Darnell claims that Nicole came back to his apartment in Sunset Plaza. As soon as they were inside, it was obvious what was going to happen. "I've been waiting for this," she told him, putting her arms around his neck and wrapping her legs around his waist.

Somewhere in the middle of it, they crank-called Paris and giggled into the phone. (As noted, Richie denies knowing Darnell.)

The next day, he got a call from Paris, who sounded worked up about something and demanded to see him. According to Darnell, at his apartment, she gave him the third degree on his afternoon with Nicole. Sensing the jealousy right beneath the surface, Darnell proceeded to narrate the previous day's agenda, demonstrating as he went, and soon, he says, he was going down on her on his kitchen counter. He reports that Paris and Nicole wore matching low-cut landing strips.

There were other parties where Paris made an appearance. One, hosted by Donatella Versace in New York, Darnell attended with Mickey Rourke, where Paris introduced him to Nicole Lenz, "the hot Playmate that has been an integral part of the twisted Rick Salomon and Paris relationship over the years," and by his account, their introduction was consummated in a spare bedroom. After making a delivery uptown, Darnell returned to the Versace party, where he and Mickey Rourke sampled the female merchandise. Another one was held at Paris and Nicky's house on Hollywood Boulevard in the hills west of Laurel Canyon, where he met models Naomi Campbell and Adriana Lima and Tasered himself on a dare for their assembled amusement. In February 2002, he even says he interrupted a trip from Germany to Prague to see the band Jamiroquai with model Erin Naas and Simone to meet Paris and her then boyfriend Jason Shaw, the Tommy Hilfiger model, who were celebrating her twenty-first birthday in Amsterdam. On that trip, according to Darnell's play-by-play, Paris made another one of her sex tapes, in addition to the one she had already made with Jason Shaw in Atlantic City. She is going down on a fashion model with a mile of legs for what seems like hours, with Jason providing the benediction in voice-over, "Now *that* was hot—I'm going to go jack off." This was some of the same footage that surfaced in the fourteen hours of Paris tapes that Darnell brokered to the British tabloids. Other outtakes from the same trip are scattered around the Internet. (Of Shaw, Darnell says, "He was the one Paris should have stayed with, but she belongs to the night, and whoever she wakes up with in the morning.")

A typical night is apparently the one described in this paragraph: "I get to the hotel room and find a sea of asses smiling at me," says Darnell. "To my delight, there are all these freshly waxed muffs of naked models and actresses loosely attached to lips profoundly talking about nonsense. All of them are caught in the moment of the utter absurdity of an escalating cocaine high. This scenario played out many, many times. Sometimes Paris was there. Sometimes Nicole Lenz was there. Sometimes both were there. Rick was always there. Typically, Paris would break out in a clumsy laugh until everyone in the room paid attention to her. If I could pry her lips away from Rick's cock, I might actually get to talk to her."

All of this formed a backdrop for the release of the first Paris Hilton sex tape.

Here's how Darnell describes it:

"It's crazy how after the first part of the Paris Hilton tape was dropped on the net, everyone tried to distance themselves from Rick," says Darnell. "It's like he had SARS or some Ebola virus, the way people tried to put distance between them. The only ones who didn't give a fuck were the guys in our boxing crew.

"We've got a sneaky friend—Don [Thrasher]. He's a weirdo, without a doubt. Balthazar took him under his wing. Don was staying with Rick off and on. This is 2002 starting up to 2003, at the height of Rick's coke binge. He had already flaked out on our boxing plans for him. Rick had already filmed the black-and-white version of the Paris Hilton tape, which was in his apartment. He would show it at impromptu viewings; it was really no big deal. Paris Hilton was not the Paris Hilton that she is now. The paparazzi weren't the beast they are now. So Don took the tape without Rick knowing and made a copy, then put the original back.

"Rick had already married Shannen Doherty, so he was living out in Malibu with her mostly. I was cleaning up all of his mess, and he was splitting time between Shannen and Paris. It was horrible at that time for him. Rick asked me to help him with the video. He wanted to sell the video to someone (April/May 2003). He wasn't originally going to do it—that is, until Paris fucked him over. In March or April 2003, she crashed his Escalade. Of course, he didn't have any insurance, or else he didn't want to report it, but Paris didn't want to take responsibility for the crash, nor did she want to pay for it. At this point, Paris was barely getting an allowance from her parents. They paid for the place she had up in Laurel Canyon with Nicole Lenz and model Jennifer Rovero. Jennifer had already moved out because she had a son.

"So Don makes the copy and Paris crashes Rick's truck. Rick is catching heat from Shannen about the rumors that he's still fucking Paris. I'm getting calls from Shannen and all the interrogations that come with her trying to find Rick. Rick is pissed at Paris and he's ready to sell the video. I know Jimmy Flynt [Larry's brother] and I set up a meeting with the Flynts. Paris had just gotten the go-ahead to do *The Simple Life*. The paparazzi start going crazy over her in a period of two or three months. But her money wasn't set as of yet. She was making appearances, but no big money. *The Simple Life* didn't pay much—it was a reality show, c'mon. She got producer credit, but that's chump change compared to my unholy offer-alliance.

"Rick was in no condition to do anything right. He had Shannen ready to divorce him. He was deep in debt. He had given up his apartment in Brentwood and moved in full time with Shannen. Shannen's parents hated Rick with a passion. He would have to hide in the bathroom when they popped in unannounced. It was torture. He had E.G. on his ass with two kids and child support. So I told him we should get some more colored footage of Paris. Larry Flynt was also concerned that Paris hadn't given us permission or signed off on the video to be released. Paris would do almost anything for money at this point, and craved the attention. So we hit her up.

"Rick's crashing at my suite; he's in and out of Paris's house; he's in other hotels, spending cash, throwing away phones, getting new ones every week. His paranoia was at an all-time high. He broke the proposition to Paris. Paris went for it. I don't know how he got her to do it, but he said he didn't have to bend her arm, she was all for it, but only if it ain't showing her like a whore. And if you notice the color version of the *1 Night in Paris* tape, she has on nice lace panties, a bra and heels, her hair is perfect and they're in a hotel room. That was the Four Seasons on Doheny. But we got her to sign off on being able to use her name and likeness. Before we could pat each other on the back, the clip Don had sold to the porn company had popped up on the Internet. Don sold it for fifty thousand. No one knew who leaked it. Rick thought I did, but had no balls to question me. It made no sense for me to leak it, since I stood to make a nice meal ticket off the full version. Everyone blamed Rick. The Hiltons called him a rapist and said he drugged an underage Paris. They had no idea she signed off on the video and was a partner in the venture. Rick was a pariah around town. Once again, I was one of the only 'friends' who had his back.

"On one of his trips with Paris in May–June 2003, after he got the Escalade out of the shop, he left Shannen in Malibu and hung out with Paris. Shannen tracked him down and put Vaseline on his windows and egged the car. Rick stayed with Shannen and Shannen was finally told about the sex video. She had no idea who she married or the debt he had racked up or the people he owed. We made contact with Red Light porn company and they released the video. I'd get ten thousand dollars a month from November 2003 up until I was arrested in March 2005."

Darnell contends that by the time the fat lady had sung, Rick had pocketed somewhere in the neighborhood of $7 million.

That the tape had been widely viewed by people Rick knew, making its release—either by happenstance or design—somewhat less than revelatory, is really not in doubt. Kristen Williams recalls its currency.

"I was having dinner and Rick was asking everyone, 'Oh, you guys want to come up and watch the Paris tape? And I'm like, 'What are you talking about? Watch your *parents*?' And he says, 'No, the Paris tape.' That was years before."

Pamela Anderson, whose sex tape crown was usurped by the Paris tape, told *Access Hollywood*, "I saw it by accident, but two thumbs up. It made me feel better that someone else is out there taping themselves." (Darnell reports showing it to her at the home of Rich Jardine, the guy behind WhoIsWillWright.com: "At the beginning, she was a bit envious," Darnell reports. "But the sheer comedy of the thing overcame her initial feelings." The session allegedly ended with Darnell exposing his own equipment to Anderson, who agreed that his was indeed bigger.)

Even Rick's ex-wife, E.G. Daily, had a copy, which she kept in a box with Rick's remaining possessions. She remembers Donald Thrasher as just off the bus from Indianapolis and a ubiquitous presence during the early years of her marriage.

"He was a guy that came from out of town, [who] seemed like an Opie type of character and hung out all the time," says E.G. "He hung out at our house and crashed on our couch. He was a sweet guy, and very smart, and he respected—or worshipped—Rick and just hung out as sort of a buddy. Don was the person who originally sold the tape. Rick wasn't even in on the signing, which was so bizarre. It was just like this random thing, and then it disappeared. And Don had been staying at his house at the time. He probably made a copy of it. He knew where everything was. But he sold it, it was out, Rick looked like a jerk, and everyone thought he was this horrible guy.

"I call him 'Dirty Don' in my play [*Listen Closely*]. Because Rick actually called me and asked, 'Did you release this tape?' Then we found out Don's name was on this thing. That was when the Hiltons were slandering

Rick . . . Rick would never have sold that tape for fifty thousand because he makes that much money in Vegas on one weekend. He's not a lowball player. He's a businessman. [Plus] if you watch the tape, it does not look like something people would want someone to see. That was not a tape that these two people intended to have all over the world." The one thing Daily disputes is that Rick wouldn't have had car insurance. But she does confirm that everyone profited equally. "I know for sure that they made money after everything was legal," she says.

According to the license agreement, dated August 26, 2003, and now posted on the Smoking Gun Web site, Thrasher licensed the forty-five-minute section of night-vision footage to the Seattle-based Marvad Corp., alongside subscription-only adult fare that included Dr. Laura "in the buff." Among the reasons the license gives for the marketing of the tape are that "Hilton has recently denied the existence of the tape" and "Salomon [referred to as "Solomon" throughout] wishes to clear his good name and prove to the public that he is honest, that the Video does exist and that the content of the Video demonstrates Hilton's desire for the same to be viewed by third parties." In fact, "Paris Hilton expressly advised Solomon that she consents to and authorizes the public exploitation of the video, and waives and releases all claims in connection therewith." The reason for such secrecy is addressed in a Confidentiality/Non-Disclosure clause, which notes, "The parties acknowledge and understand that Solomon is married to Shannen Doherty, a famous actress, and that Solomon's marriage may be put in jeopardy, and that Ms. Doherty could suffer injury to her career or reputation, in the event the public learns Solomon authorized the exploitation of the video." Marvad posted a three-and-a-half-minute teaser on its sexbrat.com Web site, presumably timed to capitalize on the premiere of the Fox Television series *The Simple Life*, set to premiere December 2, 2003—plans that were scotched when the lawsuits started flying.

On November 13, via pit bull lawyer Marty Singer, Salomon filed a $10 million suit against Marvad for copyright infringement, which in turn filed suit against Thrasher for fraud for misrepresenting ownership of the video, i.e., whether he possessed a release from Paris Hilton to market it. Singer also claimed that Rick Salomon filed a police report concerning the stolen tape. For good measure, Rick also sued Thrasher, and Rick and the Hilton family exchanged lawsuits over various charges made in anger. The Hilton family allegedly suggested Paris was underage at the time the videotape was made, although it was shot in May 2001 (according to his lawsuit) when she was twenty and Rick was thirty-one. (On the intro to the tape itself, he claims she was nineteen.) Rick also singled out Hilton publicist Siri Garber for suggesting that Paris may have been incapacitated at the time by strong drink or drugs and incapable of rendering consent. In response, Rick sued for defamation of character, a charge that inspired much hilarity in the media. Marvad, faced with an injunction, at first removed the clip (soon mirrored in hundreds of sites across the Web) and later reposted it for free as a loss leader once the film had been released commercially.

On December 13, Paris Hilton appeared in a guest stint on *Saturday Night Live*, in an interview with news anchor Jimmy Fallon rife with innuendo:

Fallon: Is it hard to get into the Paris Hilton?
Paris: Actually, it's a very exclusive hotel, no matter what you've heard.
Fallon: Do they allow double occupancy at the Paris Hilton?
Paris: No!
Fallon: Is the Paris Hilton roomy?
Paris: It might be for you, but most people find it very comfortable.
Fallon: I'm a VIP. I may need to go in the back entrance.
Paris: It doesn't matter who you are. It's not gonna happen.

This may well have been her finest moment, and was reportedly the brainchild of PR maven/crisis manager Dan Klores, himself a filmmaker (his 2007 documentary *Crazy Love* is genius). Both her parents were in attendance, as were younger brothers Barron (then fourteen) and Conrad (nine). Sister Nicky stayed in L.A, where at Shelter, the consensus trendy club on Saturday nights, she was confronted by Rick and the pair argued. At one point, none other than Thrasher stepped into the fracas to defend Nicky, and the two men squared off before Thrasher incapacitated his one-time host with pepper spray, at which point club security ejected them both back out onto Sunset at the entrance to Laurel Canyon.

Thrasher told the syndicated tabloid show *Celebrity Justice* that he had been a willing participant and acted as Rick's agent, and that he cashed the $50,000 check (an advance against 30 percent of gross) in his name and split it with Rick. (Thrasher had previously served as an officer in Mario's Broadway Deli, a corporation Rick established in 1996 with Mario Silva.) "We had an agreement to sell the tape. He gave me the tape. Period," Thrasher said in a formal statement. After the smoke cleared and it was obvious that Paris's career wouldn't be destroyed (as Pamela Anderson's had not been destroyed before her), Salomon released the full tape circa June 15, 2004, via established porn company Red Light District and TrustFundGirls.com, in conjunction with his brother Jim Salomon, a 1992 Republican candidate for California's twenty-fourth district congressional seat now living in Prague (with whom Darnell claims a friendship), arguing that as long as the film was out there anyway, the money ought to go to him.

On the commercial release version, titled *1 Night in Paris,* Rick appears on camera and sets up each new section, looking wired in a porkpie hat and chewing gum manically. Aside from exhibiting a bedside manner that borders on grating, a good deal of his narration sounds like prepared testimony: the morning after filming the night-vision segment, over shots of her filming herself topless in the bathroom mirror, he says, "Her boobs came up in a couple of shots all veiny, and in the morning she wanted to film herself to show that she had beautiful breasts, which she does." In the color section, he makes a point to say, "All this was very legal and consensual. Over eighteen years old—barely." Yet near the end, when he takes a breather from going down on her, he asks, "I forgot how to eat your pussy?" and she says, "Forgot? You've been doing it for three years—since I was sixteen." And laughs.

Paris's lawsuit against him was settled out of court July 1, 2005, when she was awarded $400,000, a portion of which she promised to donate to charity. In 2006, she announced in *GQ* magazine that she had never received a dime from the tape and urged Rick to donate his profits to charity. It is by all reckonings the best-selling adult title ever.

Thrasher provided a formal written response to my questions, most of which he claimed to be unable to answer due to a nondisclosure agreement he signed to resolve the many lawsuits that loomed in the aftermath of the tape's release. Thrasher went on to form Thrasher Beverage to release something called Z Cola, an all-natural diet soda featuring stevia, a sugar substitute extracted from herbs growing wild in Central and South America. He sold his interest in the company in April 2007 after it merged with a similar company, but still continues his research in the natural beverage field, where he holds at least one patent. And in fact, when I first reached him, he was just back from "the flavor lab," where he spends a large part of his time. That's where I want to go when I die.

About Rick, he says, "We became roommates in 1993. After he married

E. G. Daily, he moved into a house with her. I frequently stayed over in one of the guest rooms when I came in to Hollywood from the beach." And though he won't answer in detail about their alleged business interactions, he does offer the following generic comment about that chapter of his life: "I do not want fame and do not want to be a public figure. I have seen how fame and notoriety is a curse to most people who have it. My goal in life is to change people's diets for the better with products such as my stevia soda. I regret having anything to do with that Hilton tape. If I had it to do over again, I would not have anything to do with it."

The urban myth that Paris Hilton stood to inherit the $2.3 billion Hilton hotel chain fortune—regardless of what the teaser copy of her series intro claimed—had been fairly well refuted even before her grandfather, Barron Hilton, announced that 97 percent of it was going to the Conrad N. Hilton Foundation, the charitable trust set up by his father. Given that founder Conrad Hilton bequeathed less than $2 million to his four children on his death in 1979 at age ninety-one, donating the rest of it to his eponymous foundation, and that Barron Hilton had to wage a decade-long lawsuit to win back half of his would-be inheritance, it's safe to say that something must have changed his mind. Jerry Oppenheimer's 2006 exposé, *The House of Hilton*, suggests that Barron Hilton was vocally displeased with his granddaughter's public antics. It also quotes him on Rick Hilton's failure at the family business and the lingering party reputation of Rick and his wife, Kathy, sounding suspiciously like Michael admonishing Fredo in *Godfather II*: "If he can't control his wife, how can he run my hotels?"

"She had *nothing*," claims Kristen Williams, Paris's contemporary in the club scene. "All of her jewelry was fake. She had a fake watch. Brandon Davis told me that. And her family: that part of the family had nothing. They were ostracized from the rest of the real Hilton family—the father with the showgirl or whatever. [Failed singer and actress, but same difference.] He is like the playboy that never did anything with his life. They never had shit. They lived in that tiny-ass little apartment. Brandon told me this, and his family has tons of money. The Hiltons have money now, of course, because of everything Paris is doing. They had no money to even take themselves out, and that's when I knew her."

Larry Flynt even weighed in on how the story momentarily passed through his hands. "I was approached by Rick Salomon, but I told him the tapes were in such bad shape that he'd have to reshoot them," says Flynt. "They were very out of focus, and very amateurish. So he took them back and I never saw them again. He must have taken them to another distributor and made a fortune."

David Reich (pronounced Rich) is the son of a prominent sports agent and another one of the colorful (let's say opalescent) figures that surface in this story. He is writing a book prospectively titled *Under the Bus*, which promises to spill the beans on virtually everyone he's ever met. Currently laid up in a modest Wilshire Corridor apartment that belies the exotic, luxuriant life he supposedly lived providing beautiful young women for the city's score of proto-billionaires, seven years sober, his feet split open from the pernicious diabetes that has hobbled him, when given the chance he spills like a man whose tongue has been loosened by the prospect of his own mortality. One with nothing to lose, save a few last scores to settle and the final touches on his own legacy.

"I knew Paris for a very short time in her life," Reich says. "She would show up at nightclubs—how she got in there, I don't know. Can I tell you something? When they all moved in together, [Paris, Nicole Lenz, and Jennifer Rovero in the house in Laurel Canyon], it was after I knew them. That house that the father rented for them was the last time I hung out with any of them—they were partying, [which was] out of my realm. I saw them in Vegas one time with the kid Chris Williams from *National Lampoon*, who is also sober, and some girls were all doing cocaine in his room, and I saw a lot of actresses, and Paris and those girls were working him over."

He also voices an opinion I heard from Louis Ziskin, the incarcerated Ecstasy kingpin, and others: if Paris needed money, she could have come to them. "Look—her father is a real estate agent, and we know that they live off of her, not the other way around," Reich says. "If people are stupid enough to believe that they own the Hilton hotels, then they're idiots. To her credit, Paris made her own money. I don't respect Paris, but I respect that she got up every day, showed up at every party, made a fool of herself, made money, made it legally—did whatever she did. You don't have to like her or respect her. She works a lot harder than most people I know.

"Paris never needed me to get laid. She did whatever she wanted to. Nobody could tell her what to do as long as I've known her, and she certainly didn't use me for any of that . . . When she saw Oscar De La Hoya and went after him, I was there. She didn't know who he was. She just asked another girl if he had money. Next thing I know, she's dating him for a week. Doing blow . . . and he freaked out; he's not that kind of guy. But you've got to realize, to a girl like Paris, I was boring. I wasn't doing blow, I didn't have X; she went somewhere else for this, and that's part of why I wrote my book. And that's why I want to be careful here. At the end of the day, my reputation had a lot more fun than I did."

"If she wants to fuck you, she'll fuck you," says Ziskin, a sentiment echoed by Jack Ninio, Heather's husband.

"I hung out with Rick when he was dating her at Brandon Davis's grandfather's house [Marvin Davis]—a zillion-dollar house in Beverly Hills," says Jack. "I hung there when they were dating, and I definitely saw a crazy side to Paris—which I thought was fun. But it never surprised me that she let him do it [release the tape]."

Jack's wife Heather, Kristen's best friend who also appeared in the *Dateline* special, remembers a party at the home of Dipu and Nick Haque, owners of Koi restaurant on La Cienega in Beverly Hills, where Paris put on a show for those in attendance.

"Paris was laying in the back, and everyone was screaming," says Heather. "I didn't go look. I was in town visiting Kristen, and this is the first time I met Ron [Richards, the attorney for Darnell, Will, Timmy, Erin, and others], so I remember it vividly. Erin was sitting at the bar at Dipu and Nick's; Will was trying to make her jealous. We've got Ron Richards coming up. I'd just arrived at the party, and this guy is a freak show with his eyeballs to me. In my opinion—whatever. I was with Dipu talking about old times because I hadn't seen him in so many years, and then I heard, 'Oh my God, Paris is getting fucked over there. You should see this!' I said to Jack, 'You sit your ass right here.' And she's in a corner, and everyone is running over to watch Paris get fucked in a basement bar."

Holt Gardiner, a former investment banker and gambler who traveled on the rich man's L.A.-Vegas circuit until his checkbook gave out, tells of meeting her when she was eighteen—and although it's a little hazy, he thinks he might have almost had his own night in Paris.

"She'd show up on roller skates at my house at late-night parties. And I think I almost had a threesome with her one night when we were all wasted. It was before her whole media explosion. This was fucked up—we had a big party going on downstairs, I was making out with some chick who was my girlfriend. She came up to us, and she wanted to use my computer. I said, 'I don't let anyone use my computer.' And she said, 'Well, I have to check the gossip sites.' I didn't know who she was, and at four in the morning, jacked up, she was checking the gossip sites in New York to see if they'd written about her that week. That was my first encounter with her.

"And she considers herself a player, too, in the sense that she can play in this world—the world you're talking about. She thinks she's a manipulator . . . and, in fact, a girl I know, Elizabeth Jawhary—who is not a liar—claims that she was in a room with Ted Field . . . She has pictures of her and Paris doing a fucking lesbian show for Teddy. I've seen pictures of it."

"Yes, that's true," Jawhary says matter-of-factly, reached at her home in Texas. "I was present—absolutely. But with Paris, it was very low-key. She would fly down and I was there with them. We would party pretty hard. Paris was just a party girl and seemed just to be having fun. But she had no problem getting naked for those guys. That's what she did. I remember her hiding her face around some Asian guys because they might know her family."

Darnell's got his own claims of public sex with Paris—in the back seat of his Mercedes at an after-party at pro skateboarder Chad Muska's house, with two people in the front seat, or in the back room of the downtown L.A. strip club Spearmint Rhino, with a stripper-dancer, where a private lap-dance mutated into some kind of semipublic three-way. But as usual, Darnell manages to one-up everyone else.

On the day that Darnell collected money for an unpaid tab from P. Diddy at the Ivy, apparently fashion photographer David La Chappelle was dining nearby and witnessed the entire exchange. Later that afternoon, Darnell claims he received a call from Paris, who was doing a shoot with La Chappelle at one of the bungalows at the Chateau Marmont on Sunset and asked him to stop by. When he arrived, he discovered that the photo shoot amounted to grace lessons, with La Chappelle trying to teach her some signature modeling poses—the sideways glance with her mouth half open and the like. When they were alone, she told Darnell she had a favor she'd like to ask.

"Paris's problem turned out to be simple," says Darnell. "She needed to stay away from cameras. 'Okay, okay, what I'm saying is, this guy has some photos of me . . . some nude photos . . . can you get them back for me? And he's got this video of me with my old boyfriend. Well, he wasn't my boyfriend.' " She names a famous rock star—one who is on record as saying he found her attractive. As Darnell tells it, to seal the deal, Darnell and Paris had sex on the floor of the makeshift studio, with La Chappelle accidentally stumbling upon them and backing out apologetically. A week later, Darnell walked in on the man who allegedly held this latest Paris video at his apartment. After he quietly explained what it was he needed, the man turned over the contraband without an argument.

But for all the attention he spends on her, Darnell's stated position seems to be that, as far as having sex with Paris goes—really, who didn't?

"Me banging Paris was no big newsworthy thing to me," says Darnell. "I did it before she became the porn queen or the paparazzi magnet. On the tape that was on the *Dateline* piece, she acted like we only saw each other one or two times in the club and that was the extent of our world. She didn't mention the back-and-forth texting. The pet names. Me calling her rock star. 'What zip code r u in?' '10119.' Familiar shit. I believe there's enough there to infer that I've fucked her on several occasions. Not that I was the first, the best, or the last, but that it was as casual as the text messages we exchanged."

Virtually everyone I talked to for this book has some Paris Hilton story. It seems to be the one proof of service among the veterans of these foreign wars. One such source tries to put the Paris sex tape into perspective:

"I've known Paris since she was eighteen years old. Paris was the most reckless girl I ever met. At eighteen, she came to me to try and get a fake ID. I was going to help her, but she wound up going down to Alvarado by herself to get a fake driver's license so she could drink in bars. She was always unfaithful to everyone with Rick, except for Jason Shaw. They [Paris, Lenz, and Rovero] all lived together in the Hollywood Hills. Rick was seeing Nicole Lenz, and Paris is extremely jealous of that relationship.

"Rick loves to get a piece of the spotlight. With Shannen he got that. [When] Paris was with Jason, Rick and Shannen met through friends and they went and did a quickie marriage in Vegas. Rick's MO, unfortunately, is to be very manipulative. Whether Rick had money or not, he was always looking to get more money. And yes, it is fair to say he was broke at the time of the Paris Hilton tape. Paris did wreck his car—it was an Escalade. And yes, she did owe him money. Ultimately, though, there was no betrayal from either of them."

Rick and Shannen Doherty were separated in October 2002 and the marriage was annulled in 2003—Darnell says because she was worried about the threat of lawsuits stemming from the Paris tape. Doherty had at least one public spat with Paris, and in Episode #5 of the first season of *The Simple Life*, while playing Trivial Pursuit with their hosts, the Leding family, after the question, "Shannen Doherty is the star of what show?" Paris says quietly, "I hate that girl."

As a side note, Darnell claims that all monies due him for his help with the tape were paid through Rick's media company, and he always cashed the checks immediately. The one exception was the final month before his arrest, March 2005, when he deposited his monthly check directly into his checking account. It's taken five months of wrangling with Wells Fargo, but they finally released the check. Made out to "Darnell Riley" and dated March 8, 2005, it is drawn on RSTT Enterprises, LLC, the name of Rick's company, with a Las Vegas address. (At that time, it was a Nevada company: the same company name was registered in California in May 2007.) On the memo line is printed the word "Final." It makes a pretty good case they had business of some kind.

"My point being," says Darnell, on the tail end of some discourse, "it ain't shit to me to casually tell you I fucked Paris Hilton in the back of my Benz and two people got in the front and started talking, but we continued. That's high school juvenile shit, I agree, but that world is like none that you've ever seen. That's why I love the Studio 54 book [*The Last Party*, by Anthony Haden-Guest]. The photos are insane. You've got well-known dope dealers mingling in one with Liza Minnelli, Liz Taylor, Betty Ford, and the underworld of the nightclub scene, with Secret Service agents looking on. The nightlife in L.A. isn't too much different. What am I doing at a party with Paris Hilton, Leo DiCaprio, Michael Bay, et cetera? Okay, take my name out and put in Rick Salomon's. Take his out and put in Chuck Pacheco's. Now put in Will Wright's. We're all cut from the same cloth. As of right now, I'm the only one who's lost my anonymity. I'm the obvious culprit. But I'll be back."

X-MEN

*I*n the late nineties, the kings of the roost were the Ecstasy dealers—the guys who were flush with cash, who drove $140,000 automobiles, accessorized with the finest women, and always picked up the tab. And according to the U.S. government, there were no bigger Ecstasy dealers anywhere, at any time, than Louis Ziskin, Tamer Ibrahim, his brother John (later shot in the head after early release), Eyal "Al" Maimon, and a handful of associates, many of them of Israeli or Middle Eastern heritage, who imported Ecstasy from Amsterdam, resulting in the biggest Ecstasy bust in U.S. history in July 2000 (over one thousand pounds). This was part of "Operation Red Tide," an undercover multinational task force that revealed that Sammy "the Bull" Gravano, the former Gambino family underboss and enforcer, in conjunction with local Aryan gangs, had cornered the Phoenix Ecstasy market after leaving the Witness Protection Program, which he entered after serving as the government's chief witness against John Gotti (for whom he performed a reported nineteen contract hits). But Sammy the Bull was just a marquee name consigned to mid-level billing, running twenty-five thousand pills a week. These guys were bringing in two million doses at a time. After turning himself in and weathering two indictments and one trial, Ziskin was sentenced to thirty years. After fighting his way through two appeals and representing himself on the second indictment, he ended up with fifteen years.

Louis Ziskin was also Kristen Williams's boyfriend, and it was during his tenure at Taft Federal Prison in Kern County that he met Will Wright and provided an unwitting entrée for Will into Hollywood. Louis was well liked in the L.A. club scene, and when Will walked into the ongoing party with Kristen on his arm, it didn't sit well with a lot of people—even before Will started sizing up the nightclub world with a predatory zeal. Darnell relates the tale as he heard it:

"Louis wasn't even convicted yet, and Kristen had already moved on to this new character, Will. The problem was, Will wasn't Louis. Louis used to have a million in cash in his apartment. He had Kristen driving around in bulletproof BMWs. He had office space in the ICM building [the International Creative Management agency headquarters on Wilshire Boulevard], so he had a legal front to him. Kristen was the hot young model-actress with the rich boyfriend. Louis is a good guy. Everyone loved him. And just like me, the pricks turned on him once the Feds came. Even the girl. Kristen caught a little hell with people around town, but people quickly forgot when they got word of the next party. The creep Will's time was coming up.

"I had a couple of connects with the boys in the Feds, so I paid Louis Ziskin a visit while he was at MDC [Metropolitan Detention Center] in downtown Los Angeles to see what he knew about Will. I checked Will out with Louis and he tells me the whole story of how Will got to Kristen. Louis and Al [Maimon] were fighting their case and Will was about to get released to a halfway house. Louis was getting all type of pressure from Kristen for more money—she had the BMW, Benz, ten-carat diamond rings, jewelry, and a fat allowance, but she wanted more. She knew a lot of people were ratting on Louis, so she wanted to liquidate all she could from him before he got his time. Louis told Will his story, and Will just conveniently had a friend who owned a luxury car lot out in Orange County called J Star Motors. So Kristen wanted to get rid of her CL-500 Benz worth eighty-thousand dollars to free up some cash. Louis gave him the hookup and Will worked his charm. Kristen thought she had a whale in Will and she jumped ship. There were so many chicks showing their true nature, thinking he was going to put them in his movie that he had coming out. He had the doctored-up paperwork and fake indictments fudging the numbers on how much product he had. All his aces were ready. He sold his story. But he neglected to clear it all with me. Remember, I've seen his type before. I knew he wasn't kosher. People fell for his drag too easy. Initially, I thought he was a cop. It was too perfect.

"Once Louis told me how Kristen had left him for Will, I didn't like him. Louis wasn't buried yet and ma'fuckas was spitting on his grave. His body wasn't cold yet and his turf was getting cut up. I also found out from Louis that Will is a bitch. Al had to protect Will on the yard several times because of gambling debts he couldn't pay up. He lived off of his parents' money. He blamed his incarceration on them, and they felt guilty so they gave him whatever he wanted. All the cash he was gambling with was his parents' and Kristen's. So armed with my information, I knew I could play on his vulnerabilities. He was spending like a crackhead, trying to buy his way into Hollywood, like so many other fly-by-night characters who burn out before they get the keys to the city."

All I knew about Will's time at Taft was what someone by the colorful name of Big Paul Sung had posted on the WhoIsWillWright? site. "Will was at Taft CI [Correctional Institution] when I got there in 2002, and he stood out as a liar in a place full of liars," read the reverse testimonial. "He would tell a story 'he obviously heard some[where] else' and regurgitate it as his own . . . The guy's a joke."

Since Big Paul Sung wasn't in any of the corners I was looking in, it seemed like if anyone was willing to give me an unexpurgated reading on Will's character, it was probably a cuckolded drug czar doing federal time who had been the first one to see Will coming. And one thing about a con sitting in lockup—they'll receive any visitor, sight unseen. And so on a Sunday morning, I waited in a private sunlit conference room adjacent to the cafeteria on the Camp side of Taft, where low-risk inmates are housed in low-slung buildings adjacent to the main prison. The prison proper is where Louis's friend Tamer is still housed, where Will lived during his time here, and where Al Maimon spent three years before he walked on a twenty-four-year bid, which is still a sore point among those he left behind. Louis Ziskin greets me with his signature shaved head (one of his street names was "Baldy"), a healthy prison-yard tan, crisp khakis, and a clean white thermal shirt. He's short like I am, with piercing brown eyes, but much better built—although, to be fair, I don't spend much time pumping iron on the main yard.

"Who the fuck are you?" Louis says as he is ushered into my presence— less a threat than a kind of bemused curiosity, as if he can't imagine what this place has in store for him next. I run down my story, and he seems happy to get into it with me. Luckily, this is something he's thought a lot about long before I showed up. He tells me if he'd known I was coming, he would have had his shirt pressed. He's got a guy to do that for him, as well as someone to cook whatever food he orders from the commissary. He tells me he lives like a rock star; his time in the high life still throws a long shadow, and the rumor that he's got money on the outside doesn't hurt, even if he's got a $9 million judgment against him he'd have to retire before he started slinging any serious bling. The downside is that they throw him in the hole once a year for not giving anybody up, or just on general principle. (And, in fact, soon after our meeting, they shipped him off to sunny Tucson in the dead of summer, where presumably his legend carried less cachet.) He pointed to a tented area outside where visitors can gather, a corner of which can't be seen by the guard towers, where it is theoretically possible to have undetected sex with visitors. If I ever go down, I want to do his time.

Louis doesn't remember the conversation with Darnell in MDC (or, really, Darnell at all), although he does remember the day word came down about Kristen and Will. "I stood on the rec deck and screamed, 'What else can you throw at me, God?' " says Louis. "I quit smoking right then and there." Their mystery confab aside, he does confirm most of what Darnell has told me, if not exactly in the same order. He also never met Will—although word on a character like Will travels fast, whether in prison or out. With not much else available to him besides perspective, it seems like there's not much that escapes Louis's notice. His particular curse is that there's little he can do about it.

"Will used to get beat up here all the time," says Louis. "He had a black guy slap him in the middle of the unit and didn't even throw a punch. He didn't do anything. It's worse to get slapped than punched. Al Maimon met him right here. Al wants to rat. The government wants my money. Al has made a name for himself. Al and Will are hanging out here—playing ball, betting on football. They ran a [sports] book, but they got ripped off badly by the Mexicans. Once it got around that Al was a rat, it got worse for them: the Mexicans taxed them heavily. So Al tells Will to hook up with Kristen through his wife. 'Find out where Louis's money is at. When I get out, I'll set you up. We'll make a ton of money working for the government.' That was the deal.

"Will sold Maimon's car. Al needed cash—probably for his wife. How I found out about Will, the whole thing: Guy here named Stanley did sixteen years flat. He gets out, and Will owes him money for football. Will and Kristen meet him at the Beverly Center. Will takes him shopping, they have lunch, Will asks, 'What's up with Al?' Stanley says, 'Al is waiting for

Louis and Tamer to go to trial so he can testify against them and get out.' Will says, 'Old news. What else?' Stanley goes to see a paralegal. Paralegal comes up and tells me what's going on. This is why [Kristen and I] don't talk. Kristen never warned me. I understand that you're not going to jump in front of a train for me, but at least call out my name.

"To keep it fair, I was in a downswing when I met her. She took care of me, fed me, maxed her credit cards for me. And Will spent her money, stole her jewelry, beat her up. Remember: I saw him coming before he did. Ask Kristen for the letters: 'He is going to use you and burn all of our friends.' Anybody that knows me will tell you that I see angles before they are being played. He's an open mike for the Feds, and they can turn him on and off whenever they want. He's a sociopath. He's reasonably intelligent. He knows how to pick his spots well. The problem with Will was not that he was a lying, fraudulent rat; it was that he made them all look and feel stupid. But I begrudge her nothing. Don't forget, Will Wright got her what she wanted: her fifteen minutes. He got her you. Without you, she had no fifteen minutes—no *Dateline*, no VH1, no book.

"I know what Will's play is when I get out: he'll meet me with a suit-case full of cash and say, 'See? I did it all for you.' Will wanted to be me. They *all* want to be me until it's time to do thirty years." I ask him what happens to guys like Will Wright. He answers me with a joke, except he's serious.

"They become studio heads. I mean, look at the characteristics of a stu-dio head: they lack compunction, they are reasonably intelligent, and they are always willing to roll the dice. That's Will Wright. You think that your problem is your best friend is fucking your wife? That's probably the good news."

He's also very vocal on Ron Richards, the attorney for (so far): Darnell Riley, Will Wright, Timmy Iannello, Erin Naas, Al Maimon, and Tamer Ibrahim. Richards prides himself on his Ecstasy acquittals: his official bio states, "In 2000 and 2001, Mr. Richards defended more MDMA or Ecstasy cases than any attorney in the United States. His office has handled more Ecstasy cases than any other in America and has represented defendants in each of the three largest seizures in U.S. history."

"He functions as a de facto U.S. attorney for [the Feds]," says Louis bluntly. "He's the classic example of what Hollywood does to people. Ron was real tough back in the day—a known gunslinger. Now, he's turned a hundred eighty degrees: all deals, no trials, all rats. The upside is that the federal government gets what they want. His real danger zone comes in about ten years—when everyone he's fucked over gets out. I paid him $75K to help me out, and he didn't do a fucking thing. He wrote me a double-jeopardy motion for my next trial, which I lost.

"[Ron and Will] are mutually parasitic, and if the balance of power ever shifts, then you are going to see some fireworks, because it is in both of their natures to prey on people in weakened conditions. This holds true for Will's informant relationship with the government as well. As soon as his criminality outweighs his usefulness to the Rat Pack, then you may see the government pull his protection."

Interviewed separately at his Sunset Towers office, Richards remembers avoiding Will altogether in deference to Louis's feelings, until Louis finally gave him express permission. Louis responds: "Yeah, I gave him explicit permission, based on the fact that Ron Richards came up and visited me—he and I were close at that time—and he *promised* me that Will was not a rat."

But the one subject that seems to dig deep into him is his former protégé Damon Kidwell, a successful graphic designer (in a company that Louis insinuates he bankrolled) and a good friend of Rick, Chuck Pacheco, etc. I met him with Heather and Jack in their Beverly Hills hotel room when I was reporting the *Dateline* story; he had a kind of aging-club-kiddishness about him. In an article on the front page of the *Los Angeles Times* on July 27, 2000, on the record-breaking $40 million Ecstasy seizure at LAX that sent Tamer Ibrahim on the run internationally and lit the fuse on Louis's fate, it was reported that Kidwell and a business partner were both arrested in conjunction with the smuggling ring that U.S. Attorney Alejandro N. Mayorkas said had "tentacles that reached throughout the world." After Ibrahim was arrested in Amsterdam September 6, the *Times* reiterated the information in a November 23 article, now calling them "Ibrahim's alleged top associates." On December 4, the *Times* issued a correction, which stated: "Federal authorities now say that while Kidwell was arrested, he was subsequently released, has not been charged 'and is not being prosecuted in relation to this case.' "

"Damon calls me," says Louis: " 'They're behind me! They're chasing me! Plain vehicle—it's the Feds!' Damon gets busted. He calls me from West Valley Detention Center later. I'm sick about it. I've already called my attorney. It's a half-million-dollar ticket to get him out. I told my lawyer, 'Whatever it takes—Damon is out before the end of the next business day.' Damon had called that night, before eleven p.m., on the jail phone: 'My bail is a half million dollars. Get me out of here now!' I told him I couldn't do it right then but that my lawyer would be down there before six a.m. Damon said, 'I know you have the cash. You have it in your safe.' I hang up on him. [My attorney] went to the jail the very next morning and called me: 'Damon is out.' I don't know how, but . . . okay. Now everyone is saying, 'Damon said something.' I didn't believe it. I got mad at people. I punched someone over that. I never even asked Damon. Later on that night, at Dublin's, Damon said, 'Bro, I didn't say anything.' I told him, 'I never asked you.'

"There's a lot of unanswered questions about Damon," says Louis wistfully. "There is no word in the world that can describe how close we were. Maybe the Spanish word *carnal*—'the meat.' I needed him to come testify for me, and he ran off to Canada. He broke my heart more than everyone else put together." (Kidwell refused to comment.)

A week after I visited Louis at Taft, I got a call from Tamer Ibrahim, who had spoken with Louis during their regularly scheduled weekly meetings and been brought up to speed on me. A Coptic Christian born in Egypt but raised in Woodland Hills, the thirty-three-year-old former international playboy, as he was labeled in *Vibe* magazine, currently looking at the last five of a dozen-year bid, was calling to weigh in as an elder statesman of the club scene—and maybe to buff up his legacy if the opportunity arose.

"Let me tell you," he says in a practiced spiel, "if there was any Ecstasy coming down from anywhere—from Miami, Vegas, or L.A. between 1997 and 2000—we had between eighty-five and ninety-five percent of that market sewed up. My PSI [pre-sentencing investigation report] reads like a gangster novel. You talk about Will Wright and these guys claiming all these crazy stories? I'll let the paperwork and the discovery do the talking." He sounded like he was selling me my next book.

Although Will was already out by the time he arrived—trailing Louis by half a year for the time he was on the lam in Mexico and Europe—Tamer couldn't help but follow his exploits via the jailhouse tribal drum.

"The funny thing about jail is that word spreads like wildfire," he says. "When I came here, I knew what Will was up to because of what happened between him and Louis's ex. He came here, and he might be a criminal, but he has no criminal sense. He doesn't have any street stripes or credibility or anything like that. He was acting so black that the whites didn't want him.

So he was hanging out with the blacks for a while, and then he stepped out of line and he got beat up. And then he and my codefendant [Al Maimon] were running a poker table here in jail, and apparently when people lost, they didn't want to pay them, and there was no recourse for them because they're not going to do anything about it. They shut it down because they couldn't collect. This place we're at right now is like the fucking Disneyland of prisons. I'd love to sit here and tell you some hardcore stories, but they didn't happen in here. At the other prison we were at, the penitentiary at Lompoc, he wouldn't have made it—people were getting their domes split. It wasn't even blood anymore; you could see the plasma coming out on a daily basis. He wouldn't have been able to run his bullshit over there; they would have already canceled his contract.

"I ran into a black guy here, and he hooked Will up on the outside, where he was supposed to go do something. Will ended up doing it and got the money and never kicked this guy back his commission for the hookup. So the guy is like, 'Look, I don't care when I'm gonna get out'—because a little bit of money to a guy in jail is big money. If you promise somebody five or ten grand, they could be down twenty years, but you'd better believe they're going to come looking for that five grand. If that's his MO, then it's only a matter of time."

About Ron Richards, Tamer says unequivocally, "He is only where he is today because of me. When he first started out, he didn't know anybody. I brought him into the scene, I introduced him to friends who had cases. It started off with five or ten thousand dollars—you know, small cases. And then he started getting up to the forty- to fifty-thousand-dollar mark, hundred-thousand-dollar drug cases, and he won a few. He's a good attorney when he wants to be. We used to party in Miami, in Vegas, at all the clubs and everything—that's how close we were. And then this whole thing happened and I just saw his true colors.

"If Will comes back to jail, he's got a drug prior—that's a ten-year minimum mandatory on the case that you just caught, and if you have a prior they double it, and you're looking at an automatic twenty. And he's not about to come lay down for eighteen years, which is how much you have to do on that. So he's going to cooperate."

I tracked Kristen Williams down in New York, where she was now living full time. After the Will Wright debacle got her eighty-sixed from her own life for a couple of years, she briefly returned to exotic dancing—at the Spearmint Rhino in Las Vegas and, according to David Reich, Club Paradise across from the Hard Rock.

"Do you know how much I cried before I had to go fucking work there?" Kristen asks when I meet with her at a restaurant in SoHo. "I'm a grown woman now, I don't care what people know. I'm not proud of that, but after Will took me for so much money, I had to get myself out of debt. I was way down in the hole." Still a smart-looking woman, even well into her thirties, Kristen later would send a text apologizing for having been out of touch, when the mysterious call girl who was about to bring down straight-arrow New York governor Elliot Spitzer, identified only as "Kristen" (real name Ashley Dupre), was discovered to be living in the same building and (our) Kristen woke up with several hundred voice messages on her cell phone. Darnell claims she fled to New York after she and Heather were depicted as party girls on the *Dateline* special, but Kristen seems less humiliated than simply mystified.

"*Dateline* didn't show anything at all of the whole reason why we went on there," she says. "I feel like they cut out a lot of the incriminating stuff—like Will made them do it. It made no sense."

She confirms having first met Will while living with Eyal's wife, Andrea, before his release, in an apartment along the Wilshire Corridor.

"She was trying to sell their car," says Kristen. "They needed money. Eyal was like, 'Talk to Will. He knows a guy in Orange County.' That was Jared [Merrell]. We met Will at lunch, and I told Andrea that I would go with her because she was nervous about going by herself. So I did the whole transaction with her. [Louis] bought me a bulletproof BMW because he was worried about me, and that was paid off, so we ended up selling that and one other car."

She met Ron Richards at Louis's trial, where he represented Al Maimon and had recently won acquittal for another alleged Ecstasy dealer, Jacob "Cookie" Orgad. She says Ron was constantly hitting on her, "but I've met a lot of people like that."

"It's still hard for me to look at a photo of Louis six, seven years later," Kristen says. "He was so good to me. His family was wealthy, and he was a really brilliant guy. He could have continued on with college and everything, but he wanted everything right away. When I finally figured out what he was doing, I told him that if he wanted to be with me, then he had to get out of it as quickly as possible. He kept me out of most of it, because he treated me like a princess.

"With Damon, he protected him like he protected me. He invested money for him to get his business going, and now he has a successful business. Louis cared for him so much as a brother. He did think that Damon rolled over on him for a while, and Damon was blackballed from Holly-wood for a good year and a half or two years—kind of like what I went through. And then finally Louis asked me to ask him something, and then Damon started telling everyone, 'It's okay, everything is good now,' and he was sort of let back into the crowd."

Kristen's friend Heather remembers a party during one of her infre-quent visits to Los Angeles with her husband when she acknowledged the elephant in the living room to all of Kristen's old friends and Will's new ones. "Jack and I were in L.A.," says Heather, "and it was Louis Ziskin's first birthday in prison. I remember sitting in the restaurant, and Kristen was there and she was dating Will. Kristen was still very much in love with Louis. I know his birthday. Because of how great this guy has been to my family and to Jack through his hard times mentally, as a friend, I come out with a birthday cake for Louis in front of Will. With all due respect, if you have any class, you just kind of say your good-byes. It's kind of like a death. I told him, 'I'm really sorry if I was rude to you, but it's all on behalf of my friend. I'm going to go with my judgment; I have to.' That's what friends are for. So I brought out the birthday cake and Will just *cringed*. And then he kind of just went, 'Well, that would be great. It would be great to know that if I was in jail, people would do this for me.' That was classy. But then, Will would never get a cake."

Heather sees only one motive in Will's actions toward Kristen, her hus-band, herself, and everyone he ever met: "Money, obviously. He just needed more money, to manipulate more powerful people, because he used every-one as a stepping-stone: he owed Jack [an $80,000 debt he has still never repaid], and he'd get some money here and get some there, and he got Kristen's money, and then he started hanging out with celebs, and he just used everybody as a stepping-stone. I think that's why Louis wanted to get the word out to Jack. Jack is credible and wonderful and honorable, so Louis—I believe in my heart of hearts—wanted to get the word out that this is a *bad* guy—a bad egg. And the message did get out there, but so many people were like, 'No, no, no' because he was already in the works."

"Everybody loved Louis," says Kristen. "He didn't screw anybody over. He was always trying to help people. He was the antithesis of Will. And Will just wanted to believe that he could be the new Louis. I told him how everyone loved and respected Louis, but he couldn't do it. He tried to, but he got it completely screwed up."

HIGH SCHOOL WITH MONEY

s any high school guidance counselor will tell you, secondary education curriculum is designed to teach civic skills, interpersonal relationships, compassion, restraint, the public virtues—all the things
that keep the collective social order greased and running on the rails. High
school is also where you chase after the popular kids, get in fights after
school, party like there's no tomorrow, betray your closest friends, and
hopefully get it all out of your system in time to become a productive member of society.

Welcome to Los Angeles, city of perpetual youth.

"Will was new to L.A. and hardly knew anyone," says Kristen in her
formal apologia on the WhoIsWillWright.com site. "I, on the other hand,
after living here for nine years, know a lot of people. I started bringing Will
out with me and introducing him to people, hoping he could make some
good business contacts. I took him to dinner with my friends Brandon
Davis and Paris Hilton, introduced him to Rich [Jardine], who had an advertising company; Chuck [Pacheco], a movie producer; promoters that I
knew, so he could get into all the parties, and some of my very dear and
close friends.

"Will took my money, several thousand dollars at a time, and told me he
was investing it in various things. The deals would always fall through and
he would come back asking for more money. Just to let you know, I was not
blindly investing. I checked up on things, but, he always had contracts and
documented proof of the transactions (obviously made in Photoshop, but

unknown to me at the time). Come to find out, Will was taking my money and living on it . . . He bought tables at the clubs and bottles and bottles of Cristal. He even paid for hotel rooms where he took girls after convincing them he was rich and that his family owned StarKist Tuna. He bought hookers with my money. He told people that my Mercedes, my jewelry and everything in my apartment were his. He told girls that he gave me $10,000 a month to shop on. The lies were endless. He tried to take credit for everything that Louis my ex fiancé did for me.

"It makes me sick to think of it now. He screwed over many of my friends and owes some of them hundreds of thousands of dollars. He wouldn't even be in this town if it weren't for me. To my friends: I feel horrible for introducing him to you. I owe everyone an apology. I am very glad he is out of my life. I just wish I could get some of the friends I lost because of him back into my life."

Kristen confirms that Will started chasing Paris Hilton soon after she introduced them in early 2003 (his name and Pacific Northwest cell phone number appear in Paris's T-Mobile notes—a functioning Rosetta Stone—four days after Darnell's do).

"He used to chase her," says Kristen in an interview. "I'd be with him in a restaurant, and he'd be running around after Paris: 'What are you doing? You're fucking chasing her!' " Among the people Kristen claims to have been estranged from in her social group as a result of unleashing Will like a virus into their closed circle are Koi owner of Dipu Haque and his brother Nick, Rich Jardine, Heather and her husband, Jack, independent producers Scott Bloom and Giovanni Agnelli, Chuck Pacheco, producer Steve Bing, and others. "Brandon Davis still won't talk to me because of it," she says. "Paris and I have made up since then. And Nicky—we've made up since then. The whole crowd. Because everybody heard about it"—she means the Joe Francis invasion—"and thought that I had something to do with it."

Kristen reports that Will used to hire paparazzi to take pictures of him coming out of the clubs, and she also takes credit for introducing Will to Timmy Iannello. "He was like 'Wow, Will is awesome—you should marry this guy,' " she says. "But then I find out later that they're scheming stuff: Will is telling him 'Oh, I can help you with money.' The same thing he did with Brandon Davis. How he got everyone on his side was always [identifying] whatever problems they had. He was good at reading what their problems were, and coming up with, 'Oh, I can do this for you.' Even though he never actually came up with an answer, or helped them. The thing is, Will—if he needs you for a specific thing—he'll make up something to start talking to you. 'Oh, I have this going on, and I can help you with that.' And it might be for only one tiny thing that he's trying to prove, but he'll scam this whole event around that."

Kristen eventually got wind of Will's affairs with model Erin Naas and others and kicked him to the curb—apparently only $250,000 too late. She also entertains the idea that Will might have been bisexual—Darnell and others have linked him to high-profile male figures. "I think Will might have had a bit of a gay streak in him," she says. "Normally, if a guy was in jail, I wouldn't think anything of it, but he totally liked things up his ass. It's okay, but it's where it comes from, you know?" Granted, this is coming from an ex-girlfriend, albeit one who doesn't seem especially squeamish about Topic A.

("At one time Paris was Will's Best Friend Forever, but then she started saying, 'All he ever told me was that he wanted to fuck me up the ass,' " says Scott Bloom, who knew both in his capacity as a film producer and one-time nightclub promoter, and who still remembers Paris as a skinny kid on roller skates when she first showed up in his clubs. "She took an about-face on him," he adds, in a curious turn of phrase. "The worst day of Will Wright's life is the day people are indifferent to him.")

The last Kristen heard of Will, a friend told her he was moving to New York, shortly after she did. "He just wanted to freak me out," she says.

Random comments on the WhoIsWillWright.com site create a composite profile of Will. "He told me he had to go to JFK Airport to pick up forty million dollars worth of coke," says one. "I knew this guy for less than a week and he is volunteering information like that." "He shopped at designer stores and would pretend he bought everything, and would put it on hold and never pick it up," says another. "He told me he had a production company with Leonardo DiCaprio," says "Allison from San Diego." "He also told me his best pals were Paris and Nicky Hilton, Nicole Richie (he said they had sex; who knows if that's true), Leonardo, and Mickey Rourke. He said we could maybe go to a party at their house after . . . What a crazy boy! He fooled me."

One victim was Chuck Pacheco, then a club promoter at the Belmont on La Cienega—just down the block from Club Prey, another Pacheco cash cow (later the Gate, now Area), and across the street from Koi, the club kids' unofficial sushiteria—whose Wednesday karaoke night was the consensus Hump Day hang for the coalescing club elite. Pacheco was also the equivalent of a made man through his childhood friendships with and ongoing access to Leonardo DiCaprio and Tobey Maguire—something the others desperately craved but would always be denied by birthright. It's also how Darnell's and Will's trajectories ultimately crossed.

In February 2003, Darnell claims that Will had made what Rick considered inappropriate advances toward Shannen Doherty (not that Rick really had room to talk).

"The infamous Will," says Darnell. "Chuck runs him down as being this huge crazy white dude who just got out of the Feds for a huge drug bust in Washington. Will was supposed to be spending big money around town, buying up tables at all of Chuck's clubs (Prey, Shelter, the Belmont)." Darnell describes a plan they hatched, but never executed. "When Will goes to the Belmont, I'll get the keys from the valet. We will go to their apartment (Kristen and Will's), where he will have at least a million bucks or the product.

"Will fucked up with Rick when he tried to get with Shannen Doherty (before I knew him) and it had Rick hot boiling mad. As the plot to take him down was formulating, Will was hyping himself to Shannen, telling her he had racehorses. (At that time, he didn't own a horse.) He wanted her to invest money for him. The wheels were spinning, and Will was marked." (When asked about Will and Darnell, Pacheco declined to comment, other than to say, "I've moved on from all that.")

Today, Pacheco is the co-owner of Villa, the latest in state-of-the-art Hollywood clubgoing: a nightspot so exclusive that the paying public is no longer welcome. According to the *New York Times*, one hundred A-list celebrities will be given VIP cards bearing computer chips that will wirelessly alert the doormen of their arrival, and an optional tunnel of curtains allows passage from limo to lounge without interference from the paparazzi, which easily outnumber celebrities at most nightspots these days. (Gone are the days, apparently, when Frank Sinatra peeled off a crisp fifty to every doorman and parking valet he ever met.) Of course, with a comp list at the door and presumably free drinks inside, it's difficult to identify their profit stream exactly, but then, you might have said the same thing about Paris Hilton four years ago, and you would have been wrong.

(Pacheco's partners in Villa are Reza Roohi, late of club mogul Sam Nazarian's SBE company, and Vince Laresca, also a partner in the Belmont, who had a recurring role as a rival drug dealer on *Weeds*, with whom series lead Mary-Louise Parker's character once had sex in an alley. The club is located in the shadow of the Pacific Design Center, in a space that once housed the more populist J. Sloan's, a bar where I used to hang out with the *Film Threat* crowd a decade ago. Sloan's entered Hollywood lore in the mid-nineties when bartender Troy Duffy sold his spec script *Boondock Saints* to Harvey Weinstein at Miramax and became the consensus winner of the much-sought-after indie film lottery—a rumored deal point was that Miramax would actually buy the bar for him. The feature documentary about Duffy's inevitable crash and burn—titled *Overnight*, and initially bankrolled by Duffy himself—was released at roughly the same time as the events in this book. At the film's local premiere at the Los Angeles Film Festival in June 2004, someone asked the filmmakers, Tony Montana and Mark Brian Smith, why they spent so much time documenting such stupendous arrogance and prevarication, which was, after all, not uncommon in their chosen profession. Their answer went something like, "This story may well be universal, but this was our only chance to tell it." Exactly.)

Pacheco was also one of the producers of the 2006 film *Alpha Dog*, Nick Cassavetes's lightly fictionalized account of Jesse James Hollywood, a Los Angeles drug dealer and possible aspirational figure to many of those under discussion, who became one of the youngest persons ever to grace the FBI's Ten Most Wanted List after his disappearance in 2000. (Hollywood was arrested in Saquarema, Brazil, in 2005 and extradited to the U.S. to stand trial after the film was already in production.) Starring Emile Hirsch in the title role and Justin Timberlake in an impressive supporting part that guaranteed him an acting career, the film features small cameos by Rick Salomon as a used car dealer ("Hey, the Captain and Tenille, what can I do for you guys?")—looking gaunt, speedy, and ashen in his boho hipster getup and porkpie hat—and Pacheco himself as a comical high-desert stoner in a wife beater, with a marijuana leaf tattooed on his arm ("Yo, I'm going to Fiesta, and when I get back, none of you motherfuckers better be here"). Will and Kristen reportedly completed a cameo as well, but it was cut from the release version. Although he says he visited the set, Darnell opted to retain a low profile. But their stories are incorporated into the film, even if they aren't. In *The Making of* Alpha Dog: *A Cautionary Tale*, the documentary featurette released on the DVD, Timberlake sums up this tale and all those like it: "Everybody was young once; everybody thought they were indestructible at one time." Costar Sharon Stone adds, "You see them acting like they were big shots, big gangsters, but in truth they were kids." (Pacheco is listed as a producer on Cassavetes's Cameron Diaz vehicle, *My Sister's Keeper*, scheduled for release in March 2009. Nicole Lenz is among the cast.)

Darnell presents the following anecdote to put Pacheco in perspective:

"He fucked over Rich Jardine at Beverly Hills Bookie," says Darnell, "when we had him as an agent and gave him a line of credit to have his players on our roster. We had personal players—'off-the-book players,' as we called them—guys that you trusted and/or had on a short leash in case they tried to stiff you for the cash. There are guys who don't want paper trails through our Web site. So we all had our off-the-book players. Any player who had to call in or go online, they had to enter their code and password to talk and to confirm every bet. Chuck called in and said he was signing up two more players. Keep in mind, we're recording every call. So he gets his two new on-the-book players' codes and passwords, and a couple of weeks pass and he places bets for them. They win—he wins. Except there is no 'they.' He is 'they.' They lose big, he says they ran out on him (deadbeats). If it's small cash (under ten thousand), we generally blacklist a guy with all the sites and if we catch up to him, we can collect. But 'they' lost. I went over to Rich's house in early 2004. I had already felt Chuck was up to something all of 2003. But Rich finally had confirmation. Rich puffed his chest up and said some big shit, but didn't do much about it. He cut Chuck off. This is after 'they' already looted us for maybe $20K over a year."

Giovanni Agnelli and Scott Bloom were partners in Wednesday nights at the Belmont with Pacheco and Laresca. They also ran a film production company and were the ones who fell for Will's endless stories and optioned his life rights for a feature film—to be directed by first Michael Bay and then Joe Carnahan, just off the success of *Narc*. It's a decision they appear sanguine about today, albeit a good deal quicker on the uptake.

"We don't even go out at night anymore," says Giovanni of their days in the club wars. "We've had our fill. We were the best. We dominated Hollywood nightlife a couple of nights a week: Shelter, Lobby, Belmont. We had Mick Jagger at our clubs while others had Paris Hilton. Nobody has been able to duplicate what we did, and we're done." Donald Thrasher was briefly their doorman, and they later invested in his stevia soda. Like Paris, Giovanni is a scion of wealth—among the heirs to the Fiat fortune, the Italian car company founded by his namesake in 1899, an institutional fortune his proximity to which is evidenced by the $80,000 Rolex Masterpiece on his wrist. This is the same Rolex that Will tried to purloin in one of their early meetings, using one of the oldest scams in the book.

"He had the same model in a really bad knockoff," says Giovanni. "It had a green sticker on the back of it. He was looking at mine and going, 'Oh yeah, this is cool!' and when he gave the watch back to me, it was his watch. As soon as he handed it to me, I was like, 'This isn't my watch.' And he said, "Yeah, that's yours. Dude, it is.' And then he goes, 'Mine's fake—look, yours is real, it has the authenticated sticker on the back.' I said, 'No, it doesn't. I peeled mine off. Give me my fucking watch back.'"

Giovanni's partner, Scott Bloom, has racked up a dozen acting credits on the strength of his intense good looks. Most recently, he played an FBI agent in his friend Joe Carnahan's *Smokin' Aces*. But he is most prominently featured in *Don's Plum*, and odd black-and-white independent feature, almost entirely improvised, named for the late-night diner where a group of young actors collect and interact. The film began life as a 1994 short by director R. D. Robb in which Leo DiCaprio and Tobey Maguire, whose stars were just then ascendant, agreed to appear with an ensemble of actor friends in the interest of raising their collective profile, while taking the showiest roles for themselves. This ran aground once the director wanted to release the film as a feature and DiCaprio and Maguire filed suit, claiming breach of contract. The stalemate was eventually resolved in 1998 when all parties agreed the film could be released in all territories except the U.S. and Canada. Among the actors on display are Kevin Connolly of *Entourage* (who dated Nicky Hilton in 2004), Jenny Lewis (now of the band Rilo Kiley), Jeremy Sisto and his sister Meadow, Giovanni Ribisi's twin sister, Marisa (now married to Beck), *CSI: Las Vegas*'s Heather McComb (now married to James Van Der Beek), and *Buffy the Vampire Slayer*'s Amber Benson.

Giovanni identifies Pacheco as a role model for Kevin Dillon's character in *Entourage*, although any number of people have compared him to Turtle, the self-effacing fixer who is loyal to a fault.

"Oh yeah—to Leo," says Kristen. "Because Chuck lived at Sunset Plaza also, and Leo would stay over all the time at Chuck's place. And Lukas Haas was living there also. So we'd wake up and they'd be walking across the street, and Leo would have his sunglasses on. We used to hang out at Leo's table at Club Prey—it's called Area or something now. And we'd go to Leo's house afterwards to party and stuff. But yeah—Chuck is kind of like Turtle, because Chuck will not say *anything*. They know they can trust him."

"It's easy to roll like that for a lot of people," says Giovanni, "just kind of kowtow and be a bit of a BS type of guy. Chuck is not even the worst of them."

From their vantage point at the Belmont, Giovanni and Scott were also able to see Will coming. Agnelli remembers one Wednesday night when the club was at capacity and the fire department had shut them down—a CNN camera crew had taken up residence on the sidewalk to capture fleeing celebrities while pandemonium reigned.

"We're trying to get the valet in priority," he says, "getting certain people their cars first. Certain people shouldn't be sitting on the sidewalk with all the paparazzi and the cameras. People were trying to get out the back door—it was chaos. We were trying to keep people away from the press. You've got to remember that the Belmont at the time was just a little struggling nightclub."

"It was a good location, but it was just a steakhouse that was teetering," adds Scott. "And we turned it out—they expanded it and bought the place next door."

Giovanni continues: "And Will came up to me and said, 'Chuck says you're a trustworthy guy. I have five girls and I have two cars here. I can't fit all these girls into this car. And I'm drunk, and I shouldn't be driving, plus I don't trust this bitch to drive my Ferrari. Can you park it somewhere safe tonight, or can you take it with you and bring it back to me tomorrow?' I said, 'I don't think you should leave your car here overnight, and I don't think I want to take your car to my house. I don't want to drive your car.' I asked where he lived, and he said Sunset Plaza. I said, 'That's right up the street. You go home, I'll follow you, my brother will follow me and it'll be done.' So, basically, I drove his car—a Ferrari—up to his house. And I believe it had a rental key chain on it, which I thought was really strange. I was like, 'Did he rent a car for the night? Whose car is this?' But what was really strange was when my brother said, 'I know this car. This isn't Will's car. This is my friend's car, who lives up in the hills. I know this license plate, because I know this guy from the gym.' Whatever—maybe they're friends. So we go up, give him his keys and leave." When I was dropping the Ferrari off, he said, 'Isn't the Scaglietti amazing?' But the Scaglietti wasn't even in production yet. It was a Modena." (The Ferrari 612 Scaglietti was released in 2004; production of the 360 Modena was suspended in 2005.)

"I don't even like talking about Chuck because he's such a maniac," says Scott. "I don't want to hear from him, all that nonsense. But I met Will with Chuck when he first got out of prison. It was at an Italian restaurant on Sunset, and Chuck pointed him out and said, 'That guy just got out of prison and he took Louis's girl.' He was with Kristen. Chuck was immediately painting him to me as this fucked-up, intriguing guy; that's the way I saw him. And the first time I talked to him was at the Belmont, and he said, 'I've got a stack of articles this tall that you guys have got to see about my life.' It wasn't tall tales, it was, 'I've got the papers to show you guys. You guys are making movies? You want an interesting story? I have an interesting story.'

"The owner of the Belmont had some partners who were pretty notorious," continues Giovanni. "And those partners—that's whose Ferrari it was. This guy Lucky and another guy used to work out at the gym, and my brother trained them. They were always like, 'We go out of town a lot, we have this great house in the hills, we have this Ferrari, we have a hot tub, and if you ever want to bring a chick up and use the hot tub when we're gone . . . ' My brother never took them up on that, but he remembered the Ferrari. Then a couple of weeks before that, my brother found out that these guys were bad news—through this whole other thing involving steroids and human growth hormone—like dealing and stuff. Then that night at the Belmont, they were sitting with Will—the owner of the Belmont, this guy Lucky, and Will. What was weird is that, when the police came, one guy took off—he threw his keys to Will and said, 'Take care of my car.' And I think Will gave the keys to me and said, 'Take care of my car.' I don't know if there was something in the car; I don't know if I was an idiot that took the car up for them or what. But the Ferrari was a device to make us think there was something more. He thought, 'Here's a way to make the people in charge here take notice of me and think that I'm important.' And then that following Wednesday night after we met, he was like, 'Why don't you guys come up to my apartment tomorrow, and I'll show you this thing.' "

Scott tells a version of the plan to have Will robbed. "According to Will, Chuck sent somebody up to Will's apartment to break into it and steal something—a painting, cash, something—because he knew that a heist, some sort of robbery, had taken place, and whatever it was, it was in Will's apartment. And when the guy got up to this address, he calls Will and says, 'Somebody hired me to steal something, and I got up here, and I realized— I've never been in your apartment, but I see pictures of you, I see your name and I realize that it's your apartment.' And Will goes, 'Who hired you?' And he gave up Chuck. And Will goes, 'Don't do it. Just let it go.' "

Darnell maintains that Pacheco never put the plan into motion. But a month later, Darnell met Will at the same time as Jerry Rosenberg did, when Mickey Rourke brought him along to lunch in Sunset Plaza for show and tell. That was when Will told Darnell about a jack move that Chuck Pacheco had pulled instead: Will said he had paid Pacheco $20,000 for access to Leo DiCaprio's courtside Lakers tickets when he wasn't using them. Later, after the money had changed hands, Pacheco explained that what Will had actually bought with his $20K was *access* to the tickets—he was essentially placed on a list with other A-listers. Will asked if something could be done about it.

Darnell claims he spoke to Pacheco, who sheepishly admitted his subterfuge and returned the money. Then seven months later, in late August or early September of 2003, without apparent warning, Pacheco was savagely beaten coming out of Shelter, the successful Thursday night venue he promoted at the club on the northwest corner of Sunset Boulevard and Crescent Heights, right where it turns into Laurel Canyon.

"I was with Chuck when he got beaten," says Scott. "You know it was Darnell, right? We were walking back to the car from Shelter. A masked guy jumped out of the bushes, pulled a gun on Chuck, hit him with the gun and busted his lip, then kicked him. Chuck was begging for his life: 'What did I do? I didn't do anything!' I wouldn't want to humiliate Chuck on that, but it was pretty terrible."

Jerry Rosenberg was also present at the beat-down—or at least nearby. "We were waiting there in the bushes for him," says Jerry. "But [Darnell] said, 'No Jerry—you just sit in the car.' "

Kristen also heard about the incident after the fact from Will himself. "I didn't know what had happened until a year later when Will told me that he told Chuck he had him beaten up," says Kristen. " 'Oh, bro, you know you got beat up like eight months ago? That was me. I had someone hired to beat you up.' With his arm around the guy's shoulder. 'Bro, I just wanted you to know that that was me.' What a dick."

"I don't think that Chuck knew it was Will [who was responsible]," says Giovanni. "I think he was scared."

The Pacheco beat-down, as he calls it, is one of those subjects that Darnell treads softly around: conditionally absolving himself while simultaneously leaving no doubt who might have been responsible.

"Chuck got his ass whipped as he was leaving Shelter one night by a short stocky guy," says Darnell. "Guess who? The masked man sat in the bushes for two hours waiting for Chuck to leave the club after closing at three or four a.m. Everyone speculated that Will and I had something to do with it. Chuck wasn't able to make out who the guy was that beat him down, or else he was too scared to say. This wasn't one of Hollywood's great unsolved mysteries—it was just business. Nothing was taken from him. Chuck told investigators that he never saw the guy. He said the guy just appeared out of the bushes and beat the shit out of him. Well, crime don't commit itself—somebody got to do it."

But Darnell ascribes the whole incident to business as usual. "A break-in, and a whole year later to let it boil?" says Darnell. "That's revenge. That's not me. It had better be business or money connected. I wanted to beat Chuck's ass so many times, but Rick begged me not to. Chuck fucked over both Rick and Rich. But it wasn't until Will put up some cash did things happen.

"Will brought in a couple of guys from Canada—dope dealers—and a couple of guys he knew from childhood who are legit, with successful real estate or construction companies. Will would bring them down to L.A. for a weekend and show them a good time—the cart in front of the horse— and wet their whistle, and they would invest in or loan on whatever gimmick he had. He had some dope connects with guys he knew from his time in the Feds; he had a nice New York-Detroit-Atlanta connect. He was trying to be the wild party guy: played out. Seen it before. But to those who thought he was the real deal, he was the man. I didn't buy it. He wasn't a mastermind. He latched onto whoever he could. But after a year of running his game on Kristen and spending money like crazy, getting caught banging chicks, flaking out on her and on business to chase after Paris and Nicky, he was starting to rust. The shine had left the gold-plated surface. Kristen had suspicions. People started questioning. His stories were just too far out. He was telling people that at fifteen, he had a mansion in Mexico, a cabin in Whistler in Canada. He got pinched with seventy million in drug money. Too much shit. Will knew I knew his drag. I ain't one to rain on someone's parade. I felt that all the hangers-on who tried to profit off of him, invested with him, fucked him, basically deserved what they got. 'Oh, he played me.' Well, you tried to play him, he just got you before you could get him. The story goes on. We ain't re-creating the wheel; we're just hamsters running in the same squeaky one that the Studio 54 crowd ran in, that the Rat Pack ran in, after imitating the Roaring Twenties Jazz Age. Nothing new under the sun."

THE $24,000 SUNDAE

If Paris Hilton is an heiress who isn't really an heiress, but plays one on television; if Darnell is a ghetto thug who was raised in the middle-class redoubt of Larchmont and reads Eastern philosophy in his spare time; if Joe Francis thinks he's Hugh Hefner or even Larry Flynt, but he's really Fatty Arbuckle, even if he doesn't know it yet; then it stands to reason that Will Wright could sell himself to the movies as a homegrown Pablo Escobar.

Here's the last paragraph of his treatment, a ten-page document and freelance marketing tool that tells his prospective story in paragraph form, sans dialogue or camera direction. I won't burden you with the plot, ripped as it is from the manufactured headlines, but you can get the gist of it:

"For as much fun as I did have, and for as much money as I did make, I had just as many losses, my best friend murdered in my arms, kidnapped and tortured, two of my pilots dead in a plane crash, many associates killed on a monthly basis, disappointing my entire family, losing my girlfriend and eight years in prison. If I could do it all over again, would I change my life? No!"

Let's make that, "Hells, naw!"

Apparently, even Darnell wanted to be in the Will Wright business, however conflicted he appears today. He identifies *Double Down*, a two-page quasi-interview stored on his computer, as a teaser spot for Will's auto-biopic that he wrote at Will's behest. In two minutes of screen time, it attempts to capture the man, the myth, the legend:

"Four strippers stiffed on payment. One waitress pushed in the pool—New Year's 2004. Sixteen-year-old drug and money launderer/Federal Prisoner Number ___. Producer of his [own] life story. Womanizer: 'Bitches love me.—Will Wright.'"

Presumably Darnell as the interviewer finds Will on a Sunday afternoon in front of three giant plasma-screen TVs, simultaneously monitoring his sportsbook action on the weekly games and juggling his four buzzing cell phones while deigning to give the camera (and his imagined audience) a moment during halftime.

How do your high-profile friends react to your past?
Everybody knows about my past. It ain't no mystery that I'm a degenerate gambler. Drink, party, fight, fuck—that's my motto.

Like Kristen Williams, Giovanni Agnelli and Scott Bloom take a certain amount of responsibility for unleashing Will Wright on an unsuspecting world—or at least introducing him into a closed biosphere with no built-in resistance to him, once he slipped past the institutional protections. Not only did they walk him and *The Untitled Joe Carnahan Project*, as it eventually came to be known, past the studio gates, but they put out all the requisite publicity that seeds the clouds for this kind of thing, a secondary campaign waged in whispered asides and confidential assurances that softens up the hard cases with its insider cachet: something they heard directly from a guy who knows a guy.

"I'm the idiot who fell for Will's bullshit and bought his story for the movie," confesses Giovanni with a twinge of embarrassment and good-natured incredulity. "We brought Will in. We're the reason that Paris Hilton even knew who Will was, or Leo, or anyone. We vouched for this guy as interesting, cool. We were doing this movie. And we wanted to make this movie as soon as possible. We wanted talk shows to get hold of him and newspapers to write about him. We thought the bigger he is, you know . . . So we sort of created Will."

"He was really good at 'the intro,' " adds Scott, chiming in with a practiced rhythm and soothing cadence that no doubt holds them in good stead in the various pitch meetings where they do battle (they currently have a $100 million line of credit from bebe, the U.S. fashion retailer, who purchased their company last year). His word choice echoes the opinions I've heard before in attempting to come to terms with Will's complex nature.

"He was entertaining, amusing, kind of intriguing right at the beginning, but eventually it played out with everybody right across the board," says Scott. "In the beginning, it was like, 'Wow, this crazy maniac—he's kind of fun, and he has a crazy story. Why wouldn't you want to hang out with him?' . . . But I really think he has sociopathic tendencies. He doesn't understand consequences, and he feels no guilt, no remorse. He really was a cartoon character."

"He is a compulsive, habitual liar," says Giovanni. "He'll never be satisfied with, 'This is my accomplishment.' He'll have to make it bigger." He also volunteers his opinion of how Will Wright has been handled in the media. "I was so disgusted by that *Dateline*," he says. "They made him out like, 'What a fun guy to be with.' It helped him."

Okay, there's enough blame to go around.

They claim they got the option to Will's story for free, meaning they had the exclusive right to sell it to others for a fixed amount of time. Initially, Will announced that Steve Bing, his partner in real estate ventures, had wanted to produce, but now instead would write the screenplay. (Bing is a real estate billionaire who has since produced *Beowulf* and the Martin Scorsese Rolling Stones concert film, *Shine a Light*. His most recent writing credit is *Kangaroo Jack*.) Scott, Giovanni, and Will took the project to ICM, where they contractually agreed to accept equal credits and equal fees, and then shopped it on the open market, settling on Film Engine, an equity financing entity. Film Engine set the project up at New Line.

"They had the same ambition that we had," says Giovanni. "We were moving forward. We attached Michael Bay as a director. We turned down Antoine Fuqua. Michael Bay was going to do it until Will pissed him off in Vegas. He charged his bill in Vegas to Michael Bay."

"Bay told us that personally," says Scott. "We talked about it. [Will] embarrassed him. He figured Bay wouldn't care. He went too far."

At Will's behest, Scott had lunch with Mickey Rourke, who was there to size him up. Giovanni takes up the story: "So Mickey Rourke asked Will, 'Are you sure you got the best deal possible? You should come in and talk to my agent.' So David Ungar, who was at ICM, said that he got fucked. Will said, 'I want to renegotiate my deal. I want out.' We said, 'The deal is done, dude. We signed our deal with ICM, and ICM transferred all the rights to Film Engine. We're done. Film Engine sent it to New Line.' Then Will said, 'I want you guys off the movie and I want all the money you guys were going to get, and I want your credit and I want your fees.'"

"We had been very straightforward," says Bloom.

"So he started threatening ICM," says Agnelli. "He started threatening Margo [Lane, in Business Affairs], Mike Kernin, Michelle Berg—all these agents at ICM."

"I got some anonymous phone calls," says Bloom: 'You will drop the contract, hand Will Wright back the life rights.' Heavy breathing—you know, creepy calls. I was surprised when I found out he was having me followed, because I didn't know people actually did that shit over this kind of a thing. I assume that was Darnell. I don't really care anymore. Darnell was like Will's security: he was the silent one, always with Will. We wanted to call the cops, but at the time we were afraid to do it because we thought it was a good project." He laughs now at the absurdity of it all.

"This was our first movie," says Agnelli with a shrug. He maintains that Will also made threats with respect to his young nephew, Peter, who has cerebral palsy.

Mike Kernan, who was then a vice president at ICM but has since left to form a soundtrack company called Nu Media Studios and Management, is diplomatic when discussing the matter. "The story was going forward and Will wanted them off the story," he says. "They had put tons of effort into it, and Will threatened their safety. The threats were to them. I called Will and said, 'I'm Mike Kernan from ICM, and I want you to know that I've heard you want Scott and Giovanni off the project. Just so you know, that can't happen. We at ICM can't let them do that. You'd obviously understand that; when you take the time, you have to get paid for your time. Do you understand that?'

" 'Yeah.'

" 'And ICM needs to get paid for this project, and if they step off, we don't get paid. As you'd understand, we can't let them step off the project. I'm happy to talk about it, if you want to come down.' In that call, he didn't threaten me. He said he appreciated the upfront call. I talked to his lawyer [Ron Richards] and agreed that if the movie got made, they'd get paid. The confrontational part was more with Giovanni and Scott, and messages sent to them through ICM. I do think that Will is very smart. He doesn't do things that will overtly get him caught. I don't think that anybody is going to catch him that way. He didn't know if I was recording the call, but he took it as we were protecting our client."

Kristen Williams claims that she was the one who finally shut the party down, since at this point a line was forming of people who had allegedly fallen for Will's con, and she was at the head of it. "I told them what happened," she says of Scott and Giovanni. "They were upset with me at first, but I maintained that it was all bullshit. Also, the film company, Film Engine: when I saw it in the trades, I called them and told them, 'Listen, I just want you to know that the records he gave you were photocopied and it's all bullshit.' And he checked, and he was like, 'Oh my God, you're right.' It was Tyler something [Mitchell, an executive at Film Engine]."

For his part, Darnell denies any knowledge of any of this. "Regarding Will and his ICM deal, he may have used my name without my knowledge," Darnell says, "piggybacking off of what people might have talked about."

But it was director Joe Carnahan (*Smokin' Aces; Narc*) who everyone agrees finally got to the bottom of things.

"It's funny—Joe immediately figured him out," says Giovanni.

"Long before we didn't like him, he spotted shit we weren't aware of," echoes Scott.

I was an early and vocal champion of Joe Carnahan's *Blood, Guns, Bullets and Octane* at Sundance in 1998. Later, in a book on indie filmmaking, Carnahan is quoted as saying, "The first thing you need to do is get to know Mark Ebner." So I set up a lunch meeting with him.

"He is one of the most dubious characters I have ever met," says Carnahan of his brief encounter with Will Wright, the screenwriter parts of him ramping up to an elegant exegesis. "He had a guile; a taste for human weakness. Felonious doings notwithstanding, we still haven't found a suitable substitute in this town for *hustle*. You can galvanize, through force of personality and will—the way you communicate that desire—and sometimes that wins the day. Even things that are completely built on fucking sand, you can somehow sustain through pure determination, drive, and hustle. I think Will certainly has all those things in spades. They say 'Money talks and bullshit walks.' Well, sometimes bullshit talks, too. Just loud enough to be heard, to draw in the like-minded or the eager or enthusiastic.

"I think Will had an in, in a town where deception and disguise are art forms. Where people do it professionally, in front of cameras. It was pretty remarkable, the hubris and chutzpah of this guy, who was a complete interloper. A lot of starry-eyed kids get dropped off at the Greyhound station in North Hollywood and have no idea where to go. Here's a guy who came in and implemented this wild-ass game plan about how to insinuate himself into the 'upper echelon' Hollywood social scene. And right out of prison. Taking advantage of Hollywood's need to be in proximity to this criminal element, so somehow that street cred rubs off on them. They want to drink champagne with some asshole that did a ten-year bid for armed robbery. And I think my first impressions of Will, when we sat down for coffee the one and only time, were that he looked like a kid coming from hunger. He had that penal thing, where you eat your food in thirty seconds, so there was certainly a legitimacy about that part of him. But Will was also the guy who was perpetually looking around you to see who was standing behind you.

"To not have any material beyond press clippings that amounted to a glorified scrapbook was a mistake. I was skeptical when I got the scrapbook, because I started looking at the source material—where it came from—and it was like the *Edmonton Gazette*, or not even that. There's not a single national clip, and for a guy that's been extolled as this kind of wild guy, it seemed really dodgy. Everything just smacked of a Kinko's paste-up job. So I contacted a DEA friend of mine who at the time I was developing a film at Universal with. Will had seemed hinky long enough, and I had a conversation with Scott and said, 'I really want to vet this guy now, because it just stinks. I can't find anything on record about this guy. There's not a single reporter that can run this guy down.' I get a call the next day from my buddy, and he says, 'This guy did go to prison, but it's not [for] what he was saying it was.' You know, when Che Guevara was making fun of the peasants out of a passing car, and his old man gave him the what-for, he said, 'Talent is the only aristocracy.' I believe that wholeheartedly, and I think guys like that will eventually fall by the wayside."

Carnahan is currently trying to mount a film on the real Pablo Escobar: *Killing Pablo* (not to be confused with the film-within-a-TV-series *Medellin*, which dominated the fourth season of *Entourage*). But it's the last film he made—*Smokin' Aces*, a rollicking crime story that threads together a dozen Vegas characters—that may have the most in common with *The Untitled Joe Carnahan Project*. Here's a monologue, written by Carnahan and delivered in voice-over by FBI agent Ryan Reynolds, that describes the title character, played by Jeremy Piven at his sleaziest:

"Buddy 'Aces' Israel: Cardsharp, illusionist, asshole, douchebag. Five-time Vegas Showman of the Year. The Mob guys for some reason love him, think he's like a mystic or something. Now Buddy starts making friends: the Connected Kid, doing the Sinatra thing, becomes the unofficial Mob mascot. Now he's got connections, he's got pull, so he starts to make plays. Wants to live the life for real. Bankrolls a couple of B&Es on rich folks, runs smash-and-grabs on pawnshops, jewelry stores, that kind of thing. Then he gets his dick wet: strong-arm robbery; Vegas lounge act turned legitimate thug. Truth is, Buddy don't know the ball from the bounce. He's a wannabe. And like most wannabes, he starts fucking up fast and picking up speed. This little criminal foray shines a light on the entire Carlotta [Mafia] organization. Cops get curious, they start camping out and everything goes sideways real fucking quick—people get pinched, snitches snitch . . . This Israel really is the great white whale of snitches."

Displaced Jersey boy Gordon Bijelonic, Vin Diesel's long-time producer, most recently an investor in the now-shuttered Memphis restaurant on Hollywood Boulevard, reports a run-in with Will at his club one night. "In 2006, my partner Michael Sutton and I were busted by vice for selling liquor after hours at Memphis. Actually, the charges were dropped because it was simply a case of my partner having an open beer. These guys started breaking out their IDs and saying, 'Okay, you're under arrest. You're drinking after hours. Where's your liquor license?' As they're putting cuffs on him, this clown Will Wright starts yelling, 'It's okay, man. I'm going to bail you out. I'm gonna take care of this!' I see that the officers are getting irritated, so I go, 'Yo—who the fuck are you? You're making a bad situation worse.' And he says, 'I own the place.' I said, 'Wait a minute, *I* own the place.' And that's when he started fumbling over his words and everything, and got so mad that he just hauled off and punched me. This was two years ago—mid-2006. I couldn't believe it. He fucking punched me! A friend of mine said, 'Gordon, I've never seen anyone take a punch like that, and just smile.' And the detectives saw him, as they were putting the cuffs on Michael. They came over to me and said, 'Do you want to press charges?' I said no, and the cop said, 'Why not? I saw him punch you. You might as well.' So I said, 'Alright, fuck it then. Go ahead and press charges.' So then they took him and locked him up, and afterwards he called me crying like a little bitch. At that point, all the tough guy was gone."

Bijelonic indicates he eventually would have demurred on pressing charges after discovering that among the investors in both Memphis and one of partner Michael Sutton's other concerns, the Lodge, was none other than Bob Hoff, by that time Wright's financial backer. But it particularly galled him to have Wright try to leverage him through his attorney. "I got a letter from his lawyer—Ron Richards—who offered me five thousand dollars not to press charges," says Bijelonic. "I was like, 'I don't need your fucking money.' And I never signed the affidavit—it implicated that they were paying me. I never took a dime from that prick Will Wright. I just never showed up in court. I shrugged it off."

Anecdotally, Scott and Giovanni relay a lot more havoc that Will wrought on his long march to the Academy Awards—or at least profile some of the public figures he tried to use as way stations in transit. Like Penny Marshall.

"It was interesting, because old-school Hollywood didn't buy it," says Giovanni. "Penny was like, 'I don't know who the fuck you are.' It was on a plane. He came up to her and said, 'I'm a friend of Giovanni's,' and she went, 'So the fuck what? Everybody is a friend of Giovanni's. What does that have to do with me?' And he said, 'Well, yeah, I thought we could do this and that,' and she said, 'I don't fucking know you. Don't call me.' Penny was awesome. She was Penny Marshall."

I tracked down Penny Marshall at a party for her brother Garry Marshall's forty-fifth wedding anniversary. After I read her back her alleged quotes, she says, "Mark, I'm not Joe Pesci, I don't say 'fuck' every five seconds." Although she doesn't recall meeting him on a plane, she did recognize him from the *Dateline* special as someone who had bothered her. She tells me, "The last part, when I say, 'I don't fucking know you. Don't call me'—you can use that."

Giovanni also remembers several incidents where Will insinuated his involvement with Farrah Fawcett, all of which Fawcett explicitly denies through a spokesperson. ("Ms. Fawcett does not recognize the name 'Will Wright,' nor does she recall ever speaking to the person described.") But Heather relates an incident she personally witnessed in Las Vegas.

"I did see Will control Tara Reid one night," says Heather. "And, oh my God, Farrah Fawcett, too. It was at Ron Burkle's party, and Ron was with me and he loved my husband then. And Will goes, 'This is Farrah.' I'm sitting there and Kristen was with Will, and Will comes rolling up with Farrah in the front middle in the Mercedes. Jack's quote was, 'This is great. I used to masturbate to you all the time when I was a kid.' . . . We're being perverted and laughing about the seventies swimsuit edition. Give me a fucking break. Will ran her around—snapping for her at the party: 'Farrah'—snap-snap—'over here!' "

Even Darnell linked him to Nicky Hilton's godmother and O.J. survivor, Faye Resnick. (A picture of her in Will's arms appeared on my Web site.)

And then there was Belinda Stronach, a Canadian billionaire and heiress to the Magna auto parts fortune (most recently considering a bid for Chrysler), and now a Liberal member of parliament in the Canadian House of Commons, whom *Fortune* magazine ranked the second most powerful woman in world business in 2002.

"We introduced Will to her, and he just charmed her," says Scott.

"She's thirty-six years old and one of the richest, most powerful women in the world," says Giovanni. "He was telling her that he knew all about horses, and he just completely led her on, and she brought Will out to the track and was going to fly him up to Canada. He came across like a rock star. She was like, 'God, he's amazing.' And there was another thing: her right-hand guy was looking for watches. And Will sold him a watch that wasn't real—for a lot of money. A *lot* of money. He took them for a little ride, too."

"That was around the time the whole Will thing kind of jumped the shark for us," says Scott. "I don't know if it was the watch, but, you know, 'you can't meet any more people.' "

"We would introduce him to someone, and he would create a story so fast," says Giovanni. "He was really good at what he did. Once Stronach decided she was running for public office, she had to distance herself from him."

Which is why neither of them can understand how, even as they relive their experience with him for my benefit, and the pool of Will's alleged victims spreads larger, Will recently wrapped production on his first film. According to the trade bible, *Variety*, Vertigo Entertainment and Tyler Mitchell, long gone from Film Engine, in conjunction with Will's company RightOff Entertainment, are producing *The Echo*, an English-language remake of *Sigaw*, a Filipino horror film in the extreme Asian horror style of *The Grudge* or *The Ring*, helmed by original director Yam Laranas and written by Eric Bernt, the ex-Marine who wrote the 2007 remake of *The Hitcher*. According to the article, "The story involves an ex-con who becomes trapped in a cursed apartment when he tries to intervene in an abusive situation with the neighbors."

The $5 million budget for the picture was provided by Robert Hoff, according to *Variety* "a leading venture capitalist with Crosspoint Venture Partners, who puts up coin through RightOff Entertainment." Bob Hoff is an Orange County billionaire and Web entrepreneur who cashed out to enjoy his life, and their company moniker combines his and Will's last names minus the first letters (get it?) to explain what he's suddenly doing in the film business.

Among RightOff's projects in active development is *The Untitled Mitchell-Wright Project*, slated for 2009, whose logline reads: "A top athlete and National Merit Scholar is revealed as the mastermind of a narcotics empire. Based on the story of Will Wright."

Producer Roy Lee (once profiled in the *New Yorker* for his success selling Asian film remakes to Hollywood) addresses the Will Wright controversy head on. According to Lee, he was approached by Mitchell, his former intern at Alphaville and now in business with Robert Kravis (the son of Henry Kravis, the founder of KKR, a leading private equity firm and one of the protagonists of *Barbarians at the Gate*, about its hostile takeover of RJR Nabisco). "It was one of those things where they came to us asking if we needed financing for anything," says Lee. "He was looking for an under-five-million-dollar movie. It was only after we agreed on the project that Will was realized." Lee claims he was unaware of the controversies surrounding Will when he entered into business with him, and that Will's time on the set in Toronto was more a learning experience than hands-on production. "I would have no problem working with him again," he stresses. "He was professional throughout the process. Had I known before, I probably wouldn't have gone into business with him . . . He comes off a bit rough, but he has a good heart, it seems."

Lee admits that the screening process for guys bringing $5 million to the table are somewhat lax. "If you come with the money, your background really doesn't matter," he says. "Other people submit scripts to him now. They say, 'This guy is a fucking thug . . . but I like him.' I asked him how he felt when Will's criminal attorney visited the set—as Ron Richards made sure to point out to me in his office. "He brought members of the New York Yankees to the set!" Lee says. He admits to some trepidation still over the allegations that continue to dog Will. "If he was found guilty, I'd be hugely concerned," says Lee. "Given who he hangs out with, there's a chance that anyone could be investigated. But with me, he has been professional, and there has been no indication that he'd break into my place or my place of work. He has never been to my home. He acts accordingly."

Will's former producing partners also recall crossing paths with him not that long ago. "We ran into him at Eva Longoria's birthday party," says Giovanni. "We signed Eva Longoria as the face of bebe, and we threw a birthday party for her at Skybar three months ago, and Will showed up. That was the first time we had seen him, and he acted like nothing was wrong. He wanted to know why we don't hang. I was sitting with the Duff sisters, and he wanted me to introduce him. I told him, 'I don't really know them.' He introduced me to his investor. He said, 'This is my partner. I have a thirty-million-dollar fund, and he's giving me a hundred-fifty-thousand-a-year salary and a company car, and we're gonna fund movies.' I was like, 'Wow.' I didn't say, 'Yeah, well we have a hundred million.' He asked me, 'What are you doing here?' I said, 'I got invited just like everybody else.' He was saying, 'We gotta have lunch. Call me. Seriously—call me.' And I'm thinking, 'Don't you *remember*?'

"Here's how forgiving this stupid town is: Bill Block [ex-ICM powerhouse and founder of Artisan, the company behind *The Blair Witch Project*] now has this company called Key Creatives with Ken Kamins [also ex-ICM], and he's doing the distribution on Will's movie. He was a part of the whole thing from the very beginning. He was the one who sent us over to Film Engine. He was there when we were all getting threatened. Pam Silverstein was Ken Kamins's assistant, and when he started his management company, she went over there as a manager. He [Will] was threatening to run her over. After all of that, we were talking about *The Echo* and he told us, 'Oh yeah, this looks good, we're going to sell this . . . It was really fun being on the set with Will and Tyler, and everything was great.' I was kind of dumbstruck. You don't remember? Are you serious? You're telling me and Scott these things, knowing what we went through? Hollywood doesn't care."

Louis weighs in again from Taft:

"Will Wright can have all the good things in life, but he'll never, ever have a seat at the *desired* table. He needs other people like a car needs gas. He's only as good as the last people he used. He used the Feds, his codefendants, Darnell, Kristen. You see, he is not, and never will be, autonomous. True power comes from autonomy. He's relentless. He's ripped off people that did nothing to him, and he didn't come away empty handed. You combine that with the willingness to stand on a street corner and ask every hot chick that walks by for a blow job, and sooner or later, you end up with money and a blow job. He's a salesman. You've heard about the twenty-four-thousand-dollar sundae, right? Sooner or later, someone buys it. So your exposé on him, the Web exposé, talk on the streets—it doesn't matter to him. He knew that his life story wasn't going to pan out going in, Michael Bay or not. He needed to watch the story unfold. To defeat your enemy, you have to truly know who he is, not who you want him to be. If the kid wasn't a rat, I'd probably like him for his doing what he's done without a safety net."

4

SUNSET STRIPPED

D arnell told me a story:
A cop named Mike Vanags, working Robbery/Homicide out of Orange County, had come up to see him at Corcoran. He was looking for a stolen diamond—a seven-carat wedding ring worth $250,000—boosted by someone who kicked in the back door of a private residence. Three weeks later, they returned and pried the entire safe out of the wall and carted it off wholesale, along with some money and valuables. This was in early 2006, after Darnell had taken his deal and relocated north. The victim was Jared Merrell, the owner and proprietor of J Star Motors in La Habra, where Will had sent Kristen and Al Maimon's wife to unload their high-end automobiles. It turns out that J Star was less that ten miles away from Will's halfway house straight out of prison, and is where his father and brother took him to buy him a car back in 2003. Jared and Will became fast friends, and were out dirt-bike riding at the time the first robbery occurred, and Jared had fingered him for the robbery.

According to Darnell, Vanags had Will's cell phone records and showed him a list of phone calls made and received around the time of the burglary. Darnell had picked out the name of Charlie Pope as a likely person of interest. Charlie Pope was a scarecrow figure who showed up a couple of times in Darnell's voluminous correspondence and campfire tales told on a jailhouse payphone or across a game of dominos in the prison library. Sometimes christened "Crackhead Chuck," he was involved with Brandi Young—a lawyer and former meth-head, now out and clean after a jolt in a women's prison—in an Oxycontin buy that went south, resulting in an extended furlough in Lynwood Jail in South Central L.A. (where Paris Hilton later did twenty-three days of hard time for driving with a suspended license). Louis Ziskin pegged him as a rat, which accounts for his revolving-door regimen of incarceration. He was also Anna Nicole Smith's drug buddy and briefly lived with her. And according to Darnell, he was definitely in Will's orbit.

This was a hallmark of many of the burglaries Will had been implicated in—he always had the perfect alibi: when the crimes were committed, he was always in the presence of the victims themselves.

Outside of a really unconscionable number of speeding tickets, which I suppose is an occupational hazard if you're trapped in Orange County with a fleet of high-end preowned luxury vehicles you've customized yourself, Merrell's record was clean (although I noted his business logo was a thinly veiled knockoff of the puppetmaster logo from *The Godfather*). A weight-lifter and one-time Versace and Calvin Klein model, according to an article in the *Orange County Register*, Merrell was also a family man: two brothers in the business, a second lot just opened in San Juan Capistrano near San Diego, a couple of kids in the photo that ran with the article. He was a guy who would buy his wife a pricey engagement ring. Will reportedly steered a lot of his fast-money contemporaries to Merrell as clientele: in police reports, model Erin Naas was identified as driving a white Cadillac Escalade from J Star ("I'm just friendly with them—I went down one time and they slapped their license plate frames on my car," Naas says). Kristen vouched for him. Even Vicki Mallahan in Blaine recognized the name when it came up, having been steered there by Bill Wright when she was looking for a new Jaguar after her divorce. When I pulled up next to an ultimate-fighter-looking guy in Hollywood one day with a J Star logo on his plates and name-checked Merrell, I got a fist-over-the-heart salute in return. So I made an appointment.

After a forty-five-minute drive south on the 5, I walked into the original J Star showroom, surrounded by Hummers, late-model Mercedes, Porsches, and the like. I told the woman at the counter I was here to see Jared Merrell and identified myself as Mark Ebner. Across the room, a short dark-haired man in a leather jacket who had been talking with his girlfriend to a salesperson spun on a heel of his cowboy boots and faced me.

"Mark Ebner!" he says, coming toward me. "Timmy Iannello." He shook my hand. Suddenly, the whole thing smelled like a setup. As I do when faced with these situations, I immediately went on the offensive.

"Oh, yeah?" I say. "Then how come you haven't returned my phone calls?"

Immediately, he starts back-pedaling, fast-talking his way out of a corner, apologizing for being rude. "You know, I've moved on Mark," he says. "I want to put it all behind me. I'm just glad the cops never questioned me." Yeah, I bet you are. "I run nightclubs now," he adds. I thought he was about to invite me down or offer to buy me a drink, but then his companion joined him: a pretty blonde who towered over him by a good eight inches. He introduces her as Olivia. "I'm just down here buying my girl a truck," he explains, noting the coincidence of running into me like this. Taking back half the space he'd conceded, he steered the conversation back to our mutual acquaintance.

"You know, Darnell is crazy," he says in what seemed like an opening gambit. "Have you read any of those sick scripts he's been writing in prison?" Olivia asks, now his voluntary ally. I agree that Darnell "does have an imagination," and he begins to patronize me, telling me how much he enjoyed my work on Scientology—articles I've written over the years on the ersatz religion, all readily available on my Web site. I ask him if he'd sit for an off-the-record interview, and he tells me to call him and we'll set something up. As he was leaving, he says, "Write anything you want about me; just make me taller."

I laugh and tell him he's taller than me. He points to the lifts in his expensive cowboy boots, and both of them exit out the back door. I was just getting my adrenaline level stabilized when out of the corner of my eye, I see a guy who looked very much like Will Wright coming at me at a rapid clip: same physique, same shaved head, looking like he was ready to spit nails. 'Okay, this is it,' I think as I spin to face him. Instead, he stuck out a beefy hand and took mine in a massive grip.

"Mark—I'm Jared Merrell," he says. He told me his father-in-law would be joining us for lunch, then ducked back in his office to take a call.

On the walk to the restaurant, I ask him what the chances were of running into Timmy Iannello. "Yeah, I wish that had never happened," he says. In fact, that had been Will on the phone, already tipped off by Timmy less than thirty seconds later, telling him to "get that Ebner guy the fuck out of his office." I ask him if Will was in town, since the last I heard he'd been on the film set in Toronto. Jared tells me he was.

"Are you scared?" he asks me as we all took our seats at the Mexican restaurant a few doors down.

"I'm not scared of anything," I say. Then we ordered.

As near as I can tell, Jared Merrell embodies the American dream: a hard worker from a modest background who started out selling motorcycle parts for his dad at fifteen, then turned a love of tinkering with engines into his own business, which catered to sports figures, motocross enthusiasts, and the odd celebrity. He was born and raised in Anaheim, just around the corner from Disneyland, where his family "never even locked the door, and business was done on a handshake—which means nothing in Hollywood, apparently." Now thirty-two, he calls Will "like a brother to me," a rangy, animated kid who told a hyperembellished boys' adventure tale about "getting busted with a truckload of marijuana" and being ratted out—*Young Indiana Jones* or *Terry and the Pirates* for pot-friendlier times, still perfecting his criminal résumé even on his off hours.

"He said he was getting back the money that the Feds took from him," says Jared. "He wound up buying several cars from me over time. He established contacts in Hollywood, and they bought cars from me. He stayed in my house and I stayed in his." He also got a taste of the storied nightlife most people only read about in lurid headlines at the supermarket checkout stand. "I was in Hollywood with Will one night," he recalls. "Nicky Hilton was on my lap, Paris was on Will's. Brandon Davis was driving, and he got pulled over. He got a DUI that night."

Merrell was robbed twice in early 2006, three weeks apart, both on a Friday night when he was scheduled to be out.

"The first time they robbed me, they kicked in a back door, tampered with the safe, and knew my house enough to go right to where my wife's jewelry was," he says. "They did not ransack the house. In fact, they took my wife's yellow seven-carat wedding ring and an expensive diamond-encrusted watch. My little brother Jeremy and Will were at my house. I talked to them from Islands restaurant. They were calling for a pass code to get into the garage. They both left the house—I'm not sure if they were in separate cars or not, and fifteen minutes later I was robbed. He missed my own cash—about three thousand dollars that I left for my father-in-law in a drawer in the kitchen. The second robbery, they came in through the same back door that I had screwed shut. It must have taken two or three of them to get the safe dollied out. It was big and heavy. There was nothing in it. Will knew about the ring, and the value of it. I went to his jeweler to appraise the diamond: Sam at Prima Diamonds in Los Angeles, down-town."

"You know what I told him?" asks Kristen, who after she split from Will remained friendly with Merrell and his family. "Why don't you ask Will, 'Who did you go to to sell my diamond? I'd pay good money to get it back.' Will would probably get it back for you just so he could make some money off of it, and make you like him more."

Merrell is still in touch with Will. In fact, Merrell's father-in-law, Barry McKinley, says that Will just bought an off-road bike from him—a pur-chase he would only approve if Will paid in cash and paid him back money he had owed him "forever." He acknowledges the contradiction by repeat-ing what Vanags told him. "Mike Vanags believes Will *is* a good friend," he says. "To Will, this is just business."

"Will always had money," Merrell tells me as we say good-bye outside his dealership. "I know how hard I work. I don't know where the fuck Will gets his money from. I hope you can answer that question."

On the drive back to L.A., I called Detective Vanags to see where his case stood. "There is no doubt in my mind that Will stole that diamond," he tells me. "However, that case is back-burnered because I can't prove it. But I can tell you this: when that diamond turned up missing, Will had no money. What better way to get started again?" He also confided something Merrell wouldn't tell me himself: that Merrell *had* confronted Will on the theft. Will shouted, "You think I took your shit?" Merrell told him, "Just call and settle it with the cops." Will promised to, but never did. Vanags called it "a spiderweb of crimes"—most of which he didn't follow up on because they didn't pertain to his case—and wished me luck, patience, and time enough to solve it. He had a meeting set up with Charlie Pope, but wound up talking to him on the phone instead. "It was pretty sterile," he recalls. He also interviewed Bob Hoff, as the most likely person among Will's associates to be able to afford such a ring. "Hoff may have backed Will Wright in some things, but I can assure you that Hoff is an upstanding businessman." He also took a drive up to Sammy Mesica at Prima Dia-monds, who told him, "Will is a great guy and I can't imagine him ever hurting anyone—and he never sold anything through me." Mesica said they knew each other socially. Said Vanags of his meeting with Darnell up at Corcoran, "He told me that when he's out, he's going to produce movies, and he has the money to do it."

I asked him if he thought that Darnell was being cagey to avoid a snitch jacket inside, the mark of the informer that amounts to a kiss of death in the insular world of penitentiary status. "Hell no," the detective tells me. "He'll be a rock star—a legend in prison—if his snitching makes it into a book. You only get the jacket if you talk to cops."

"I believe Darnell would kill you," he says, using two decades of police instinct to sum up this motley cast of characters I had inherited. "I don't think Will would, because he's a pussy. And Timmy—well, he's just disreputable."

After I hung up, I called Detective Koman to inform him of my interview with Merrell—and would-be ambush by Timmy Iannello. He told me, "You're dealing with a class of people you should not be involved with unless you're packing something."

Later, when I tracked down Charlie Pope, he admitted to being questioned by the police, and that he knew Will, but denied he had anything to do with the break-in. "I've been approached by the Justice Department on some of these things—so I mean, I just don't want to fuck myself and have the Feds on my ass," he explains. However, he did volunteer the following: "I know that he took a diamond, and I know where he took it and who he sold it to and all that kind of stuff," he says. "Sammy Mesica. That's who Will took his diamonds to."

I found a Sammy Mesica affiliated with Prestige Diamonds on the Internet, located in downtown Los Angeles, as well as a company called Orka Mesica, founded by "Israeli artist and jeweler Orit Mesica, a gorgeous half-Spanish and Bulgarian beauty and ex-Israeli Army," according to a Web site associated with Prima Diamonds. She produces the beaded friendship bracelets seen on the wrists of Nicky Hilton, Lindsay Lohan, Lauren Conrad, and Audrina Partridge from the MTV reality soap *The Hills* and "all the Young Hollywood Celebs" according to promotional materials. The two companies share an address. (In fact, Orit Mesica is married to Shy, Sammy's brother.) I stopped by on my appointed rounds.

The California Jewelry Mart at Sixth and South Hill downtown boasts "Nine Floors of Jewelry Stores," and Prima Diamonds occupies the penthouse. I'm buzzed into a cramped foyer with framed eight-by-ten glossies of a bald-headed man posing with celebrities that even to my trained eye are completely unrecognizable. From behind (no doubt bulletproof) glass, a pretty Asian receptionist informs me neither Sammy nor Shy is in. As I'm trying to boil down my message to notepad size, the door buzzes and the bald man in the photos joins me in the now even more cramped alcove. He's a tall sharp-dressed man in a gray flannel suit and polished black spats, with big square-framed black glasses that make him look like Robert Evans or Junior Soprano, and he's eyeing me the way the hawk eyes the field mouse. I ask him if we can talk here in the lobby, and he spreads his hands, palms up, and says, "I have nothing to hide." I ask him about his relationship with Will Wright, and he shrugs and says, "I met Will in a club and he was a nice guy. He came here with his girlfriend to sell her ring." (He identifies her as Kristen Williams.) When I ask him if he bought the J Star diamond as well, he answers, "No. I have heard bad things about Will, but he never did anything to me. I don't think he is a thief, and I don't think he would steal from his friend. That's what I think, but I may have misjudged him." With that our meeting is over.

Charles Timothy Iannello, according to Darnell, possesses both the gift of gab and a Napoleon complex, which conspired to deposit him in the world of professional nightlife where traditionally, hawkers work the sidewalk outside to lure the suckers in and goons stand at the ready to toss them back out just as soon as trained professionals have labored to separate the fools from their money. He promoted nights at the Key Club on the Sunset Strip (formerly Gazzari's and Billboard Live) in the mid-nineties, events at the Whisky and the Viper Room (both also on the Sunset Strip), promoted the band No Doubt, and eventually bought his way into the Garden of Eden, the still-successful club at the western edge of the Hollywood Strip—although how and to what extent varies (widely estimated at 1 percent)—for which Darnell claims he did some work. Timmy subsequently was involved with the clubs Bliss (now Republic) at La Cienega and Melrose; Central, where Ketchup is now—a spectacular flameout intended as the linchpin nightspot in Sunset Plaza that opened in November 2004; and Citizen Smith in the Cahuenga Corridor, now under new management on a month-to-month lease.

"My buddy Timmy 'I Own It' Iannello was one of the original owners of the hugely successful club Garden of Eden in Hollywood," says Darnell. "Everyone nicknamed him 'I Own It' because Timmy had his hands in so many nightclubs around town. Timmy loved strippers who robbed him blind and hated any man who was taller than him. He had an incredible knack for putting lucrative deals together and an unbreakable streak of burning every bridge he helped to build. He would round up a group of investors who get all juiced up about the pitch he's sold them and feel warm and fuzzy, like one big happy family. Afterwards, just like the drunk dad from every story with a drunk dad, Timmy turns Charlie Manson, shoots himself in the foot, and then slaps his wife and kid around. Timmy is scared of his own success. He blows it every time. I've picked Timmy up from more strip clubs, after he's pissed off a meeting with investors, only to wallow in his own (and some skanky chick's) filth. Timmy and I have been down many roads together. Before we teamed up, a lot of people around town didn't have too much respect for Timmy the man, but knew he could put together business. He was his own and everybody else's worst enemy. But he was always a stripper's best friend."

"Remember," says Andrew Belchic, owner and general manager of Citizen Smith, who is currently embroiled in a lawsuit with Timmy and won't address their business dealings in any detail, "if Timmy meets your daughter, he's married to her and he's her protector. If Timmy drives your car, it's his car. When Timmy has it in his mind that he has a piece of something, he's the creator, the financer—he's everything. Now, it's sneaky how he gets to that point, because he ingratiates himself with you so well. I've always said the reason why Timmy is around people and people put up with him is that he has the ability to make you laugh. He can make you feel so special and so good about yourself that you enjoy having him around you. And for me, when I was going through a really tough time, that was good for me. I didn't even realize what was happening, but I knew that when I was with him, it seemed like everything was going to be alright. And that is a talent. He makes people feel really secure and good about themselves while things are crumbling around them. And when things crumble, he takes."

It seems like Timmy is one of those galvanizing figures that everybody on the scene has an opinion about, neatly and concentrically divided between those who were close enough to have business with him and those who merely enjoyed him from beyond the footlights. Heather met him as a college student when she went on strippers' junkets to New York, picking up enough cash in a weekend to finance a semester.

"At the time, he was great, outgoing—kind of like the Will personality," she remembers. "Very enticing. A great guy then—always had a crush on Kristen. Always. He and Kristen and I were going to buy a house together, but Kristen and I backed out because we were reluctant about his sketchy ways. We didn't even ask about that because it was better not knowing."

"I met Timmy at Gold's Gym back when I met Mark [Wahlberg]," says Kristen. "He lived maybe three blocks away from there. I met him twelve years ago, and he was friends with the Haques [Koi owners Dipu and Nick]. I thought he was a really good guy back then; I guess I was a very bad judge of character. He was in his twenties and he was promoting [clubs], but I'm very disappointed that he turned out how he is now. And of course, I introduced him to Will." She laughs.

"I've known Timmy forever," says Brandi Young, the lawyer and re- covering meth addict. "Timmy was always a character. He was known as a chronic exaggerator, so a lot of people just never took him seriously. He was more comical than anything." In fact, according to a number of people interviewed, Timmy even had a brief career as a stand-up come- dian.

"Timmy is exceptionally smart," says Belchic. "He is one of the wittiest people—he can put word to thought instantaneously, so he's never at a loss for words."

Ex–party girl Elizabeth Jawhary, who dated him and still remembers him fondly, can even quote his act: "Timmy's big stand-up joke was, 'I've been married three times. Never engaged.' " (Among Timmy's three ex-wives is the porn star Chasey Lain.)

But like Will, Timmy found that a tough-guy persona is more easily aspired to than embodied: a limitation that made Darnell handy to have around. Timmy claimed he was mobbed up—the nephew of Matty "the Horse" Ianniello, a one-time acting boss of the Genovese family and for- mer owner of the legendary Umberto's Clam House in Little Italy—even though their names are spelled differently. Darnell buys into it (while ad- mitting his story is no doubt embellished), but Belchic claims that Timmy once confessed he was adopted and hailed from Pittsburgh—this during a Steelers game at Hooter's when some of Timmy's high school friends spotted him. And then, people in a position to know ridicule the whole idea.

"You can quote me," says Alex Vaysfeld. "I don't give a shit if he was saying he was Genovese, Sicilian, mobbed up, whatever—they would cut his fucking tongue out just for saying that. If you ever ask me if I'm mobbed up, even though people think I have connections, I would deny it on my deathbed. That's that. Nobody who is really, really mobbed up would ever say they were—Russia, America, wherever. For somebody to come out and say they're mobbed up—I mean, that is fucking stupid."

And then one of the two legitimately connected guys I talked to in the course of this story tells me, "There is no way that Timmy Iannello is mobbed up—not a chance—that's been checked and it's a lie," which to my ears, at least, sounds fairly definitive.

"The real motherfuckers don't talk that shit anyway," says Jerry Rosenberg.

Timmy does have a criminal record—or at least he did until Ron Richards had it expunged: attempted murder, or 187 (A), in 1992, for which he claims to have spent time in county jail. "It was a bar fight over a chick being slapped by another guy," says Darnell. "He was defending the honor of a female friend who was being harassed. He probably told the cops one story, but the story he told me was he got a year in L.A. County as his eventual disposition, and this was in '93 or '94. Timmy was/is stupid and a tiny man, so he had to make a name for himself in town." As Belchic remembers it, "Timmy was on his way out, heading back to the parking lot to his car [from the Garden of Eden], and he saw a girl getting pulled into a car. And he said he took out his pistol and hit the guy with it."

In fact, he was waiting in the valet line at the Roxbury, Bob and John Long's seminal nightclub at the corner of Sunset and Crescent Heights (and the future home of Shelter), on the night of February 28, 1993. The club was immortalized in the film *A Night at the Roxbury*, which, according to Darnell at least, featured a spot-on impression of Bob Long by Chazz Palminteri, whose catchphrase in the film is, "Did you just grab my ass?" Timmy and some friends were drunkenly arguing about Mike Tyson, just then serving what would amount to three years in prison for rape. Two patrons behind him in line joined in the discussion, and after his friends left Timmy became heated on the subject. At some point, one of them said, "I've heard enough," at which point, Timmy began "swearing and just getting real annoying," according to court testimony, eventually pulling a 9mm pistol and leveling it at the two men, threatening to kill them. They defused the situation, but when Timmy became agitated and drew his gun again, one of them tackled him and security rushed in to control the fray. Timmy was sentenced to sixty days in jail, two hundred hours community service, and three years probation. In August 1995, he received a special dispensation to travel to Vancouver, Canada, to act in an episode of *The X-Files*, for which he reportedly earned $23,000, although there's no record of his credit anywhere I can find. (Of Timmy's attempted murder and the possibility he served time, Richards says, "Maybe County time, I don't remember. Not serious time.")

Darnell claims that in 1998, Timmy sold Richards a surveillance video from the Garden of Eden for $10,000 in a case involving his client John Gordon Jones, the notorious Limousine Rapist. The tape allegedly refuted testimony that Jones's victim had been administered a date-rape drug and had to be carried to their waiting car. (Richards said he got the footage through a subpoena.) Jones was eventually acquitted; he avoided a subsequent civil judgment by transferring his assets to the Cook Islands, a tax haven in the South Pacific; and the suit was settled for an undisclosed amount. Richards was also offered a point in Citizen Smith for performing legal work, but declined—he says because it was too much work, and owner Belchic claims it was due to a falling-out between Richards and Timmy.

"He had the management contract at Bliss," Belchic says of Timmy. "He would tell me how Ron would sit at the bar every night. Timmy's gift is that he gets guys like Ron laid a lot. Get them laid, and they're happy."

Darnell also recalls a former Playmate named Angela Taylor, an ex-girlfriend of Timmy's, who showed up with her new fiancé at Shelter. "Timmy asked me to bump into the guy and then crack him," says Darnell. "Timmy would have had the guy thrown out. I left. Timmy knew he pissed me off—to try and use me, first off, but also to not have respect or care for the fact that I am a trained fighter. It's a skill I don't just throw around. I don't take it lightly. I've got several buddies who are fighters who have gotten stretched out in the courts for abusing their skills. I'm no bully or brute walking around punching on people. That's not my style."

Central closed within six months, just in time for Timmy to come to the attention of Belchic, who had relocated to Los Angeles after selling the family business, jumped feet first into the club business, and was looking for investors to cover cost overruns. Belchic says he bought Central's assets for his new club Citizen Smith—kitchen equipment and the like—and was introduced to Timmy, who agreed to try to bring in additional money. "I thought he was a much bigger player than he was," Belchic says.

Many people, some of them investors, accuse Belchic and Timmy of spending the club's assets on an extended bender in Las Vegas. Darnell, who says he applied back-channel pressure on investors at Belchic's be-hest—a claim that Belchic denies outright, although he does admit that Timmy would frequently make the offer—reports meeting with the pair while the club was still under construction and Belchic was bouncing off the walls. Although Belchic concedes that the period was a low point for him and he certainly is no stranger to cocaine, he attributes the longev-ity of these rumors to Timmy's efforts to destroy him after they parted ways.

"We don't talk, and frankly I'm happier for it," says Belchic. "I truly feel bad for the investors he brought in." Belchic believes that once he and Timmy became estranged, Timmy had bad-mouthed him to his investors. "That's the day that my life became difficult," he says. "He did that with everybody. And to this day, I haven't recovered from that. It's really hurt my reputation.

"Timmy has always had the gift of knowing people with money, and he knows the right time and the right place to strike. You've got money, right? We'd go out, party, get you laid, and you'd want more of that, right? Who wouldn't want more of that? And in the back of his mind, there's a deal that he'll hook you up with and he'll take a piece for himself. He's amazing like that. I always said if he could take that and use it in some-thing legitimate . . .

"At Citizen Smith, I'd be at one end of the bar, and Timmy would be telling me how much he loved me, and that I was his brother. This is not an exaggeration. He would walk to the other side of the bar—and in four or five seconds, he'd be saying, 'That piece of shit.' And the bartenders would walk over and ask, 'Why is he talking shit about you?' He's an amazing, amazing creep."

And yet, that's no match for Timmy's assessment of how he and his friends felt about Darnell:

"Timmy used to tell me that Will hated Darnell, and the only reason he hangs with him was because he was afraid Darnell was going to kill him," Belchic tells me. "Basically, Will was friends with all the fucking Paris Hil-tons and everybody else, right? He had those contacts. This is Timmy's story to me: It wasn't good enough for Darnell that he was kind of in the background. He wanted to be high profile. It wasn't good enough that he just stole from these people—like guns from Nick and Dipu and all that shit—he wanted to be in the group. The joke was, When you have a bunch of starlets and one black guy there, it's like not knowing you're the sucker at a poker table. Right? If you can't spot the sucker at the table, you're the sucker. And Timmy would say that there were a bunch of these debutantes like Paris Hilton and all of them running around Hollywood, and there was this one ghetto black guy hanging around with all these rich white people. So it was only a matter of time before something started to go wrong."

5

CHROME HEARTS

interviewed former Elite model Erin Naas at Ron Richards's office in the Sunset Towers, where I was thinking of renting a pied-à-terre to cut down on my driving. She showed up right on time, in black jeans and a black top, and she looked—well, however good would get her a million bucks back in change. Erin's been linked to a couple of shelves' worth of trophy suitors, from Pamela Anderson's ex Tommy Lee (she's in the Fuel video for "Bad Days," on which Lee is the guest drummer) to Joe Francis to latter-day reality star Brody Jenner. Darnell links her to New England Patriots quarterback Tom Brady, NASCAR driver Jeff Gordon, and a number of other professional athletes.

"She's been around," says Darnell. "She gets bored and don't wait for the truckload of money to back up and drop the load. She'll wake up at thirty and it'll all be wrinkled, used, and sunburned, and she'll have to settle for a mere millionaire instead of the Big Kahuna."

Among Darnell's stored possessions is an eight-by-ten headshot of Erin, on the back of which is written with a Sharpie, "You are a real man, I can vouch for that! Love, Erin." Jerry Rosenberg believes they had a sexual relationship (one he characterizes in more dramatic terms). In his letters and the stories he tells, Darnell refers to Erin frequently.

"Erin has always been my muse," he says. "Her passion for living life to the fullest is intoxicating." He claims to have met her at the Hilton-Lenz-Rovero house in Laurel Canyon, and they quickly fell into a sexual relationship. "As far as her criminal enterprising with me, it all started with her being pissed at her moneybags boyfriend at the time, Lukas Haas," says Darnell. "He is one of DiCaprio's friends, and Chuck Pacheco's roommate. A great actor but I knew him from my pre-YA days. Lukas Haas was seeing Natalie Portman behind Erin's back. Erin was just with him for the access into Hollywood, so that was her cue to fuck me more, as well as others."

Erin has worked for the Elite and Premier agencies, posed for Victoria's Secret and Frederick's of Hollywood (as well as Abercrombie & Fitch), and appeared in *Playboy*, although she never technically posed for them as I once claimed. Instead, she can be seen in the September 2004 issue in their Grapevine section, a two-page black-and-white photo layout in the back alongside Beyoncé, Serena Williams, and Mandy Moore. She confirms she was once "the biggest earner in town"—that's how she's referred to by Peter Hamm on the Oxygen reality series *The Janice Dickinson Modeling Agency* seconds before Dickinson is cruelly dismissive of her. (Erin says they're friends and the scene was set up beforehand.)

During our hour-long interview, Ron Richards was virtually perched on her shoulder, at times physically cutting her off when the story she wanted to tell differed from the one he wanted me to hear. I brought up the name David Reich.

"You're not a friend of his?" she asks. I assure her I'm not. "He makes up really mean stories about me being on hooker Web sites—escort Web sites—and I would go to the men's house and have them robbed and stuff . . . He's crazy and controlling, and if you tell anyone what he does to you, that he tried to hook up with you, if you say anything, he'll try and ruin your life and scare you. He's just one of those bad people."

"I met her at a hair salon," Reich says of Naas. "She was with a kid in a purple Lamborghini, and came up to me and gave me her number. I was with some girls, and she said she wanted to be a model." He claims to have provided her with, in quick succession, a haircut, a wardrobe, an agent, and a boob job, and sent her to the Wilhelmina Agency in New York, which quickly signed her.

"I have the first photo shoot she ever did," he says, "that I paid for out of my own pocket, because she was apparently in trouble, and she had all these horses to pay for. And the funny comment on Erin Naas is: she doesn't have any horses, she's never been to rehab. But every guy that she dates—if you want to use the D word, which I never would—any guy she fucks pays for her horses, the horse food, or for rehab." ("Erin Naas, who I'd met earlier, started hitting me up for money right away," says a prominent Century City attorney who comes up elsewhere in the story, after running into her one night at the Mondrian. "She needed money for her horses. I was like, 'I'll give you a couple of dollars for a hamburger.' ")

"I can literally put eight guys on the phone right now that will tell you the same stories about the horses and the rehabs—we've all been worked over by her," says Reich. "She hustles chips in Vegas, she cashes them in, and goes shopping."

He dialed an outside source for corroboration. "Just give us a short description of her for as long as we've known her," Reich says after laying out the setup.

"Beautiful, loves coke, loves to lie," says a gruff male voice.

"What does she lie about, for instance?" asks Reich.

"I'm losing my horses . . . I'm going to rehab."

This went on a bit longer but made the same point over and over. He also read me a section from his upcoming book (*Under the Bus*), which he said Erin begged him not to include her in.

"Erin is what David calls a starfucker. She's willing to do whatever it takes to walk down the red carpet on the arm of a star at a movie premiere . . . [so] she will be mentioned as the star's new girlfriend in one of the gossip columns."

"I was driving down Wilshire once, and she rolled down her window while I'm driving and yelled, 'Did I fuck Enrique Iglesias?!?!' " he says. "Because she had met him with me and I wouldn't help her out. And she fucked him, and she fucked Tommy Lee, and she fucked Kid Rock, and she fucked all these people . . . I think you should look into who she's been dating, because he also just got out of jail for murder."

And in fact, in July 2007, the *New York Daily News* reported that Erin was dating ex-Miami-based nightclub impresario Chris Paciello, and was three months pregnant with his baby. Paciello famously dated Madonna, partnered with Madonna's reported lover Ingrid Casares in businesses, and was undisputedly one of *The Kings of South Beach*, the name of a Nicholas Pileggi–scripted cable movie on his life, before his high profile led authorities to arrest him for the murder of a Staten Island housewife seven years before as part of New York's Bath Avenue Crew, an offshoot of the Bonanno crime family, for which he served seven years in prison. (Mark Wahlberg reportedly turned down $10 million to play Paciello in the prospective feature film version, *Un-Made Men*.) Erin admits dating him but not being pregnant, and fingers none other than Paris Hilton for feeding rumors to the press.

"I dated her ex-boyfriend Jason Shaw and she's hated me ever since," says Erin of Paris. "I knew her back when she was doing really crazy things . . . She's evil. She's not a nice girl."

Richards emphasizes that his client has never been convicted, in custody, or prosecuted. "And I don't have a porn video," says Erin. "I'm the only one without one of those, I think."

She doesn't deny rumors of wanton drug use because she doesn't have to; Richards volunteers as much almost as soon as we start.

"Unfortunately, like a lot of people in the United States, she had a drug problem, and it caused her to fall out of touch," says Richards. "She's now totally sober and has been sober for over a year, and is doing great. The irony is, she was so loaded during this time, she wouldn't leave the house. I'd have to go to her house. That's what's so sad. She had no life."

"I was too paranoid," says Erin. "I would lock all my doors and stay in my room and do drugs all day by myself. I couldn't drive anywhere. And I certainly wasn't looking to get anyone in trouble, because when you're doing that many drugs, you're scared of everything. I started using them to lose weight. I wasn't doing them for fun." (This is obviously the story behind the February 19, 2005, message leaked on Paris Hilton's T-Mobile Sidekick, from financier Bert Dweck—one half of "the Berts"—whom Erin now calls "a very good friend of mine": "By the way you gotta see erin naas in miami she's worse than ever".)

"I think I was having a bad troubled weekend or something," says Erin.

"It's weird, because Erin is one of the nicest people you'll ever meet," says Richards. "It's why I've been extremely protective of her, because I've never seen so many people pick on someone that never bothers anybody. She's never given an interview, ever, and she's never said a mean thing about any of these people. All she ever wanted to do was not get involved in their personal issues."

Darnell claims to have traveled widely with Erin: to Munich in 2002, in the company of Simone, the Austrian model; from there, a road trip in a G-Wagon Mercedes via the Autobahn to Prague for a Jamiroquai concert, with a side trip to rendezvous with Paris Hilton and then beau Jason Shaw in Amsterdam. He claims Erin was on the yacht when they saw P. Diddy in Saint-Tropez in July 2003 (he traveled on to Moscow alone at the behest of Alex Vaysfeld). He says they visited Italy in early 2004 and stayed with model Natalia Vodianova at Lake Como. He claims to have bought her an expensive Hermès saddle for her horses. He insinuates three-ways and other misadventures—tantalizingly holding back incriminating details and key participants in deference to various statutes of limitations. Here's his description of one such nefarious errand up in Harlem.

"So I'm headed uptown with Erin in one of New York's gazillion taxis. The cabbie is giving me a couple of looks as the number gets higher and higher, knowing that we are heading into Harlem and the sun is steadily continuing its descent. 'Where you say we going again?' the Brooklyn cabbie asks me while staring me down in the rearview. 'Jefferson and Wagner Projects, Spanish Harlem—the Jets,' I say nonchalantly, like I was telling him to go to the Upper East Side. I relayed the information as if going to El Barrio after dark was a normal request from the passengers he picks up at the Waldorf-Astoria.

"Erin had taken plenty of rides with me, but not too many to Harlem. She's in full hooker-fashion model regalia—stiletto heels, micro-mini, and my V-neck T-shirt on. All of this was under a fur coat that gave the Dark Angel gangster bitch cockiness as she stepped out of the taxi. The greetings came in unison: 'Oye, Cuba.' '¿Que paso, Cuba—tu tambien?' This was a friendly greeting. No pistol placed to my dome. No stick-up kid trying to gain a rep by taking a shot at us. No one was dissing Erin as she strutted down the walk like she was walking for Chanel or Karl Lagerfeld in some fashion mecca. No bullshit, no worries, as Erin kept it all gangster. 'Oye, mira—mami, tu es fucking hot,' my boy Hector responded as Erin leans in to kiss him on both cheeks. There's no doubt about it—the Dark Angel from Sylmar is hot as hell."

"We had a P.O. box together [now closed], and several times she's called me and told me to go check it," Darnell says elsewhere. "When I would, in it would be a Patek Philippe, a Cartier, a Daytona Rolex—whatever. Or a couple of times I've gotten calls from her when she was shopping with the moneybags, she would call to ask what I wanted. So by proxy, I was fucking the moneybags, too."

For her part, Erin tells a very different story.

"He was friendly with Paris and all those people, I'm very sure," she says of Darnell, "and he used to e-mail me pictures of puppies sometimes and talk about his dog or something that I would try not to respond to, because I knew that I didn't really . . ." She trails off. "There would be a weird comment once in a while that would make me uncomfortable, so I just wouldn't respond. I'd go, 'Oh, cute puppies.' He seemed like he had this other side, he liked animals. I didn't know him in any personal way at all."

She denies dating him, sleeping with him, traveling with him, and certainly being part of any criminal conspiracy. Basically, she denies everything.

"Darnell Riley, even though he's a former client of mine, admittedly, he sometimes embellishes certain things," says Richards.

And yet, whatever their relationship, their names are continually linked—at times furtively—in the secret folds at the heart of this story, and in the motivations behind some of the more inexplicable actions in Darnell's public legacy. Case in point is the Tommy Alastra incident.

"When I said we need to figure out a jazzy way around the statute of limitations, I mean stuff like the Tommy Alastra situation," says Darnell. "Jazzy" is Darnell's word to designate literary artifice or artistic license. "Being that I've never been charged with the crime nor accused by Tommy Alastra, I wouldn't talk about it. It would be tactfully unwise for me to poke my chest out with pride for having tapped Tommy Alastra on his ass."

According to the police report, on June 19, 2004, club promoter Tommy Alastra returned home to his four-story apartment building on a wide, manicured street south of Franklin in Hollywood with his friend Erin Naas, whom he had known for between two and four years, identified throughout as "Suspect 2." In the underground parking garage, Alastra reports that Erin introduced him to a black or Hispanic male named "Javier," who suddenly materialized, entered the elevator with them, and followed them to Alastra's ground-floor apartment. At that point, Javier produced a small-caliber handgun and forced his way inside, tied Alastra's wrists behind his back with nylon wire ties, removed his shoes, socks, and pants and told him to lie down on his stomach. He then asked for and received the combination to the wall safe.

As depicted in the report, "Suspect 2 [Erin] told victim [Alastra] to return some unk(nown) items that she had accused him of taking. [Alastra] denied ever taking any property from her. Suspect 1 ["Javier"] returned to [Alastra] and pulled out a stun gun from a blue bag and stunned [Alastra] two times on the neck and possibly on the back. [Javier] told [Alastra] to remain quiet and not say anything. [Javier] also pulled out a knife and threatened to 'gut him open.' "

As Alastra lay prone naked, Javier asked Erin if any of the jewelry in the safe was hers, which she denied. He then ransacked the apartment while Erin tried on Alastra's hats. She eventually covered Alastra with a pair of blue jeans, telling him he didn't have to be naked, whereupon Javier remarked, "I was just going to play with him a little," and laughed. Before leaving, Javier cut an iPod cord, which he presumably took to be a phone cord, and took Alastra's cell phone, which he left outside. He also pocketed a Rolex watch, which later proved to be fake and which Alastra told police he was keeping for a friend, no trace of whom exists anywhere. He also claims that Javier smoked cigarettes throughout. (Darnell doesn't smoke and claims they were "props.") Alastra left town the next day for two weeks for a funeral in Florida, and didn't file a police report until he returned. A day later, Alastra reported that he had received the Rolex back from Damon Kidwell—Ecstasy dealer Louis Ziskin's one-time protégé—acting as an intermediary for Erin. He also told police where they could find Erin celebrating her twenty-first birthday: at the Havana Room in Beverly Hills. When police arrived and questioned her there half an hour later, "Naas stated that she had never hurt anyone." She claimed not to know any Javier, and when asked who had accompanied her to Alastra's apartment, told officers "she did not know his real name," whereupon she was taken into custody. A week later, Alastra was caught in a routine traffic stop in Beverly Hills with a registered gun in his car. His bail bondsman was Alex Vaysfeld.

After Darnell was arrested in the Joe Francis break-in in March 2005, Detective Koman began to work backward through his rumored crimes, including this one. "I went to look for Tommy Alastra five, six, seven times," Koman says. "He never returned my calls; he was never there. Maybe he was there and didn't return my calls, but I can't force victims to testify. Everybody knew the problems that these guys were creating on the street, but nobody wanted to step forward to deal with it."

He also had a close encounter with Erin herself when he went looking for Will and Kristen at the Sunset Plaza address, although he didn't put it together until later. "I door-knocked the place, and a woman answered the door," says Koman. "By the time I got to the office, I had a call from an attorney—fill in the blanks—and I realized that the woman was probably Erin Naas." When I suggest that she may have been behind the Tommy Alastra home invasion, Koman says, "It don't take a whole lot to figure that one out."

In my early back and forth with Darnell, he continually suggested there were things he would tell me in person that he wouldn't commit to print, and so during one of our face-to-faces at Corcoran, I asked him to explain the Alastra incident to me. He wouldn't come right out and admit it. Instead, he narrated the entire story, start to finish in excruciating detail, in the third person. It doesn't represent a confession in that the word "I" never comes up in his account. But by the end of it, he left no doubt in my mind at least as to who Javier was.

The story he told me, reconstructed from memory without notes, is this: Alastra and Erin were out partying. Alastra had gotten word from Florida that his best friend had committed suicide. At a small gathering at Erin's apartment, Chuck Pacheco, who worked with Alastra at various club venues, showed up unannounced, and he and Alastra went outside to talk. Later that evening, some antique jewelry left to her by her grandmother turned up missing from Erin's safe. She called "Javier" and told him what had happened. Javier told her, "Well, if Chuck Pacheco showed up, then he and Tommy are the ones who took your jewelry." Javier went to Alastra's apartment, waited for Erin and him to return, confronted Alastra at gunpoint, and cuffed him, telling him, "This is for your protection, not mine; I don't want you swinging at me."

Darnell speculated on why Javier might have stripped Alastra from the waist down.

"This is exactly what I did to Joe Francis," he says. "The reason why is, these people all think they're entitled, because they have money and all these things. They all think they're privileged: 'I can do whatever I want.' Well, if you strip them down naked, now they're the way they came into the world. Now we're equal. If I'm talking to you, it's just us: we are men before God. You're naked; if you want to run, run."

As Alastra was crying and carrying on, Javier would zap him with a Taser and tell him to calm down. At that point, Erin returned to look for her stolen jewelry. When they left, they took the Rolex as collateral. And yet, this was not the last Alastra heard from the elusive Javier.

"I get a call from Alex Vaysfeld telling me that a young Hollywood guy was getting bailed out after getting popped [arrested] for driving with a pistol in Beverly Hills and did I know him?" says Darnell. "Rick had called Alex. He knew Alex through me—'I got to bail my buddy out'—but when Alex called me, I couldn't make out the name, so I didn't know it was Tommy at first. Then Erin called me within minutes of me hanging up with Alex. She told me Tommy got popped with a pistol, and she was laughing because she had just had her run-in with the fuzz. I go by and see the photo Alex took for his records, and it's Tommy. So Tommy came back by at Alex's request, and that's when Javier surprised Tommy at Alex's office as a way to let Tommy know to shut up, and that he could be touched at any moment—that Javier's reach stretched far. But I can't confirm anything, being that they believe Javier and myself are close."

Erin denies any run-in with Alastra, any stolen jewelry (she never knew her grandmother), being present at Alastra's during any part of the home invasion, and virtually everything in the initial police report—the one rendered moot when Alastra refused to press the matter.

"[Alastra] didn't identify the person that took his watch, which then turned out to be fake, and then he got his watch back," explains Ron Richards. "My client was there. The police arrested her to question her about what she knew, and then no charges were filed . . . That was the end of it."

"I was shocked, and I was hysterical," says Erin about the night she was arrested on her twenty-first birthday.

"You're making this so dramatic," says Ron.

"It was," she insists. "They said they were arresting me for having something to do with a robbery. I was in a tiny dress—that was really bad. It was not a good jailhouse outfit. They didn't have a police car, they had a black car—they're like detectives. And I had this tiny, tiny little mini-dress on with my boobs hanging out. It wasn't a very classy way to be brought in."

"I happened to be there separately," says Richards—not as a guest at her birthday party, but as a dues-paying member of the Grand Havana Cigar Room. "And someone said, 'Oh my God, Ron Richards, your client is getting arrested.' And I see this girl that I recognized screaming and crying as the police are taking her to jail. I'd only talked to her on the phone. So I ran over and had her assert Miranda at the scene. I followed her to the station, went in the interview room, reasserted her Miranda, and posted her bond and took her home. It was a hundred-thousand-dollar bond, and she paid ten thousand to the bail agent and paid my fees."

I told them that Darnell had as much as admitted he was the perpetrator.

"Great. He can admit to any crime he wants," says Richards. "If he wants to admit to some felony, that's great, let him go do what he wants. My position today is the same as it was five years ago: she didn't participate in this robbery, she was with Tommy Alastra, and she's not going to assist Tommy Alastra or corroborate this bizarre admission of an uncharged offense . . . [Darnell] commits all sorts of offenses and then he tries to bring everybody else in."

"The stuff with Tommy Alastra was public knowledge," says Darnell.

"Everyone talked and laughed about it around town. Tommy and I hung out on the scene all the way up to two nights before I was arrested for the Joe Francis shit.

"I was in Vegas with her when Tommy saw her after the event and she started running," says David Reich, who claims that Erin was living at his apartment when the Alastra thing happened. "She ran to the bathroom to get away from him. Tommy said, 'Stop, you bitch!' And she ran into the bathroom at the Bellagio and screamed that she needed protection. But we didn't know what happened with that until later."

"He was giving her problems, so Darnell checked him out for her," says Jerry Rosenberg.

"Even after that whole incident, we'd go to the club [Prey] that Tommy was promoting, and Darnell would be there," says Kristen. "He'd have to look at him after everything happened, and they had to let him in the club. So he must have been scared."

"Everyone was saying that she was so wickedly out of her mind on drugs as this was all going down," adds Heather.

"When it came to saying no to her, people ran," says Giovanni, then the promoter of Lobby.

"They used to call Erin Naas 'Bubblehead,' " adds Scott.

"Every single guy, every single club owner, everybody was so afraid to tell her no because of what happened," says Giovanni. "I liked her, and I thought she was really sweet, but everyone was terrified that she would rape them."

After a dozen or more calls over many months, Alastra finally called me back and told me in so many words that he couldn't comment on any of it. He wished me luck with my book.

ACTS OF DEPRAVED INDIFFERENCE

It's L.A. Everybody comes from somewhere. Darnell slipped like a ghost up from South Central, through the collected shadows of old Los Angeles—the brittle Cubism of ash and noir, leeched of color, etched in chiaroscuro—closing one door as quietly as he opened another. Will caught the mainline down from land's end: a pretty-boy hustler with a manic spiel and no restraint mechanism. Timmy found his way out from South Philly, a mob comic with a fast line and a glad hand—buy you a drink, tell you a joke, slip in the blade, and then scurry for the darkened corner. The worlds they passed through, just an exit ramp away off the fast lane, are ones we recognize from forties movies and suspect in the present day, but whose inner workings seem to have eluded the documentary record: gambling, boxing, drug trafficking, prostitution, pornography, organized crime, shady lawyers, mobbed-up nightclubs, rich women with poor judgment, skip-tracers and high-end muscle—a subterranean transit through all those things that facilitate the business of celebrities at play. Chart their movements, and it's a huge spiderweb of crimes and sporadic violence, cross-leveraged between power, access, money, and fame.

Every ten years or so, we get a look at it—when they kill a Kennedy, say, or when O.J. fucks up—the cross-section of all those convergent worlds that operate at any given time beneath the consensus narrative. You'd think the sheer number of paparazzi trolling the clubs and alleyways off Holly-wood Boulevard would guarantee saturated coverage, bring it up to a bilious froth, and yet it doesn't: we get a tenth of the story documented in blinding light and debilitating detail, while the nine-tenths beneath the surface carries on with impunity, safe in its anonymity.

"You know Hollywood from your point of view—professional people, fame, the Joe Francises and Paris Hiltons of Hollywood," says Tamer Ibrahim, the Ecstasy dealer and one-time king of the nightlife. "But in the underlying current of Hollywood, the things that make things click are always in the underworld, because that's where all the cash is coming from. The running of these big clubs—the protection money, the profits—that's where everything goes down."

And that's the story I'm trying to tell: what happens when real criminals—sociopaths wielding acute violence in the service of authentic crime—get inside the party and run riot, brutalizing the guests. Andrew Brin, the doorman at Les Deux Café and another longtime Hollywood nightlife fixture, says, "You should be asking why this doesn't happen every day."

But don't take my word for it. I'm late to the party. Ask Darnell's ex-wife.

"I know Will, and I've heard conversations on the other side of the phone with him—he was a friggin' nut job," says Ashley. A twenty-five-year-old Canadian and statuesque blonde with a dancer's body, Ashley met Darnell when her boyfriend ran in the AIDS Project L.A. marathon. ("Legs for days" is how Darnell describes her.) Six months later, with the boyfriend long gone and faced with the prospect of deportation, she finally agreed to marry Darnell for a green card in July 2004, even though they were never romantically involved. After his name surfaced as a person of interest in the stolen Paris Hilton tapes, she put distance between them, and finalized her divorce in 2008—but not before observing the cast of characters around him at close range.

Of Timmy, she says, "I'm trying to get the right words for it. You know in L.A. how you think everybody's sketchy? He was just kind of sketchy. They were sketchy. The two of them were weasels, but I didn't know how deep they went. If you were to think of the trio: the smart guy, the weaselly friend, and then you've got the one who's got a few screws loose and is kind of stupid; that would describe them. Darnell was the smart mastermind who is kind of a sociopath; the weaselly friend who would kind of do anything but would break under pressure was Tim; and then you have the one that was the crazy friend that's got a few screws loose and that's kind of fucked up—that was Will. That was my interpretation of the situation."

● ● ●

"The agreement Timmy, Will, and I had on deals that came our respective ways did equate to a partnership," says Darnell. "Will brought in a good connection with his Canadian guys—connections he had from years back, before his Fed time—and some good dump-off points in L.A. versus my connects back in New York. Will also brought in the hype. He liked being out front and running around the country to cozy up next to Paris Hilton, so why not? Well, it became a liability, as we can see by my current home. Timmy had all the connects to the club scene. He had plenty of legitimate [film] industry connects. He knows nearly every agent/manager to whatever celeb you may want to deal with. They've been in to one of his clubs, or is an investor. Other people believed the hype of his Genovese connections and his uncle, Matty the Horse. But that's his weak way of getting people around town to think that he has weight behind him. Timmy is a character. He has weaseled his way out of a lot of situations around town.

"As far as Erin being the Shirley MacLaine to our Rat Pack, that's pretty accurate. She let Will buy her shit. She let him try to protect her like he was her man—just to get next to her and meet her friends, and try to piggyback onto another connection. She let Timmy hang on also. But Timmy isn't a trick like Will. He does have the balls to tell a chick to blow him or get the fuck out. And unlike Will, he had history in L.A. So Will needed Timmy. He needed me. We legitimized his existence in L.A. Timmy fed Will at his restaurant, Bliss. As far as Will introducing me to Hollywood, that's the furthest thing from the truth. My life in Hollywood predates Will's arrival by four years. Now, if you count my younger years, I've got eleven years of history with Rick, Balthazar, Chuck Pacheco, et cetera before Will ever got out of the Feds. Will was never the mastermind, the oracle in the shadows calling the shots. He has always been a two-bit chump."

But it took a leggy model with druggy eyes, a razor sneer, and a heart of purest platinum to pull them into a single criminal braid—or at least to goad them into administering a rough kind of frontier justice, one that in the end only made sense to criminals like them.

Cherchez la femme. Always look for the woman.

"The reasoning behind me having to play Spiderman through Bel Air on January 22, 2004, stems from two sources," says Darnell. "Erin Naas and Joe Francis. Erin Naas was attacked by Joe Francis, and Joe owed several wise guys big money, and I stepped in to settle his debt. But then Joe happened. Like always.

"Joe gambled on all USC games (his alma mater). He bet religiously with me on SC games since 2002. But he had always paid up with me on any win/loss. He owed two bookies from back east over a million each. In 2003, he lost big to two of them and played Casper the Ghost for the whole year. I went back to New York to tie up some loose ends before Xmas of 2003, and the bookies/wise guys asked me to step in and straighten out this Hollywood prick, Joe. It was either that or he would be getting a visit that would have left him hearing footsteps before it all went black forever. I agreed for several reasons. One being, if Joe got the axe, that would bring unnecessary heat onto my stomping grounds, Hollywood, and there would have been a mass exodus of wannabe movie star tough guys shacking up behind bodyguards and gated communities. Maybe I should have let the hounds loose so that young Hollywood could see what can happen when they try to play in the big leagues. Also, Erin Naas was dating Joe and she seemed into him, for the moment at least. I also wanted to keep myself in the best of respects with these guys. I knew that by stepping in to clean up the drama, I would be able to call on them if I needed to. And that favor is still available.

"So leaving New York, I got back to L.A. days before Xmas. On Xmas eve, I get a call from Kristen Williams. I was finishing up a nice dinner with Nicole Lenz. The night was perfect, and Kristen tried to maintain her composure, but I could tell that there was trouble. She briefed me on what had just happened with Erin. Erin had broken it off with Joe days earlier, but they were still on fucking terms. Erin goes over to give Joe his Xmas present, when he attacked her. Erin broke away and was able to get to her car. Will was in Washington with his family, and Kristen knew Riley would take care of it.

"I arrived over at Erin's apartment (Sunset Plaza) and Kristen was in the living room with Timmy. Erin was trying to pull herself together. She saw me and burst into tears. I had already called up some of my reservoir dogs and had them standing by in the car. I saw how broken up she was, so I took her into her room and gave her time to tell me what happened. She said the prick Joe had been high and like usual he believes the world is his. He goes off and starts pulling at her clothes and tries to pin her down. He digitized her through her panties and punched her a couple of times. She says she blacked out for a couple of minutes, and when she awoke he had most of her clothes off and had his war chest of dildos and anal lube out, and she bolted for the door in her panties with whatever clothes she could grab. She had her keys in her truck, and nearly broke down his security gate backing out. Joe didn't even come out of his house, he just buzzed the gate open and she sped away.

"I know Erin's bullshit and her drama, but she wasn't bullshitting."

In her interview in Ron Richards's office, Erin claimed she didn't know Darnell when she was dating Joe Francis, that she never invited him into his house or car (Darnell's explanation as to how his fingerprint could have ended up in Joe's Bentley), and that Darnell and Joe were strangers to each other. She maintains that she had nothing to do with the Joe Francis home invasion (or any other crime), and that she has no lasting enmity with Joe, although she is a little less certain when asked if she claimed Joe Francis physically attacked her.

"Joe and I were friends after any incident like that may ever have happened," says Erin. "Joe and I were always friendly. We spoke on the phone. We actually communicated well. After any time I'd ever been upset with him, he would call me the next day, and we actually made up, we were fine. I had no hard feelings against Joe, I never even said bad things about Joe, and I would never want to see anything bad happen to him ever."

"Let's just say that at the time, Erin was doing drugs, and you know, there were a lot of allegations made, but at this point, she doesn't have any bad feelings toward Joe Francis," says Ron Richards, interceding on his client's behalf. "My whole office was on call," adds Ron. "She'd come by, people would have to calm her down, let her sleep it off. It was terrible— one of the worst cases I've ever seen. So, you know, she may have had a conversation with Kristen Williams about it, but to now make a spurious allegation while she was in the middle of that cocaine/methamphetamine-induced paranoia, it's silly, because sitting here today she doesn't have any negative feelings about Joe Francis."

"And I would never tell Darnell about any problem I ever had," says Erin.

"Erin called me *bawling* one night," remembers Kristen. "She had gone over there. And yeah, this was at the time when she was doing lots of drugs, so, now that I look back, I don't know if I should believe it or not. But she called me bawling—'Oh my God, oh my God! He just tried to rape me! He held me down, he pinned me down!' And I'm saying, 'It's okay, it's okay—don't worry.' Will had told me that Darnell was like a bodyguard— 'he can protect you.' So, I rushed home, called Darnell over, called Timmy over, I was crying with her: 'Oh my God, this is my friend, this is horrible!' It freaked me out. I think she had something to do with the Joe Francis break-in, because she knew his house really well. Everybody thought it was Erin"—the girl heard at the end of the videotape.

In a statement made to police on April 7, 2005, in response to previous allegations made by Darnell, Joe Francis told Detective Koman that "he does not know Riley" or even who he is, "that he has never met Riley for any type of deal," "that he does not owe Riley any money for any sports bet" or anything else and that, in fact, "he does not bet on sports," although he does gamble in casinos. He said specifically that he never invited Riley to any party, although he can't say Darnell never attended one, that "he never partied with Riley at any of the local bars," and that if he did know who Riley was, "he would have turned him in immediately."

"I've handled plenty of things on his behalf," says Darnell today.

Any number of people come forward to attest that Francis and Darnell were at least acquainted. Joe Campana, the actor and club patron, said he had met Darnell a handful of times. "I was invited to a dinner party Joe Francis had at Shelter," he says. "I went to the dinner, saw Darnell there, and we shook hands. Joe Francis's dinner party was the first time I had seen him since the initial time we met. I called Joe after everything happened, and said 'Yo, that's the guy who did that to you?' It was only after I saw Darnell on TV." Both Jerry Rosenberg and Alex Vaysfeld reiterate much the same. Jerry claims to have hung out with them together at a nightclub on La Cienega, and Alex, who was prepared to testify on Darnell's behalf if the case went to trial, says in typically colorful fashion, "*Fuck* yeah. Look, that motherfucker, he knew from way back—they went to parties together."

Kristen says it's highly unlikely they wouldn't have known each other, at least by the time of Joe's statement, since, "By that time, Darnell was already hanging out in the crowd and stuff. He was at Nicky Hilton's birthday party. He was already hanging out at the parties. I saw him out everywhere."

And Jaime Weinberg, who dated Darnell briefly, says, "There were pictures. And he had like thirty videos of him filming with *Girls Gone Wild*," as well as photos of him and Paris Hilton together. "Just that crowd. He had a lot of pictures of him and them."

These "*Girls Gone Wild* videos" purportedly include footage that Darnell says he shot in Rio de Janeiro on the set of the Snoop Dogg video for "Beautiful," a song written and recorded with Pharrell of the recording/producing entity the Neptunes and released in February 2003. Snoop Dogg was the first "celebrity host" of a *Girls Gone Wild* video—*Girls Gone Wild: Doggy Style*, filmed at Mardi Gras in 2002 and released in May 2003—and Francis was present for the filming in Rio.

"I went down to Rio to visit a buddy who fled the U.S.," says Darnell. "He is Brazilian and he got arrested for busting some guys up in a rumble. He is a jujitsu fighter, and he was only here for some matches. None of us could get any chicks—they was all circling Snoop. I was the one with the camera—just a little hand-held thing. You can hear my voice, though." (That footage was not among the video returned by Koman, although evidence exists that an additional mini-DV tape is still being held by the police.)

And there are photos from a Halloween party that Francis hosted in 2003 at a rented mansion, in which Francis and Erin Naas (both dressed as angels), Mario Lopez (as a Spanish toreador), and others are posing for the camera. "He had guys that worked for him dressed in orange jumpsuits with Bay County Jail on the back as a way to mock his arrest months in prison," says Darnell.

On the stand at Darnell's preliminary hearing, Francis vehemently denied that he ever participated in sportsbook gambling. Among Darnell's papers is a spreadsheet printout of gambling client payouts, returned to him anonymously while he was awaiting trial in L.A. County. It lists a dozen players by shorthand code: director Joe Carnahan (listed as "Tarnahan"), Fred Durst, Michael Madsen ("Mad Scene M."), and Rick Salomon, who Darnell says bundled ten to fifteen players after cashing out of his sportsbook investments following his *1 Night in Paris* windfall. (Carnahan denies he gambles.) For the period depicted, Francis ("JJWild") is shown having won $4,000 on the USC-Arizona State game October 4, 2003, $1,000 on USC-Notre Dame October 18, $2,000 on USC-Washington State November 1 (plus $1,000 on the over), another $1,000 on the over for USC-Arizona State November 15, and $8,000 on USC-UCLA November 22.

Rick Doremus, in his brief pre-DEA dealings with Will, says that Will told him Francis owed him a $150,000 gambling debt, and promised him half of it if he could collect. "I made a phone call to Joe Francis and said, 'Hey, you owe us some fucking money, you better pay,' " he says. "He sort of blew us off, and I wasn't going to expose myself for that little amount of money, so I made an attempt and that was it." (In my VH1 interview, Francis denied this ever happened, and to be fair, it could just as easily have been some boneheaded extortion ploy.)

In the course of making his rounds, Darnell claims to have stopped by a dinner party at Francis's house two nights after the break-in, attended by Nicky Hilton and others, to drop off gambling receipts. "He acted nonchalant about the robbery," says Darnell. "He did say, 'The ma'fucka won't be able to get me now.' He was like a little bitch, thinking the security was a deterrent. I wanted to do it again just to show him I could. In fact, Timmy and I talked in late 2004 about doing it again. We joked about Joe Francis Number Two." (Joe Francis is currently being sued by Wynn Las Vegas Casino for $2 million over a delinquent gambling debt from February 2007.)

Darnell also claims to have been instrumental in structuring offshore shell companies to divert taxable income for Francis, something he did for clients with unexplained cash to launder. This involved a couple of companies through which Francis allegedly purchased multiple homes in Southern California and leased them back to himself as legitimate business expenses, claiming instead a Nevada residence. According to Darnell, these were "accounts to bounce funds off of in Panama banks to PayPal accounts to Costa Rica, and everything ending up in Euro accounts and clean to withdraw." When this line of questioning was brought up at the preliminary hearing, Francis refused to answer on Fifth Amendment grounds on the advice of counsel, who was present in the courtroom. On April 11, 2007, one day after being jailed on contempt of court charges in the ongoing Florida civil litigation stemming from his 2003 criminal charges in Panama City Beach, Florida, for having filmed minors in sexual situations, Francis was indicted on federal tax evasion charges for illegally deducting in excess of $20 million in illegitimate business expenses during the calendar years 2002 and 2003. The charges, which carried a maximum of ten years in prison and a half-million-dollar fine, were brought in U.S. District Court in Reno, Nevada, to which he was eventually extradited while awaiting disposition in the Florida civil matter.

"I had my mother call the IRS when I was in L.A. County and give them the thorough breakdown," says Darnell. "So if he's up on tax evasion charges, as he should be, you can attribute that to me. Our whole plan was to dirty him up so much—collateral damage—and then get it to a point where they could offer me something, which is what happened."

During his stay in a Nevada prison, Francis and his attorneys created a Web site to help turn public sentiment in his favor. (He was also interviewed in prison by journalist Martin Bashir for ABC's *Nightline*, and by weekend *Extra* host Mario Lopez, a frequent guest at Francis's Bel Air estate.) On the Web site, amid cuddly dreamboat photos of Francis, he shares his fabled biography and glowing testimonials from his friends (neighbor and mentor Quincy Jones, Lance Bass, Peter Guber, Kim Kardashian, Lopez, producer Adam Fields), all the time almost having to pinch himself to prove it's really real:

"It might be a stretch to say that I'm just your average Joe," he says on the opening splash page, "but as you explore this site, I think you'll come to find that my desires, dreams and disappointments aren't terribly different from your own. I suppose the particulars of my life might seem remarkable, even unbelievable to some people. But that's the reason for this website. Because if it hadn't happened to me, I never would have believed it myself."

Okay, he had some time on his hands. But compare this to the contempt citation in the Florida civil trial for which he was eventually incarcerated for seven months: at a court-ordered mediation on March 21, 2007, Francis arrived "wearing sweat shorts, a backwards baseball cap and was barefoot," "put his bare dirty feet up on the table, facing plaintiff's counsel," and "repeatedly shouted vulgarities and threats at plaintiffs and their counsel," including "We will bury you and your clients," "I'm going to ruin you, your clients and all your ambulance-chasing partners," "Don't expect to get a dime—not one fucking dime," and the terse yet elegant "Suck my dick!" at which point intermediaries were forced to intercede.

Along with the footage he shot in Rio, Darnell claims he got an unexpected bonus when the tapes were shipped over to him: *Girls Gone Wild* master tapes. The tapes were seized by authorities at Darnell's arrest, and Francis claims they were taken during the burglary, although, as Darnell points out, they appear nowhere on the stolen property report. This may or may not have to do with Francis making his impromptu acting debut.

"The video goes like this," says Darnell. "Joe is on one of his *GGW* shoots. His team coerces four chicks to give this one chick a tongue lashing for about thirty minutes. All the chicks are stoned and probably underaged. The chicks are poking at the one girl like she's a pin cushion. Mister Dick Head Joe doesn't like what he's seeing; it's not raunchy enough for him. So he jumps into the camera shot, mad like a prick, and starts digitizing the horizontally stiff chick. He's ramming his hand in her with reckless abandon, and then he realizes that he's on camera and tells the camera operator not to get his face. He tries to step back, but his hand never leaves the frame. But it was the way he went about digitizing her that sparked my interest. He obviously hates women. He was jamming her like she was a turkey and he was putting stuffing in her. All I wanted to do was show that to the court, to demonstrate the pathology of this guy. He is a brute and a sexual deviant.

"Once again, I had to take things into my own hands. I had people contact the district attorney in Florida, where [Francis] was up against seventy-two charges, and let them know that my D.A. was in possession of those tapes."

Outside of the underage speculation, which is pure conjecture, that's a pretty good description of what's on the tape.

At one point, I put a link up on my Web site to a story that ran in the *Los Angeles Times Magazine* in August 2006 by Claire Hoffman called "Baby, Give Me a Kiss." Assigned to profile Francis, she unavoidably broke the cardinal rule of newspaper journalism and entered the story when Francis, having been asked about his 2003 arrest in Florida, in an ill-advised bid for sympathy wrenched the reporter's arm behind her back and slammed her onto the trunk of a car. The title was taken from his parting words to her minutes later, which he apparently considered an apology. That's the post where I first wrote about Alex Vaysfeld and the Joe Francis trip to Moscow, where he allegedly tried to order up a twelve-year-old girl off room service. But it was a published comment from a reader that stayed with me.

"Living in New Orleans, I can't tell you how many times, during Mardi Gras, I've seen girls leaving the 'back room' that *GGW* sets up in a club, crying hysterically. *GGW* pays girls to go over to groups of drunk girls and tell them it's fun and cool (they're decoys), and then the drunk girls end up on tape and leaving the back room in tears. It's the girls' fault for the bad judgment, but the way that the company goes about taking advantage (when you see it in action) is just foul."

But then, it's not like Erin is the only one to accuse Joe of outright rape. Here's a story that ran in *Radar* magazine in October 2007.

"According to several sources, days before [*New York Post* editor Richard] Johnson's April 8, 2006 nuptials to Sessa von Richthofen, the editor and a half-dozen of his friends were crashing in the living room of Francis's $25 million, 13-bedroom estate in Punta Mita, Mexico, nursing hangovers when the porn auteur came home and disappeared into a bedroom with a reluctant young woman. Eyewitnesses claim that a few hours later the young woman burst out of Francis's boudoir, groggily crying, and yelling, 'That motherfucker raped me!' She staggered off alone after loudly threatening Francis that her boyfriend in Oklahoma was a lawyer who would 'sue the fuck' out of him.

"Johnson and fellow revelers were left dumbstruck. But Francis—who has been accused of procuring underage prostitutes, promoting sexual performances from children, drug trafficking, racketeering and rape—was quick to calm their nerves. 'Guys, relax,' he told Johnson and others, according to witnesses. 'We're in Mexico.' " ("I never saw anything of the sort," Johnson responded to *Radar* through a *Post* spokesperson.)

But John Connolly, the reporter on the story, says, "There is no question. None. I talked with someone who was there."

If those who were at the bachelor party—and here's the guest list: hotelier Andre Balasz, Niche Media CEO Jason Binn, producers Bill Block and Adam Fields, novelist Coerte Felske, John Flanagan (no clue), *Post* writer Braden Keil, talent manager Mark Russo, Lionel von Richthofen (a runner-up on ABC's *The Bachelor* and the brother of the bride), and *Men's Health* editor Dave Zinczenko—in fact witnessed a cry of rape and failed to intervene or report it to authorities, that would be an act of depraved indifference.

Block, the distributor on Will's movie, e-mailed back, "I cannot discuss what went on at the bachelor party." Russo confirmed he was there, but won't comment. Nobody else called me back. But that woman is out there somewhere. Her boyfriend is a lawyer in Oklahoma. And she didn't sound to me like a shrinking violet. She should give me a call.

Darnell claims it was a not-so-well-kept secret that Joe Francis may be gay. He says that over New Year's Eve 2004, the following year, Erin and her boyfriend, Brody Jenner from *The Hills*, were in St. Bart's (at first he says Saint-Tropez, but later he corrects himself). "Joe had his new flaming boy-toy with him," says Darnell. "He had just bought the boy-toy a Porsche. He was nearly fully out of the closet. It was never a secret around Hollywood. Every chance I got, I clowned his ass with the kidnap video. He definitely hated me."

Of all people, Erin Naas lends credence to this theory.

"Well, if I was to say he was gay, I'd be answering wrong. He definitely— if anything, he would be bisexual. But I really, I think he's just kind of like a tortured human being, maybe. And he's a little bit . . . he has issues. But I don't think . . . I never thought of him as liking men. He travels with men, he has close guy friends, but I think it's a trust issue or something.

"I'm sure Darnell told you that he had a sexual relationship with Joe," says Ron Richards, clearly skeptical. "That's a hard one to believe."

"Yeah. Maybe," says Erin.

Pushed on the issue of Joe and his très young companion, Erin finally identifies him as also named Francis. "You know what?" she says. "If I had to guess, I would say that there was definitely promiscuity to Joe's sex life, and he was never that interested in [traditional] sex. Which probably made me like him more. He always had a male friend with him, and then his other friend was always living with him or driving his cars. And Joe was pretty careful with his money. I wasn't dating him for shopping or anything like that, but you know, he would just loan out his nice things to his male friends a lot or help them out. When a woman asked, they'd get denied more."

"I've heard rumors," says Holt Gardiner. "But then again, I've heard a rumor about every person in Hollywood who gets laid a lot being gay."

And this being Hollywood, probably more so than anywhere else. Too much money, too much time on people's hands, too many beautiful women, a low threshold of inhibition. Hef's girlfriends say he needs gay porn to get off. After Pamela Anderson, Tommy Lee admitted to bisexual affairs. Paris Hilton and her million-minx army certainly don't seem to let gender slow them down. At this point, what does it really matter?

And in fact, there are plenty of people in the book who are gay, some of whom would rather I didn't know it, and I wouldn't think of outing them. Maybe even me—who knows? But the ones who mistreat women, or who are repeatedly accused of being serial rapists, I think we can probably make an exception.

Darnell certainly thought so.

FRESH PRINTS OF BEL AIR

Darnell says he spent New Year's Eve 2003 with Mickey Rourke and Will Wright in Miami, Rourke's old stomping grounds, where he spent most of his time babysitting an incorrigible Will who was wreaking even more havoc than usual: upending a party at a sheik's mansion on Millionaire's Row, tossing one of the midget waiters in the pool (and soaking a serving platter heaped with cocaine), eyeing the prop camel grazing on the sloping lawn. When Rourke confided he was starting to regret the invitation, Darnell sent Will back to their hotel—where he pestered the waitress at the Shore Club (home of the South Beach Skybar) so much that she kneed him in the stomach. The next day, Will showed up at Darnell's bungalow, suitcase in hand, pleading poverty. Darnell paid for the room another day and took off for New York.

"Once back in L.A., I did some recon work on Joe's pad," says Darnell. "I have a chick that is a Realtor, and at the time, Joe's place was on the market for six million dollars. So I set up a tour when I knew he wasn't going to be there. His Realtor gave my girl access, who took us through the clusterfuck mansion. I just really wanted to know what security system he used. He didn't have the sign in the yard. He went through ADT, and I just happened to have a guy in ADT's main office. I'd have him available to kill the alarm and give me time to pick the lock. I'm not as good as I should be, but I haven't found one yet that can hold me—with the exception of this beautiful gated community that I'm in now. But with the tour, I got the layout I needed. There is a roof access I could've used if need be. I had just gotten a plasma cutter and several torches to do some welding, if I wanted to bust through the roof exit. Just options. A big sliding door could be taken off its track. More options. With my guy at the company, I knew he could take the place offline for three minutes, and I'd have plenty of time to enter.

"I had a couple of dry runs—I had two of my reservoir dogs come out and we were going to move on it that night. Joe was at a Lakers game with a chick, but I didn't want any civilians involved. Also, I didn't like the feel: too many uncertainties, and if it feels off, you gotta cancel it. This is the event that Rich Jardine gave to Koman as his knowledge of the event, and then he refused to take the stand. Stupid prick.

"So a week later, I was at Erin's house, and I checked with her once more to see if she wanted to turn this rapist in. And she didn't.

"We got a game plan in place. Will would ask Brandon [Davis] about Joe's movements. Will and Joe were having problems. Will punched Joe months earlier. I told Brandon to keep me posted on Joe and I'd give him a break on cash he owed. Joe picked up Brandon from Will's house, and Will followed them to Concorde [the club du jour for Wednesdays, at Franklin and Cahuenga in Hollywood].

"I met Timmy at my buddy's gym and he had these two civilians in the car, Chera and Khalil. One of them is a stripper chick I know well. The other is a stiff who loves my style—a cool dude, but not one to be part of a crew. Tim was dropping me off to go do my magic, and was heading to the club himself. I'm in full Navy Seal gear ready to go on a covert mission.

"I make a call to my ADT guy, he switches off the alarm, I do my magic, and I'm in in less than thirty seconds. Not bad, huh? I surveyed the pad and then made myself a sandwich. I knew I had time to kill, so I took a shit in the bathroom and sanitized afterwards to ensure no DNA was left. I watched TV and some *GGW* videos. I spoke to Tim and Will: Francis was enjoying himself. No chicks with him. Tim had a walkie [and a cell phone], and Will [was on cell]. So that answers who was on the other end [of the walkie-talkie], right?

"I got the call the chump was coming home. Brandon had been dropped off and all, and I'm on standby. By the way, he never saw my face. Believe that. I had a mask on the whole time. If a robber (especially me) robs you and takes off his mask, you better start praying. My fellow criminals would kick me out of the union. I gave the prick water throughout. I ate ice cream in front of him, so he didn't know what to expect. By the way, he also had a sack on his head. The only time it came off was when it was showtime for him. The whole dildo and being filmed was to bring him down to the level that he's tried to bring so many women to. To feel completely helpless and at the mercy of someone else. The whole time, he kept asking, 'Are you going to fuck me?' Maybe he wanted it.

"When Timmy returned, Khalil didn't come back with him. Chera did, and she walked up the driveway to pick up some paintings. She was the chick you heard [on the tape]. She wanted to bang him in the keister! She was a wild child. I loaded some stuff in the Bentley and took off, [then] dumped the car. We laughed. I gave Chera all the Louis Vuitton luggage and about five thousand dollars. I gave Tim five thousand. I don't know why Joe didn't report more missing, but then again, he didn't mention a lot. He was high. I got busy with Chera that night. Her and Timmy were casual hookup buddies, and we had a great time with Chera. Afterward, we laughed watching the Joe Francis video."

Just like when the Manson family swooped down on the Sharon Tate house in Benedict Canyon, there were those on the periphery who just barely escaped being dragged into the whole Joe Francis incident, rescued by either foresight or happenstance. One of these was Jerry Rosenberg. Without hesitation, he refers to Francis as a "faggot" and a child molester. He recalls Darnell stopping by his gym.

"He said, 'Come on, let's take a ride.' I said, 'Where you going?' He said, 'I'm going to Bel Air.' I said, 'Nah, I can't ride witcha.' I knew what he was doing. But he called me from there like three times." He reports hearing Darnell talk about the incident a couple of times with Timmy and Will, and fielded a call from Darnell days before he was arrested.

"I lived in Valencia, and Darnell had a backpack that he left in my house with all that shit in it. You ever seen that documentary on the TV about all that shit?"

I told him I helped produce it.

"You seen where they had all that shit laid out with the backpack? Well, that whole backpack was in my garage. So he called me up and said, 'Bring that backpack down here.' You know, all the guns and everything. I said, 'I'm not taking that shit no motherfucking where.' Because with my luck, I'd fucking get pulled over, and with all that shit, I'm gone. Doc was living with me up at the house in Valencia, and so Doc took it down to him. I kept on telling him, 'What the fuck do you want that shit just sitting in your house for, with all that other crazy hot-ass shit you got there anyway?' And then, the next morning, the police busted him there, and he went to jail. He should have listened to me, as much older as I am than him, and the shit that I done did." After Darnell was arrested, Jerry says he had a word with Mario Lopez at the gym, asking him to persuade Francis not to testify by suggesting that Joe didn't want to be looking over his shoulder for the rest of his life.

Numerous sources confirm that Timmy was the voice on the other end of the walkie-talkie during the home invasion. Andrew Belchic says Timmy talked about it openly. "He said, 'We fucking rolled up and did this to this guy Joe.' It was totally creepy," says Belchic. "And I guess Darnell said that he should have killed him, because once he put him in the trunk and carjacked him, 'that's life without parole.' That's what I heard."

"Timmy personally told me that he was the guy in the room," says Holt Gardiner. "I heard about it the day it happened, from Timmy, because he was high as a kite. I saw him at a restaurant, and I put two and two together." Brandi Young, a close friend of Timmy's, confirms it was him.

But Will's alibi has always been that he was back home in Washington during the time of the break-in, and so couldn't possibly be involved. He claimed in the *Dateline* interview that Detective Koman had exonerated him (a claim that Koman himself was quick to take issue with).

"I know the two parties that were involved, and they were not Will Wright or Erin Naas," says attorney Ron Richards, who has represented all four of them (Darnell, Will, Timmy, and Erin). "I've had admissions by both parties to the crime—one of which, Darnell Riley, admitted it in open court; the other one is still undetected." Of Will, he says, "I know for a fact he wasn't even in Los Angeles."

Darnell's Verizon phone records for the night of the break-in reveal numerous phone calls to Timmy. They also show eight separate calls to Erin Naas's cell phone number between 10:07 p.m. and 1:27 a.m., none for longer than two minutes.

The two civilians who inadvertently wound up at the crime scene were identified by Darnell as Khalil Olmstead, a one-time publicist for NBC who worked on the Sylvester Stallone reality boxing series, *The Contender*, after moving here from Boston, and Chera, who currently lives in Las Vegas. (Olmstead, it should be noted, left the scene before any crimes were committed, and did not return.)

"I know Chera very well," says Holt Gardiner. "Chera is like the hot, female version of Timmy. She's a hustler, she'll do anything for a buck, and she's very hot. At least she was twelve years ago. Chera was very tight with [Hefner's former girlfriends] the Bentley twins."

Gardiner reports that Chera danced at Club Paradise in Las Vegas, worked for the escort service Nici's Girls, and can be found any Sunday afternoon at "Rehab" around the pool at the Hard Rock. On her MySpace page she is pictured with Hugh Hefner and Cedric the Entertainer, her occupation is listed as "Model/Cold Ass Ninja," Michael Bay is on her friends list, she's featured on the cover of *Street Customs* magazine, and she's got a bumper sticker posted that reads, "I don't have a short attention span, I just . . . oh, look a kitty!"

After Darnell's arrest, Erin Naas was widely thought to be the mystery woman heard laughing at the end of the tape, and according to police reports, Naas claims that Francis confronted her at the Spider Club on April 4, 2005, and demanded that she go to the authorities, believing that she knew the identity of the real assailant.

"He said that he thought that I knew who did this to him, and he was gonna do whatever it took to get me to come forth," says Erin. "He basically threatened me, and it made me cry, and I left the club . . . He didn't know for sure if I knew or not, but he thought he had an idea. And he's that type of person that's willing to do whatever it takes—for himself, and for his own personal gain. That's how he built his empire. I mean, he's a smart guy, but he's not above threatening someone to get them to be quiet, [or to] say what he wants them to say. Joe is very much like that." Francis initially suspected the break-in was the work of Mohammed Hadid, a contractor on a Mexico resort property he was developing with whom he was embroiled in a lawsuit, and who he claimed at the preliminary hearing had stolen $6 million from him. The day before the break-in, Francis had shown up at Hadid's offices unannounced and berated his employees. Darnell says Erin's only involvement was letting them know when Joe Francis was in town.

In addition to the Louis Vuitton luggage and accessories that Chera reportedly got, Darnell claims that one of Francis's stolen Picassos circuitously wound up with a professional gambler who lives in one of the beach communities south of Los Angeles, a fact he discovered completely by accident a year later when they were meeting on unrelated business.

Darnell also denies they had his fingerprints from Joe Francis's Bentley, claiming Koman told him as much by laughing when he asked about it during their last visit. "No fingerprints were found," says Darnell. "Come on, I watch *CSI*. If my prints were found, with my record, they would have been at my door before the sun came up, let alone a whole year later."

A week after the incident, Darnell began making extortion phone calls demanding money in exchange for the salacious videotape he had made, and which he threatened to dump on the Internet if his demands were not met. After the first one (which Darnell claims was made, with Timmy and Will huddled around a payphone, from Hamburger Hamlet, adjacent to Ron's offices), Francis contacted the FBI, and three such calls were subsequently taped. Darnell claims there were approximately forty such calls in all. A voicebox designed to mask his voice was discovered among Darnell's possessions at the time of his arrest.

In the first call, they had obviously expected Francis to still be in Mexico, and Darnell has to momentarily recover. His tone is chatty and at times patronizing, especially when Francis becomes willfully obtuse or combative in the interest of stretching out the phone call as long as possible.

"You freaked me out when you came in my house to kidnap me," says Francis, not at all telegraphing his desire to have his caller incriminate himself.

"I'm starting to believe that you and I aren't the only ones involved in this situation," says Darnell. He makes reference to "our friend Mr. Pellicano": Ron Richards worked with Pellicano on a number of cases, including the Limousine Rapist case, according to a writer doing a book on Pellicano, and Darnell says their paths crossed on occasion. Darnell gives a time for his next call and promises to provide instructions on how to transfer the money.

The second call, Darnell is quick with the repartee—"I still love you, though, kid," he says at one point. He directs Francis to a pay phone on Hilgard, a mile west on Sunset, which runs along one side of the UCLA campus (all three of the taped calls were made there), but Francis blanches when informed he'll be making a wire transfer.

"To guarantee that you get the tape, I have a mutual friend of yours that I will give the tape to," says Darnell. Francis speculates that their friend is in fact "Mohammed" [Hadid]. "No," says Darnell, seizing the opportunity for some business development. "If you want this Mohammed guy, I can take care of that for you later—we can work that out. But this Mohammed guy is not connected."

When Francis demands they meet in person, Darnell first tries to up the price to half a million from the $300,000 they had originally agreed on. When Francis readily agrees to the higher figure, the wind goes out of Darnell's sails. Meanwhile, Francis tries to take any opening to press his advantage. "Well, here's the deal, man," he begins. "You came to my house with a gun—"

"I don't know what the fuck you're talking about, brother," says Darnell, cutting him off. "We had a relationship going. You got mad because you wanted us to suck each other's dicks. I'm gonna call you a little bit later on today."

"Well, it's either now or never," says Francis.

"Have a good day," Darnell says acidly.

In the third taped phone call, Darnell provides explicit instructions on how to package and convey a half-million dollars in nonsequential twenties. ("A half-million dollars weights twenty-two pounds," he helpfully imparts.) He also raises the possibility of using a mutual friend again as an intermediary. When Francis adds a further condition that the meeting be face-to-face, Darnell asks, "You got the Feds talking to you? Because obviously you're not in charge here." The call ends soon afterward.

"Had he made the transfer," says Darnell, "the funds were set to go into a BHB gaming account after it went through another gaming operation and then into two Panamanian banks. Koman's team knew that if he made the transfer, the money was gone and they'd never be able to grab me. That's why they foolishly showed their hand and had Joe ask me to meet up with him to exchange the cash for the tape, which is when I knew we would not be making any deals."

The tape was eventually seen by probably several hundred people, including Alex Vaysfeld, who screened it for friends in Moscow and pointedly referenced it when he had to take Joe Francis in hand during his brief but eventful time in-country.

"Timmy has said time after time that the Joe Francis situation is a victimless crime—a rapist getting his just due," says Darnell. "It was something that had to be done, that was all. Someone has to dispose of the trash. With no Davids in the world, the Goliaths would rule unchecked. Timmy used to joke how I should be getting kickbacks from all these security guards who are getting work from all these rich people we spooked. And with that thinking, aligning myself with that thought process—self-deception, justification—I was seduced once again into thinking I had done something that would enhance the well-being of others. I know right from wrong. But I allowed myself to be deceived, and I justified my actions. 'It's a victimless crime. It's Joe Francis—he deserves it.'

"Dealing with Will and Timmy was a waste of time. I know that. Some cash came out of it, but nothing compared to what I made legitimately, and illegally, on my own. And here is this little prick Will, living my life now, being a producer."

In one of his first letters to me, describing Joe Francis, Darnell said, "Success will take you where character may not be able to sustain you."

There is nothing I have seen since then that causes me to doubt that.

FLAKE AND TREES

M e and my buddy Timmy—Joe Pesci wannabe—started calling Will 'Will Ain't Wright,' " says Darnell. "He lies, and not about big shit, but about nothing. He lies to start his day." This comes as a welcome diversion in Hollywood, maybe, where original stories are after all in short supply. But like a lot of theatrical constructs that look good on paper, it often runs into problems once you take it on the road. "The not so obvious reasons I allowed myself to be around this character, setting aside my better reasoning, is in large part due to him bringing in some solid connects for me to dump off some soft white," says Darnell.

In 2002 and 2003, Darnell was looking for new markets and connections to offload product. When Will showed up in March 2003 and set about trying to scam anyone who would give him the time on a slow news day—including those same wholesale connections he brought with him from his tenure inside the criminal-industrial complex—Darnell saw an opportunity to employ his unique skill set.

According to Darnell, Will claimed that a drug shipment he had on consignment from the Black Dragon Triads in Vancouver, run through the middlemen of the Grizzly Adams Nomads, a biker group also out of Canada, had been seized by the cops sometime in 2003. As with his profit-loss statements for Kristen's investments, he Photoshopped documents to confirm his story. Once the Canadians figured out what had happened, they put out a contract on Will with some local San Diego bikers. Darnell got wind of the hit through restaurateur J. T. Torregiani (who also currently dates Paula Abdul), who had a relative who was affiliated with the San Diego crew, and who put in a call on his behalf, unbeknownst to Will. From there, Darnell stepped in and brokered an introduction.

When reached by phone, Torregiani says he has family in San Diego but denies having served as a go-between with San Diego biker hitmen.

Later in early 2004, they did it again, this time incurring the wrath of an Atlanta crew. This time, the situation was amicably resolved by a single phone call from a mentor of Darnell's, a Los Angeles businessman with reputed ties to organized crime. He had also arranged an earlier meeting with the Nomads that took place on New Year's Eve 2002, conducted at LAX.

"Will would fake a shipment about once a year, which was his primary business," says Louis Ziskin.

"The Black Dragons are the Asian mafia," explains Darnell. "The Nomads are the father organization for the Hell's Angels. The Nomads are out of Canada. [Will] fucked with both groups. All of my connects came into play, but when I had to meet with these guys, I didn't poke my chest out and try to be a suicide missile. I met with them when I flew into Seattle—SeaTac Airport—and when I flew into Vancouver, and two times when they flew into LAX. The security of the airport came in handy. I knew they wouldn't be packing just getting off a flight, and when I met them, I never left the airport; I caught the next flight back to L.A. I helped him, and in return he had to give me access to all his connects that he dumped the coke to—Atlanta, Detroit, New York. So it was a business deal for me. But that's how Will became indebted to me. That's why he started using my name to strike fear into people. What he didn't realize was that these Black Dragons and Nomads knew who I was, and they weren't scared of me. They respected me. They had to—just the way I had my connections set up, the meetings with them let them know I wasn't a street thug. They knew I had weight if Italians were calling for a sit-down on my behalf. Also, I never advertise. Advertising is what gets you pinched. Case in point: all the pillow talk by Will that got me in here. Need I say more? I could have just thrown him to the wolves and been on my way. But I got a heart. Silly me."

Rick Doremus, my DEA-affiliated source, says that all these groups do exist, in roughly the same relation as Darnell says. "I dealt with the Asian Mafia," he says. "I haven't heard the Black Dragon name, but the Asian mob does exist. They were important drug kingpins. The ringleader was an Asian guy named K-Man. He was moving drugs through casinos in the Seattle area, and the money was being laundered through a jewelry store in Newport Beach, California. The Grizzly Adams Nomads also exist. Known more commonly as the Nomads, they are based out of Vancouver and have chapters all the way down to Huntington Beach and San Diego. They are known drug traffickers: meth, ephedra, Ecstasy, and coke mainly. The Asians do the weed, and have turned out to be some real big growers, and became real popular in the last five years. The Asians grow all the weed up in Canada now, and have grow houses throughout California. They bring the dope down, find groups to sell the dope, collect the cash, and turn the cash back to Canada as coke or heroin to maximize their profits by about thirty percent. The Nomads broker a lot of the stuff coming through from Mexico for the Asians. They also broker the ephedra going to the super-labs to make meth."

Mike Vanags, the Orange County cop, heard the same story from Darnell when he visited him up at Corcoran. "Darnell was telling a story about bailing Will out of trouble with the Vagos; Will ripped them off for something, and they were going to kill him," he says. "I think it was the Vagos, because that's the gang that runs down here. But they don't really get along with black people, so I'm not sure."

Darnell's business mentor—whose name we won't be using—has little patience for Will, who seems to be the kind of criminal upstart who gives professional criminals a bad name.

"Will Wright burned a friend of mine for several hundred thousand dollars," he says, "but [the friend] talked to his lawyers and was advised that there was nothing he could do about it. He can't catch Will. Will Wright is working for the Feds; there is absolutely no question in my mind about that. He is an arch-criminal: a loser that should be doing a million years in prison. Check that Web site about Will Wright; it's all true—to the letter and then some."

"Darnell is my boy," he continues, "but he is not innocent, either. The mistake he made was getting caught up with those losers Timmy and Will. Loser plus loser equals loser. You know what I'm saying?"

Doremus crossed paths with Darnell and Will as well sometime in 2003. His first encounter with Will was when he went behind his friend's back to make Doremus his supplier. "I gave him five pounds, representing fifteen thousand dollars, and he came back with seven thousand and said that the guy held him up, and he'd make it up to me," Doremus says. "He talked the talk. He tried to introduce me to some coke dealers, but it wasn't good stuff, so I passed on it."

One night, Will suggested they go to the Belmont, where Doremus saw Mark Wahlberg and Mariah Carey and sold Brandon Davis some Ecstasy and gave Will ten Vicodin for Paris Hilton. When Doremus slipped out and went home early, he saw a strange car parked on his street. Rounding a corner, he was struck on the head with a blunt object, probably a hammer, and watched a light-skinned black guy disappear up the hill, laughing. When he tried to chase him up the hill, he fell down a ravine and broke his shoulder. Fearing a DEA raid, he called some people and moved three hundred pounds of weed and all his cash out of the house. Later, he found Zeus, his attack Rottweiler, dead, and poisoned meat all over the backyard.

"I started questioning who knew me and who had been to my house," he says. "And Will was right there, saying, 'I'll help you find out who did this.' Then I found out that Will was talking to my driver and trying to move drugs with him." He is convinced Darnell was the muscle who clocked him, a charge that Darnell denies vehemently.

"That ain't my style," says Darnell. "I don't run up behind people. I don't snake on people. I realize what I can physically do, and I don't abuse it. So please tell Rick Doremus I ain't the one. But for fairness sake, when I get out, I'll give him a shot in the ring, or if he wants to get gutter with it, we can go *Fight Club*–style and bare-knuckle it in the alley."

Before Doremus was arrested in February 2004, he had already started handing over his operations to his underlings—his six-foot-four driver, who went by "T", and his right-hand man "Rod," who soon followed his Swedish porn-star girlfriend into the relatively classier environs of porn and pimping. One of the deciding factors was his dealings with Darnell, who came to him as a customer of Ruben Hernandez, known to him as "R," who had been one of Doremus's main buyers. They met at the Spearmint Rhino strip club in Van Nuys, where Darnell was to acquire a "fifty-pack," or fifty pounds of weed, worth $150,000—a violation of protocol in that Darnell was buying from him directly, but one preferred by Ruben. Darnell was fine with the arrangement, except that he chose not to pay.

"There was some sort of reason," says Rod, "but mostly it was just because he could. R used him as muscle in some other situations. And when you use someone for muscle, you have to realize that they're stronger than you are. I was stuck for a while, but I went to the person who I got it from, who is connected with the Hell's Angels and the Asian Mafia up in Canada, and I let him take over. [When] they started doing business together, which is not supposed to happen, I said, 'Fuck you, and your debt.' And they accepted it, because they were making money . . . I don't want to be racist or anything, but [Darnell] was so whitewashed. He had like a fucking vest on—a dress-up vest—and he spoke really eloquently. When I heard that he was a fucking gangster—a murderer—I was surprised."

Now born-again and out of the life, Ruben tells a harrowing tale of dealing with Darnell and Will: one that he says triggered a profound reassessment of the path he was on. He met Will through Doremus's driver T at Kristen Williams's apartment at Sunset Plaza, where Will immediately began running his game on him. Will asked if he needed anyone to do collections, and claimed he had a crew. The crew was Darnell.

"Darnell started telling stories about how Joe Francis was untouchable at the clubs with all his bodyguards, and Darnell started laughing about what he had just done to him. We went over to see the guy who owed me money. This guy owned a TV store. My intention was to have them give him a talking to—to posture as the Canadian guys I was in touch with who I owed money [Asian Triads]. So, they went in, and after a bit, they came out and said, 'Come on in. We want you to talk to the guy.' I went in and saw that they had tied the guy up. They had punched him out, and Will and Darnell were taking plasmas off the wall. I realized they were doing a robbery, and I was thinking 'Whoa, they are really taking advantage of the situation.' So they grabbed his keys and took his Hummer and the television sets. He wasn't even the guy that owed me the money directly—he was connected to him. Will and Darnell were acting like they represented the Asian Triads and were there to collect. Yes, the guy owed me two hundred fifty thousand dollars, but I could have handled it better, without force. Darnell got the guy and his partner's phones and started calling them, saying, 'We'll get you your stuff back when you come up with the money.' "

After receiving a $20,000 down payment from the principal debtor, and another $20,000 from Rich Jardine at BeverlyHillsBookie.com, where he had to leave his Escalade as collateral, Ruben accompanied them to a boxing gym. "I was rolling with them, and they had some white-trash-looking guys pull up in a white truck," says Ruben. "They took the Hummer and the TVs and said that they were getting paid with that stuff, and I wasn't getting anything. So, basically, they were jacking me. I never told Darnell where I lived, but then all of a sudden he showed up at my doorstep to try and blackmail me. He was like, 'Do you want me to come in, or do we want to settle this outside?' I said, 'Let's go outside.' I knew what kind of guy he was, and I didn't want him at my house. He had a green metal box on him. Darnell said, 'If you don't come up with fifty g's, I'm coming back to burn your house down with you and your family in it.' He hit me, I went at him, and he opened the box and pulled a gun out of it."

Ruben took his grievances to Will, who told him, "Darnell's upset with you, and you need to pay him." Their suggestion was to give them ten keys at a time on consignment to work off his "debt": an arrangement that eventually went through $250,000 of product.

"They did it for their own money and their own selfishness, and still wanted money from me," says Ruben. "All of a sudden, some girl calls to tell me that the undercovers got Darnell, and he was locked up. It was the tipping point of my life: hundred fifty-thousand-dollar CL 55 Mercedes, two Range Rovers, an extended cab Dodge truck, an SL500 Mercedes, a high-end BMW, and a '96 Tahoe. I had my girlfriend, my child, and a supermodel on the side. I had lost money, and all this stuff with Will and Darnell had started happening. I started driving around looking for Darnell. I was going to kill him. My wife went to dinner at Koi. I went by the boxing gyms, the clubs, and then, just by chance, I spotted him on Melrose. He was driving with Quincy Jones's daughter. I recognized her because I knew her from a lounge/restaurant she used to work at on Sunset, across from Mel's Diner. I pull up next to him and say, 'What's up? Aren't you supposed to be in jail? Pull over.' He kept driving, but he finally pulled over. I said, 'What's the deal? Why aren't you in jail?' He gave me a bunch of bullcrap—telling me he had aliases, and showed me something on the tips of his finger that changed his prints. He had someone bring him a gun. He said, 'Meet me at Koi,' because Will was at Koi and saw my wife there. He was trying to scare me by threatening my wife through Will. My supermodel was there, my wife to be was there, my friend—a UFC fighter I knew that would handle things with me—was there, and Will was there. I get there, saw Will, and said, 'Let's go.' I grabbed him, Darnell showed up, and we all went into the alley. They all had guns. I was trying to put them all on Front Street. Will pulled a gun on me, and I said, 'Shoot me.' Darnell had tried to flip the tables on me, and nothing made sense. I left.

"I told my girl I was cheating on her with the supermodel. I was trying to get away from her so she would not get hurt. I moved into a penthouse suite at the Wyndham Bel Age Hotel. I was drinking Jack Daniel's out of a bag on Sunset near the Hustler store, and I was bumping into things. I called my girl and said, 'I'm sorry. I love you. Can I come over?' She was like, 'No, tomorrow when you're not drunk. And I'm going to church.' I went into the hotel and started thinking. I turned on the church channel, and it was like they were preaching to me. I heard the word. The next day, my girlfriend got saved. She told me, 'All you've got to do now is give it to God.' I said, 'He doesn't know the game, and He doesn't know that I have Triads and Hell's Angels after me.' She started taking me to church. I squared things up, came home, and I have been fed by the word of God ever since. God told me that I had to forgive Darnell. I didn't think I could. How could I ever forgive a guy that tried to blackmail me and threatened to put my family in harm's way? I watched *The Passion of the Christ* and saw what was done to him. The Lord kept pressing my heart. When I forgave Darnell, things started happening in my life that I could not imagine. And then I went looking for Darnell again. I told the guys at the gym I had some money for him, and they were like, 'Oh, Darnell is gone. He's in prison.' I called the jail, and realized that the Lord had handled Darnell."

When Ruben's name first came up, Darnell says, "He was a good mover of flake and trees (green ones)." But once their stories diverged, Darnell's admiration began to subside. Darnell says they first met when Will brought him by Erin's [also Kristen's] apartment at Sunset Plaza with a couple of Playmates. "I didn't like the guy too much," says Darnell. "He was flashy and loud, like Will." Darnell's version is that they should have been paid $100,000 upfront, the going rate for collection work on that scale; he never threatened Ruben in front of his kids, but did crack him in the jaw and lay him out in his front yard; and their rather elegant solution, whereby they would take over his retail distribution, broke down after the first load.

"People knew he was a bitch, and people he dealt with had no intention of paying him until they heard I was taking over all his debt and the payments started coming in," says Darnell. "The Asian gangsters he owed were about to close his accounts, so for him to try and play me, I had to remind him who was the big dog. He paid up $50K that day and flooded us with weed. He dropped one hundred pounds in our lap, and I had had enough of him and took the whole load. I had one of my guys dump it off and I washed my hands of Ruben. Had he been a straight-up dude and paid me my $100K, that would have been it, but I wound up draining him for about $400K: the flat screens, the pounds of weed, the Hummer. But it was all unnecessary had he just done right by me. His fault."

Even Bolo makes a return appearance: "I called Bolo to back me up on a job involving Ruben when some dope slangers jacked Ruben for a couple hundred grand and I got it back for him in one day—with interest. He and Will rolled with me to pick up Bolo so we could have safe passage into an area where the guy wanted to meet us to pay the debt off.

"In hindsight, I was out of my fucking head," says Darnell, "shaking these characters down with twenty paparazzi in front of Koi on any given day."

"Darnell had ripped off Ruben, and he made sure that everyone knew he had murdered two people," says Doremus. "So everyone basically ate the loss and moved on. Ruben was scared to death of Darnell. If I was still in the game, I would have taken Darnell out."

Darnell tells another story involving "a trust-fund baby and deadbeat gambler," a friend of Brandi Young's, who tried to skip out on bail that had been secured by Alex Vaysfeld. "I had to slap up her whole crew after they tried to slip out on payments," says Darnell. "Will was there and was a scared bitch. We jumped in the elevator, and I told him that if the security or cops are at the door when the elevator opens, we are gunning our way out. He was shitting his pants."

Young confirms the incident. "I had to actually have a friend of mine's dad fly into town to be able to pay it," she says. "Darnell was upset because it was days later than it was supposed to have been . . . It was a stupid situation."

"My feeling is, fuck it: if you're a Navy Seal, a Mafioso, or a thug—are you bulletproof?" says Darnell. "I never bought into the so-called tough guy bull, or the Mafia tag that scares people. I don't do shit to get in the line of fire, but if the shit hits the fan, then fuck it—let's blow the bitch up. They can take a hit just like me. I've never tiptoed around people because of a title or a perceived threat. I always incorporate Sun-Tzu's teachings in *The Art of War*: 'Do what is big while it is still small.' Move first, strike hard."

Sources also remember drugs moving through Timmy's place at the Palazzo Apartments next to Park La Brea during this period, where Brandi Young recalls Will was living while he was between places.

"There was a couch and a bed in the living room—that's where Will stayed," says Andrew Belchic. "Boxes all over the place, and Timmy was upstairs in the bedroom. I remember [Will] just lying on the bed. I figured he was slinging some weed or something. I didn't really ask. I guess at some point, Will had a gun: a Sig Sauer. So Tim was freaking out because [Will's] parole officer would come over." One of the women quoted in this book, speaking off the record, remembers ending up there at the end of a long night against her better judgment.

"[Will] said, 'Oh, I got a bump for you.' " A bump is generally a couple of lines of coke that comes in a little baggie, one inch by two. Instead, she saw duffel bags packed with cocaine, ready for transshipment. "I couldn't breathe," she says. "I panicked. I thought, 'I could be in serious trouble here tonight.' And I left."

Jaime Weinberg is a pretty thirty-year-old brunette graduate student who dated Darnell briefly in the summer of 2004, just before Ruby. She met him at the Enterprise Rental Car where she worked, which Darnell frequented. "He was an all-cash guy," she says. Weinberg also remembers visiting Timmy's apartment, and also saw plenty about Darnell around the margins that didn't seem kosher at the time.

"He was a man of leisure," she says. "I knew he was shady, that there was something wrong. He went in to take a shower one day and I opened the desk drawer and there's like two guns in it. He just said, 'I like guns. I like to protect myself.' She recalls an incident leaving dinner at Caffe Med in Sunset Plaza when he got into a screaming match with another driver over an apparent money transfer gone awry. Later at two in the morning, he said he had to go out to a meeting and took his guns with him. Another time, Darnell showed up to meet her friend at the Grove carrying a heavy black duffel bag, inside of which were guns and $100,000 in cash. (Darnell's explanation: "I couldn't leave it in the car.") That was the same night she met Timmy.

"He was a fucking loser," she says. "He was really rude to my friend, and really disrespectful and really high on coke. My friend was drunk and wanted to do some coke and was kind of hinting towards it, and he told Darnell, 'Get this bitch out of my house.' And then, four seconds later, he totally hit on my friend. I was like, 'What the fuck just happened?' Darnell was basically chauffeuring us around—we were barhopping and drinking a lot of champagne. It was right across from the Grove. [The apartment] was completely empty, with a big purple circular couch in the middle, and that was it. It was very strange. And we were sitting on the floor in the middle of the living room."

Weinberg, who says she learned of Darnell's criminal past from reading the *Radar* piece, recalls watching the *Dateline* special with her mother, who quipped, "I'm so proud of you! Look at what you've accomplished!" Now back in touch with Darnell, after he wrote her in January 2008 and she visited him at Corcoran, Weinberg remembers the Darnell she knew as mean, arrogant, threatening—something he remains oblivious to and deeply apologetic about to her.

"Darnell is a very intriguing person and there's a lot beneath the surface that a lot of people don't get to see," she says. "He's very smart and has a lot of good ideas; he just doesn't know how to implement them in the correct way. If you're in his life, and you've proved yourself to be somebody he can count on, he will kill somebody for you. Literally. I mean, *literally*." She says that Darnell has proposed to her in prison and claims he's too old for the criminal life. But she also sees his preoccupation with Paris Hilton, Joe Francis, and the rest of them as something unresolved in his character.

"I know that he was around those people," she says, "but from how he would tell the stories, I don't believe him. I think he was totally full of shit. 'Nicole Richie this, and Bijou Phillips that.' As we're dating, he's telling me about certain people in Hollywood doing stripteases for him and all these things, and I'm like, 'If all these girls are doing all of these things—why are you here with me? Go fuck them. You're the one pursuing me, and they're pursuing you? I don't think that's how it works.'

"Infamy is what he wants, and that's the most dangerous thing ever," she says. "He wants to be famous. He wants his name in the papers. He likes it. It makes him happy."

In November 2002, in the interest of furthering his imagined film career and operating from the maxim "write what you know," Darnell initiated what he terms a "docudrama" about the overland transport of pounds of marijuana from Los Angeles to Omaha, Nebraska, which he directed and starred in. "I interviewed a great mixture of citizens, cops, dope dealers, truckers, hookers, transvestites, addicts, and victims, and I mixed all the real interviews with a fictional character (me) who is a struggling actor/producer who decides to go on a dry run to finance his film career," says Darnell. He claims he had the Sundance Film Festival and the Showtime Network standing by for it, which is to say he alerted them he was sending it. Principal photography was largely completed by the time Darnell was arrested in Wyoming on drug charges—in fact, carrying out the very actions he was fictionalizing in the film.

"The project was called *24 Hours to Omaha*," says David Gil, the cameraman who shot the Omaha run. "It was about these guys who would run marijuana from Los Angeles to the Midwest, where they could sell it for like four times the amount. And the way they would do that is to drive around the clock to get there. I never questioned how he got these connections, because he told me it was his cousin or something like that. But we shot some wild stuff. The guys who were helping us were very open about what they were doing. They had all these scams going—one woman had a day care center as a front for where the drugs were being stored. It was wild."

Gil insists he checked the production van thoroughly ahead of time and alerted Omaha authorities that he would be in town filming—just in case. But he is shocked to learn of Darnell's incarceration and the Joe Francis break-in—especially since he once worked on a two-week *Girls Gone Wild* shoot at Mardi Gras. "I didn't realize he had this potential," Gil says. "I didn't even realize he was somebody who had gone straight. He just seemed like a regular guy. But after he was arrested in Wyoming, he was all jazzed that they [were going to give] him back the footage of his arrest. I was freaked out that this had happened, but he was exhilarated. After that, I backed away from the project."

In approximately forty hours of footage, Darnell casts himself as a down-and-out filmmaker "trying to make a dollar out of fifteen cents" on a one-time Hail Mary weed run to Omaha. Filmed on a handheld consumer-model digital video camera, the movie looks like one of those one-man opuses that proliferated in the wake of *The Blair Witch Project*, where immediacy and no production values are supposed to guarantee authenticity. Starting at the late Mo Betta Meaty Meat Burger on Pico and Fairfax, where I used to see actor-magician Ricky Jay every day, Darnell narrates his odyssey to the camera. They leave the L.A. skyline for Las Vegas, then Utah, and finally Omaha, where they meet Spank (although his alias changes randomly), the local drug kingpin. Whether a professional actor or gifted amateur, he looks like he knows his way around breaking down a brick of weed, which he then sells by the ounce out of a convenience store. At the nominal end of the story, Darnell interviews Spank's girl Essence in the front office of a chop shop, the top dog objects to the presence of a camera crew, and Darnell gets caught in the crossfire. Along the way we get Jerry Rosenberg at his gym, Ludo Vika as a hooker, and Darnell waxing poetic at Malcolm X's grave (also in Omaha). Most telling line: "I think I was switched at birth. I don't look like my mom or dad. I think I was a mistake. I'm still waiting for the Rockefellers or the Gettys to come and get me."

Following his arrest outside of Laramie, Wyoming, in early 2003, Darnell sat for two weeks in a jail cell, unable to post a cash bond because it would be traceable. Jerry Rosenberg finally put up his ranch as collateral, and Darnell found an out-of-state bail bondsman from neighboring Idaho who took a 15 percent fee instead of the standard 10 percent. Jerry never mentioned that in fact he had sold his ranch, leaving the bond unsecured. Following the arrest, Shelly kept the tapes in her capacity as producer and financier, returning them to Darnell in June 2004. They were confiscated by police at the time of his March 2005 arrest in the Joe Francis case. According to court documents, the Laramie district attorney dismissed all charges in November 2006 since Darnell was already in custody.

"The day I got busted," says Darnell, "I was going through Wyoming, following a shipment to Iowa. I was following an old-school Suburban truck. It was packed down with probably fifty kilos and about fifty pounds of leftover weed. We had already stopped in Denver and made a drop. These guys I was with were from L.A. and Canada. My L.A. drivers had our coke from L.A. We met up with our weed connect out of Canada in Denver, made our drops, and combined our loads in the one Suburban. I had done the documentary in November of 2002, so I did some more filming of this dope transfer. I was too late to get to Canada to get the footage of the Canadians cutting the fresh crops. I wired funds back to L.A. and we carried on up I-75 into Wyoming on I-80 East. I had a stop-off chick whenever I was in Laramie—I'd meet her and her roommates who were twin sisters from Utah, ski or snowboard for a weekend, and then I'd head back to the hustle of L.A. I put my guys in a hotel room. I was going to finish our drop in Iowa, stay there one day, and break the cash into traveler's checks, then hop a flight back to L.A.

"I got busted in Cheyenne, which is east of Laramie on I-80. I fucked up and forgot I had five pounds of weed that I had put aside for a buddy's personal stash. I put that in my trunk—my car is always clean. I get pulled over and the dope car—the old-school Suburban—continued on. I ran my drama about picking up the weed in downtown L.A., which could happen, but the cop doesn't understand L.A. I just needed them to allow me bail. I was an outsider with no ties to Wyoming, so they didn't want to allow me bail with my drama. I had a rental car from Enterprise. They charged me a thousand dollars a state that I took it out of California. They sent a guy out to Wyoming to pick it up. The next morning—Super Bowl Sunday—I flew back to L.A., dropped my bags, and then flew down to San

Diego and met up with Rick for the Super Bowl game. We flew back on Joe Francis's jet."

"Darnell had indicated that he was going to rat on other, higher-up drug people," says Len Propts, an agent for the Wyoming Attorney General's office and the arresting officer. "I called them and said, 'Listen, this guy is going to help you out.' He did not uphold that. He was a real manipulator. I've called a lot of people shitbags, but he's bad news. He said he was doing a documentary when I was interviewing him. He actually tried to get the video of the arrest for his documentary. I've heard a lot of stories in my time, but that one took it."

Kristen says that Will was a drug dealer, at least during the period she knew him in 2003 and 2004. "He didn't tell me a lot about that," she says, "mainly because of what I went through with my ex-fiancé, but yeah, I found out that that's what he was doing—and probably doing with all my money, too."

"Will did not smoke weed," says producer Scott Bloom. "He drank Red Bull and vodka like a maniac, and always had cocaine around for girls, but he did not smoke pot. [He] pulled a big bag of cash out of his closet to show me one time. Bills were bound in rubber bands. A lot of money."

"He had me take drugs to Vegas once," says Giovanni. "GHB [the date-rape drug]—gallons of it. I didn't even know what it was, but when we got there, he was like, 'Where's my GHB?' I thought it was water or something. And then he was putting it in people's drinks. I didn't drink that night."

All of which raises the question: if this many people knew these guys were dealing this many drugs—and this is just what lingers residually four years later—how come they're still walking around, living the life Darnell used to? There are only a couple of possibilities.

"What Darnell is doing is a walk in the park compared with what's going to happen to Will," Detective Koman told Shelly. "There is a major federal investigation going on right now pertaining to high-level drug dealing," he told me when I asked him the same question, choosing his words carefully.

That's one explanation. The other is that they have a Get Out of Jail Free card. In the case of Timmy, there is a widespread consensus that he has had too many close calls to have gotten by on luck alone. "He has survived too many things around town," says Darnell, speaking specifically about the Ecstasy busts of 2000. "When guys like Louis went down and he didn't . . ."

Kristen Williams believes Timmy has served as an informer in the past.

"Timmy is just one of those guys who somehow, it seems, everyone around him is always getting in trouble, and he never does," says Andrew Belchic, his former employer. "How is that?"

"When I first met Timmy, he was dealing a lot of drugs," says Holt Gardiner. "He should have gone down fifty times in deals that everyone else has gone down in. I remember there was a big bust with a guy named Dino, and Timmy was involved in that deal and he never did any time. And if you see that over and over and over again, it just seems weird . . . I think he has some sort of government or police out. He's pulled the old Heidi Fleiss deal. He's just been giving information about everyone possible to someone who has kept him out of jail."

As for Will Wright, Brandi Young suggests I have a talk with Charlie Pope, the person of interest in the Jared Merrell/J-Star Motors diamond heist, as well as Anna Nicole Smith's former lover and ex–drug dealer. It was Pope whom Young was with on her ill-fated Oxycontin buy that landed her in Lynwood on the basis of a parole violation (she served thirteen months for identity theft and grand theft auto). She repeats the consensus view that he has an ongoing relationship with the DEA. "No one I know wants to touch him," she says of her codefendant. "He ran around town telling people that he was working for the DEA, [like] he was going to scare people into being nice to him or something."

"Charlie Pope is a slippery character," Darnell warns me. "Tread lightly with that guy."

Pope agrees to meet me at the Starbucks on Melrose, around the corner from his house. He's not a bad-looking guy—he looks like the actor Luke Perry—and in fact one of the first things he does is show me his Screen Actors Guild card. He's whip-thin, wiry, and in constant motion; one leg pumps resolutely, and we have to sit outside near traffic so he can chain-smoke Parliaments. Pope describes himself as "the ten-thousand-dollar millionaire," meaning that with ten grand in this town, he can look like he's got a million bucks. He has a trust fund and tried working for his family's commercial real estate company in San Diego before he segued into retail: selling Ecstasy for Tamer and his confederate Eyal, always with a buffer. He also wants me to know that he has "hung out with Paris Hilton." Good to know.

Charlie Pope is the king of the switchback, meaning that the things he's telling you always seem like they're in danger of a head-on collision with the things he just told you ten minutes ago. He says he can't talk about the Brandi Young case, but later volunteers that he sold pills to an undercover agent. He's not familiar with Jared Merrell and J-Star, but then volunteers the name of Will's fence and reports that he has kept authorities informed on the matter. And he seems genuinely surprised when I tell him that most people have him pegged for an informant, but then later tells me he has worked undercover for the San Diego Gang Task Force, and that on his last arrest—the one with Brandi Young—"the DEA bailed me out."

"If I was an informant for the DEA, I would be under a very strict and written obligation not to disclose that," he says, sounding like assassin Martin Sheen in *Apocalypse Now*.

When I ask him about Will Wright, he says, "I spoke with him about a week ago—we're friends." I tell him that I'm looking at Will in relation to some unsolved crimes, and he says, "Do you want some help? I hate that son of a bitch. I'm getting ready to put a tracker on his car." They've been out driving recently in Will's 2008 Twin Turbo Porsche (he also has a black Chevy Super Sport, apparently), after Pope spotted Will on Santa Monica Boulevard talking to a transvestite. "I called him up and said, 'Yo, what were you doing talking to that tranny?' " he says. "Of course, he denied it. I said, 'Yeah, dude, it was you.' "

About Will's long-term involvement in the drug trade, Pope says, "Will wasn't so much in the business of selling drugs as he was about stealing loads. Every couple of years, he'd steal 'two hundred.' " "Two hundred" is a common package size for weed: two hundred pounds. "Twenty-five hundred was the price per pound, and he'd wholesale it out for three grand." Pope first met Will at Timmy's place at the Palazzo Apartments when a friend of Pope's sold him fifteen pounds of weed. Two years later, Timmy brokered a formal sit-down at Caffe Med, and Pope stopped by their apartment at the Cosmo Lofts in Hollywood, around the corner from Citizen Smith.

"The whole apartment was full of drugs," says Pope. "And I mean full of drugs—everywhere: in closets, in hat boxes—everywhere. Weed, ton of Ecstasy. Will said, 'This is what I have. Let me know if there's anything I can do with it.' I took four pounds and had to bring it back. I couldn't sell it. I did the same thing four weeks later: took four pounds, showed it, couldn't sell it, brought it back. Timmy was kicking him out, and we started hanging out. We went surfing, played golf. I was still trying to sell weed for him. I got robbed a couple of times, and that's how we stayed in touch—I owed him."

"He would sit in his apartment at Ohio and Camden ordering hookers off of Craigslist.com, have them come over, show them boxes full of cash, and treat them like shit," says Pope. "He was always bragging about how much cash he had." According to Pope, two assailants showed up at his door, beat him up, and held him at gunpoint, demanding, "Where's the fucking money?" Will jumped off a three-story balcony, shots were fired, and he ran down the street (a plot turn that echoes the last season of *The Wire*). "I saw the bruising," says Pope. "I saw the physical evidence from his three-story fall. He should have been dead, but a table broke his fall.

"I know four or five Feds that are looking to bust Will now. I was at the federal building four or five months ago, and they wanted to know about Will and Timmy . . . I'm aware of the [federal] investigation, and I am aware that the focal point is home invasion, home robbery, and drugs. They did not elaborate too much on the drug investigation, but I know a lot of inside information on the wheelings and dealings of Will Wright." When I ask why they haven't moved already, he says cryptically, "Maybe the Feds are moving as we speak."

He says Will was always on the lookout for buyers for his "millions of dollars in paintings," particularly Warhols, as well as any new, unexplored wrinkle in the enterprise. "Will was very interested in celebs," he says. "He once asked me if I could broker some photos of Brandon Davis." But it's his fallback plan that has Pope offering to wear a wire, and for which he reserves his greatest enmity. "I think Will is an informant," he says.

"Will Wright is very charismatic," says Pope. "That's Will's in—his ability to get women." Explaining the allure of Will to a billionaire like Bob Hoff (or David Reich to Ted Field, whom he was also conversant in), he explains that they not only need them to introduce the girls to them, "they need to get [the girls] to leave as well—so Bob and Ted can be nice guys and keep their hands clean of kicking them out." As quid pro quo, more important than even money itself, the friendship with Hoff offers an explanation for the money. Of Will's dealing, Pope says, "His cover was that the money came from foreign film markets." This on a movie that cost $5 million, all in. I know seven out of seven studios in this town that would like in on that action.

"Will doesn't need a lawyer," Ron Richards reassures me in our interview. "Will Wright has never been involved in drugs since I represented him. He's pled guilty to one drug offense." He admits that Will's frequent sightings in Las Vegas, Blaine, and elsewhere constitute a clear violation of his parole, but argues that a lot of federal prisoners don't stay on supervised release. (This fact is confirmed by Will's parole officer, Alex Guevarra, who seemed powerless to ensure compliance. He admitted that for Will to leave the state for purposes other than employment—say, to pour champagne over his head at a party in Vegas—he would need specific approval from his P.O., and told me, "We have a saying around here: 'An individual can sit in your office twenty-three hours out of the day, and they are always going to do what they want in that one hour away—even with an electronic device around their ankle.'") Ron Richards even had Will come to speak to his class at San Fernando College of Law as a reformed drug dealer. In fact, in our entire two-hour interview, that's the one thing that seemed to get under his skin. "Why is that significant?" he demands to know. "Is that illegal or something?"

"Timmy and Will had plenty of dirty dealings with each other once I was busted," says Darnell. "They had to deal with each other, because people were on to how they had left me out to dry. [Darnell's mentor] told me plenty of times to turn over on them; he said he would go before any council and speak on my behalf." And he suggests they still have business between them, even if one of them is "a legit producer."

"Will and Timmy need one another, even now," says Darnell. "It'll be cool until one decides to pinch from the pot."

"Maybe deep down inside, he wants to get caught," says Tamer of Will Wright. "So he can be the producer that went to jail and get the ultimate publicity . . . And the Feds may well be coming down on him very soon. He will automatically get twenty. I'm ninety-nine percent sure he'll roll on anybody and everybody."

Rats don't have a very good reputation with sinking ships.

BOOKIE NIGHTS

W hy don't I play cards?" Darnell writes from prison. "Simply put, I am not willing to kill someone. If I win at cards or on a bet and a guy refuses to pay, then I'm in a position where I can end his career in here. With the racially oriented gang culture, I wouldn't have to do the work. If I bet with a Soreño, a Southern California Mexican, and he refuses to pay up, I would just tell his crew and they would handle him, and they would get me what I'm owed. So by my word, a man would be hurt. I'm not ready for, nor do I want, that responsibility. If the guy's crew says he doesn't owe, or there is conflict with the deal, I now have involved my crew. It's sticky. It's stupid, but this is the world I live in. I didn't make the rules, nor am I trying to change them. I abide by the basic ones that keep me out of shit. I don't gamble because of its problems. Like an alcoholic who shouldn't drink, because to an alcoholic, there is no such thing as just one drink, there is no understanding in my world for 'I ain't gonna pay you.' "

Darnell claims he first made his bones in the gambling world in early 2000 when a savvy gambler sent shills in to lose $10,000 a game during the March Madness college basketball playoffs, collectively moving the line in the direction he wanted. When Darnell noticed a similar pattern among other bookies he did collections for, he knew a fix was in somewhere. "Five guys lose ten grand each; five win a hundred grand each. The twist is that the five guys who bet the ten stacks all bet on the underdog." Darnell tracked down the gambler through one of his henchman with a penchant for exotic dancers, ingeniously got a message to him, and convinced him to repay pennies on the dollar, rather than wade into a philosophical debate on the propriety of what he'd done. The "boys back east," at whose doorstep apparently all criminal roads converge, were reportedly very happy.

In mid-2002, Darnell claims he invested in Beverly Hills Bookie, the brainchild of Rich Jardine, whose marketing company Clear Media provided the Beverly Hills offices on North Cañon, which he sublet from producer Frank Mancuso Jr., along with financial adviser Parrish Medley and publicist Heather Cohen. The Italian Renaissance complex also housed the Grand Havana Room cigar club and bar, where Erin Naas was arrested and Ron Richards was a member.

"Clear Media was a legit company that had legit business. It also provided services for Beverly Hills Bookie," says Darnell.

Jardine later offered a refuge of sorts to Will, whom he met through Kristen, providing him with employment through Clear Media to satisfy his parole obligations; work as a sometimes bookie; and a future victim, leading ultimately to WhoIsWillWright.com, after the whole thing had come crashing down.

Like prostitution, identity theft, bank fraud, extortion, the traffic in sex tapes, Nigerian con men scams, and probably any number of crimes of opportunity, the Internet revolutionized gambling, and for the early years of the decade, offshore sportsbook gambling, in particular, presented a gray area for law enforcement. It could easily have been companies like Beverly Hills Bookie (along with BetOnSports of New York/New Jersey, now defunct, and others) that forced the issue, with their NASCAR pit crew girls outside of clubs (Kristen was one), TV commercials (examples still exist on YouTube), news reports on CNN, and billboards prominently placed throughout Beverly Hills proper. Their flagship billboard overlooked Sunset and Laurel, a block from Shelter, which for much of 2003 featured Pauly Shore with a milk moustache and the tagline "Got Bookie?"

"We killed with that," says Darnell. (Shore claims he did it as a favor to a friend.)

As federal authorities began to clamp down, sportsbook proprietors were often forced to physically relocate abroad, beyond the territorial reach of U.S. gaming laws. Costa Rica emerged as one such destination (along with Panama, the Dominican Republic, Antigua, Aruba, and Curaçao), and that's where Jardine lives today, apparently retired.

Heather Bernardcyck, her husband, Jack Ninio, and their two children also divide their time between Costa Rica and a resort town in Mexico. Ninio ran several successful sportsbook operations (with some down years) before transitioning out of it as U.S. gaming laws went on the global offensive. (He says he finally sold the last of them for pennies on the dollar.) Well liked, and without the cutthroat demeanor the job description would seem to entail, Jack supports his family's immodest lifestyle now as a high-stakes gambler. He also retains a Zen-like serenity in lieu of collectors like Darnell (Will, for instance, still owes him $80,000, despite his $5 million in "foreign sales" from his film).

I spent a weekend with Jack and Heather at their beachfront town house in Mexico, where they prefer to spend most of their time after their hilltop mansion in Costa Rica was broken into by a gang of gun-toting bandits who overpowered their armed security team. Old friends Rick Salomon and E. G. Daily have visited them there, separately, and Heather's best friend, Kristen, is a frequent visitor. In fact, when Heather picked me up from the airport in their bulletproof late-model Mercedes, her eight-year-old daughter asked me, "Why did Will Wright take all that money from Auntie Kristen?" Momentarily taken aback, I told her that some people can't keep their hand out of the cookie jar, but this only seemed to frustrate her more.

"She doesn't like your baby answer," Heather says. "She wants to know why. She has questions."

Heather and Jack first met Darnell at Nicky Hilton's twenty-first birthday party on the weekend of October 16, 2004, at the Hard Rock Café in Las Vegas—the same one where Will's whispered confession to Paris Hilton about the Joe Francis break-in started the chain of events that put Darnell in prison five months later.

"That night was the first time I met him," remembers Heather. "It was at the bowling alley. He was dressed beautifully, in a beautiful gray Prada suit—very suave. I called Kristen and he talked to her. Will looked like the pimp of all pimps—like a young David Reich—and he was telling everyone, 'I'll hook you up . . . ' We don't need any more hooking up, thank you. At the end, we were all sitting around—Nicky, Kevin Connolly, Darnell, Will, Jack, and maybe a couple of other people. Jack was speaking to Darnell, mostly. And he said to me, 'I've never spoken to a more eloquent, erudite guy.' "

Somewhere in the conversation, the Jack Daniel's flowing freely, opulence giving way to abandon, talk turned to an event in Heather's childhood in small-town Texas where a neighbor had lured her into his house and put her in a closet, entered the closet naked, covered in Vaseline, and robbed her of her innocence at the age of seven. He sent her home with a heart-shaped crystal inscribed "I love you."

"Jack was very upset that night," says Heather, "and when he told Darnell, Darnell was upset. Visibly upset. Jack got pumped and said, 'I'm really angry. This guy took so much from her—I want him taken care of.' He reacted the way a father would to a child. The way my father wanted to kill the man himself, and didn't act on it. Darnell embraced it with all his heart, and he was sickened. Jack's original idea was far worse, but Darnell said, 'Why don't we just do a reenactment of what Heather went through?' And I went, 'Yeah, killing someone doesn't do justice. You lock him up in a closet for an hour, and leave him there with Vaseline all over his body.' Darnell has a conscience and a heart. He said, 'Yeah, this guy has it coming.' Then when it came to the day and he called me, we came to our senses and realized that this isn't the way to go. I went through twenty years of therapy. So we called it off."

"Considering what I heard about his past, I thought he would be this really caustic, shady guy," Jack tells me later. "But he was nothing but polite. Someone had told me that he'd killed his family. But, looking in his eyes, I didn't see that type of rage. He exuded a real warmth. I was really impressed with him.

"Basically," he says, "I decided that I'm not going to play God."

When I talked with Ashley, Darnell's contractual wife, she reported that two years after Darnell was arrested, she met a friend of a friend who was shocked to learn the identity of her mystery spouse. "Did you know that he planned to kill you?" she recalls him saying. Soon after they were married, Darnell took out a life insurance policy on her. Weeks later, Darnell told her he had a boxing match scheduled in Russia and invited her to go with him. "I'll pay for you to go," he told her. "It will be really fun." She decided she needed to resolve her visa situation before traveling abroad.

"Let me ask around and see what I can find out," she reports the acquaintance telling her. "And then this guy—who I've met literally twice at this point—comes back to me and says, 'Yeah, I don't know whether it's true, but he was going to take you to Russia, you were going to disappear there, and he was going to get the money from it.' Now, to this day, I don't know if that was true or not. I don't *want* to know if it's true." (She never filed for a green card, and returned to Canada once her visa expired.)

I keep thinking about something that Darnell said in trying to corroborate the wild story he's told me: "Just know that whatever I disclose is what happened. No need for dramatizing or making myself seem bigger, because there is more that I left out than what I've put in. Some that the statute of limitations hasn't ended on, and some where the limitations don't exist (if you get my drift)."

Jack confirms a character whom Darnell calls Big Ted from Tennessee (although he says he's from Louisville, Kentucky, hence Bluegrass Sports, the name of his company), who inadvertently led to Darnell's estrangement from Rich Jardine and the effective demise of Beverly Hills Bookie.

"Rich was the only prick to ever look down on me, as if I was a hired hand," says Darnell. "Out of all my jazzy friends/associates and their lofty names, this guy tried to play me. It was after my dry run of the Joe Francis situation. I couldn't get confirmation where Joe was, and when we got a visual on him, he had just come out of the Lakers game and was headed home with a woman. So we called it off. I had a couple of my reservoir dogs with me. [At Rich's place,] he had the nerve to say, in his drunken stumble, that he didn't have time to get involved in this shit anymore. He had 'too much going on.' Now, the Joe Francis job went down for a variety of reasons. One being that he owed plenty of bookies. Bookies that had been good to me, and, by association, had been good to Rich. Joe also owed us. Joe transgressed boundaries with Erin and countless other chicks, so that was just an added bonus, but this thing was business, and this prick acted like this business was beneath him. It stung me. My control is what kept me from sending Rich to the hospital that night."

Enter Tennessee Ted (or maybe it's Kentucky Ted, given his provenance) and Blue Grass Sports, a sportsbook company that offered to underwrite their losses soon after Super Bowl 2004, as the first step toward taking control of Beverly Hills Bookie (and its desirable domain name). Darnell says he heard from Will, then on the books as a subcontractor, that Ted was entered in a poker tournament at Binion's in the old part of Las Vegas, and using the $800,000 he owed the company as his personal bankroll. As vice president in charge of collections, Darnell flew to Vegas, eventually cornering his quarry in a particularly unguarded moment in the men's room at the tournament and extorting a promise to submit the $800K claim to arbitration—which Jardine informed him three weeks later they had lost. When he discovered that three-quarters of the money had indeed been paid, Darnell carefully planned his response.

"After I came back from Las Vegas, when Rich claimed that Ted won the mediation, I went by to give Rich a chance to make it right, and he squandered the opportunity. It was my way of extending my hand before I made my move. So when he didn't stand up to do right by me, I left, and a week later I came by with Doc and Desir Alexis [a boxer Darnell briefly managed] to clean up. But the time I went by with just Desir Alexis, I took Rich in the back to talk, and Desir was in the living room with Rich's girl. She said he started asking her questions about whether Rich was satisfying her sexually or not, and if he was gay. Now, this guy is black as tar with a deep South American accent, and he talked in broken English/Spanish. His hands look like gorilla's paws. Seventy-inch arms. Deep red bloodshot eyes, always. He looks like how you envision death to look.

"A couple of weeks later, I went into [Jardine's] place and took certain things that I knew would drive him crazy, and then 'someone' went into the offices at North Cañon and looted several Warhols and later had Timmy return the paintings for cash. This is after Rich and everyone in the office—Frank Mancuso, Parrish Medley—had already called the Feds. So Rich had some explaining to do. How did the paintings mysteriously reappear?"

"I don't know if it's true or false, but I heard the story," says Jack.

This effectively marked the end of their partnership. Jardine soon took off for Vancouver, where he relocated briefly, and then eventually moved to Costa Rica, where the company kept a second office. Will took off for Las Vegas, where he hid out to avoid Darnell's wrath. This was roughly akin to the drunk who hides out at the corner bar, and Darnell kept close tabs on him in exile. "Will ran, but he wasn't hard to find," says Darnell. "He's a degenerate gambler living in Vegas."

One of the Warhols taken, a Paramount Pictures logo, actually belonged to Frank Mancuso Jr., son of the legendary producer and ex-Paramount head, and an accomplished producer in his own right, who held the lease on the suite of offices.

"Whenever all that shit started happening," says Mancuso, "I said to Rich, 'Whatever you're paying in rent isn't worth the aggravation . . .' When the painting got stolen, I went nuts on Rich. I said, 'I know it was one of those clowns hanging around here. I don't care what you have to do, get me my painting back.' "

Earlier, his friend and tenant Parrish Medley, later the victim of his own mysterious robbery, had brought Mancuso an investment opportunity: a legendary drug dealer named Will Wright who was prepared to sell his story to Hollywood. Says Mancuso: "I met Will and told him, 'With all due respect, making movies about drug dealers ain't my gig.' At this point, I said to Parrish, 'I don't want this shit in my life; I don't want these guys around me.' I didn't mind Rich, but I wanted nothing to do with the world he was in."

An investor in Giacomino Drago's Panzella restaurant, Mancuso reports that just recently, "I was at the restaurant, and a guy approached me: 'Mr. Mancuso, I'm Bob Hoff, nice to meet you, blah-blah . . . ' Two weeks later at Il Postaio [another Drago restaurant], Bob Hoff is there. And out of the corner of my eye, I recognize that guy Will. I'm thinking, 'Who the fuck is this guy Bob Hoff hanging out with Will?' Well, the second Will saw me, he split. I ask Parrish and find out that Will and Bob Hoff were hanging out at the [Havana Room] cigar club. I gotta say something to this Bob Hoff guy about who he's hanging around with. I don't want that fucking scumbag [Will] around me."

"You would think that someone in his social set would have the decency to advise him," says Koman about Hoff. "This guy [Will] is known for stuff like this. Everyone who hangs around with Will knows what he has done, and what he's been accused of doing, especially with the media publicity. You would think that somebody would take Hoff aside and say 'Hey, this guy is bad news.' I find it hard to believe that Hoff doesn't know Will's past.

"Or he may know and be very accepting of what's happening for the same reason that celebrities [always] hang out with bad guys: 'He's my friend; he'd never do it to me.' "

After Darnell was arrested, Jardine approached the police as a confidential informant, giving them much of the same information that later appeared on the WhoIsWillWright.com site. After his identity was turned over to Ron Richards as part of the discovery process, Jardine claims that Will began labeling him a police informant on THERX.com, a popular gambling message board, after which Jardine severed all contact with police.

"I have my feelings about Richard Jardine," says Detective Koman. "I don't think that he's the most highly ethical individual in the world, and I really question his manhood, if you will, because he could have assisted in the criminal prosecution of some bad guys, but instead he opted to run. Not only would Will Wright have been in custody, there are all kinds of things that could have come out if Jardine had assisted in this thing. But he opted out."

(On WhoIsWillWright.com, which he ran anonymously, Jardine went so far as to write a letter under his own name, appearing incredulous at these findings: "Now I look at this site and understand why Will was so excited to call someone else a rat. I mean WOW! He's a TOTAL RAT. He got busted and straight snitched on the main guy! He was like 'super snitch,' blaming everyone but himself. I can't believe it! . . . Now he thinks this site is my doing. Oh well, this site has made me laugh soooo much that I don't care if he blames me . . . Please don't ever stop posting his stories!" Word.) After Will was interviewed for the *Dateline* special, Jardine reports that Will called him and told him that he "pimped his company" on camera.

During roughly the same period, Heather encountered Will in Las Vegas, where he was "incognito."

"[Sacramento car dealer] Chuck Peterson threw this wonderful party for us at the Hilton in Vegas as a birthday gift," says Heather (her thirtieth and Jack's fortieth). The Hilton was also the source of the *Dateline* footage where Will can be seen shaking hands with Timmy Iannello. "We were fighting about whether or not Will should be invited. Jack was saying, 'He's coming to the party, he's my friend,' and Kristen was going, 'I'm your *best* friend; he's not coming.' They had recently broken up. I don't believe he should have been in Vegas.

"So Will, Jack, and I were in a cab, and Will was being a little weird with me in the cab. It was a very peculiar evening, because I did not respond to Will's passes. He was wasted, but his hands were moving. I told the cab driver to take care of me if something happened. Jack is not a fighter. We were going to visit Chuck in his suite. This was after we had already met Darnell, but it's also where Darnell's name rung a bell again. Will was yelling through the casino while we were walking up to Chuck's room. I said, 'Don't embarrass me. Don't embarrass my husband.' Jack's drunk, and when he's drunk, he's not getting this. I run into Chuck in the hallway of the suite at the Bellagio, and Chuck Peterson had all his guys there—they all loved me; I was Jack's wife. Will comes strolling down the hallway, walks into Chuck's beautiful suite like he owns it, and says, 'Heather is a bitch.' I'm in the hallway with Chuck, and his guys, who have known me for years, they *pounced* on him. Furniture was flying, and they ripped on Will like no other. Blood is everywhere, they hide me, and Will is screaming at Jack, 'I'll have you killed, motherfucker! You're dead! I have a guy that will kill you!' All I remember from the bathroom was Will screaming, 'I'll fuck you over, I'll kill your family!' My family!

"When he threatened my family, Jack left with him to calm him down. 'Who is this guy you're talking about?' It was Darnell. When Will made those threats, I said, 'Chuck, this guy scares me.' And when Chuck saw that side of Will, he was afraid too. I have a family to protect. Chuck warned me, 'He's a bad egg. I knew it when I saw those sick eyes. He was sick.' "

"I really liked Will," says Jack. "I think a lot of people did. And in the same delusional way, I think he'll pay me back someday. I know he's done a lot of bad things, but anyone who knows me knows that I'm a softy to a fault. I always try to look for the good in people, even if it's not there, and in my mind, I think there's some good in him. Maybe I'm wrong. And my moral code has certainly cost me a chance at being very rich. Had I had more of an image as a tough guy, or been a little more aggressive, I would have a lot of money." (At one point, when considering the road not taken, Jack recounts a phone message that Louis Ziskin, one of his oldest friends, left on his answering machine a week before he was arrested: "Hey bro . . . I made more money than Shaquille O'Neal this year . . . Oh, there's two white vans outside. I'm going down. Anyway, I just called to say hi.")

"There's a bookie in L.A. who is a friend of mine," says Jack. "Every time he gets stiffed, he loses sleep for days trying to think how he's going to get his reprisal. And you know, I try to teach him. I'm like, 'Buddy, it goes with the business. If you want to go after people who are stiffing you, the FBI is going to be up your ass in two seconds. You either have to delve into a new vocation, or you can't worry about it when people stiff you. I used to let stiffs bother me big time, and I would stay up nights figuring out how I would fuck them over. But I always had the philosophy that I wasn't going to strong-arm to collect money. Several lawyers that I spoke to, including a guy from the Justice Department, said, 'If you're not hurting people, they're not going to bother you.'

"One of the worst ones that ever happened to me was Brandon Davis: paying him out an astronomical amount of money, and then having him just turn around and pay nothing. I was with my wife in New York two years ago, and we were in a limo with George Maloof [the owner of the Palms Casino in Las Vegas], Joe Francis, Brandon Davis, and a few other people that I didn't know. And somehow, I'd heard that Brandon was doing great: he bought a million-dollar piece of art, and he won like five hundred thousand in a poker game with Joe Francis, and Joe Francis paid him. And then later on, he lost and he paid Joe Francis. I'm thinking, 'Well, it seems like he's viable.' Everybody warned me, 'Dude, that guy is no good.' And I still like the guy—again, in some delusional way, I think that someday he's going to pay me. He just got hot for three weeks and won an obscene amount of money. Then when he started losing, I figured, worst-case scenario, I know that he's friends with George Maloof at the Palms. So I figured maybe he went to the Palms and blew some of it. So I called him up, and he said, 'Yeah, I don't have any of it.' When I was a younger man, I might have really done something to him. That's a situation where, if I had a lower moral code, I would have had him killed. Now that I've got a family, I can't do that."

And so Darnell doesn't play cards in prison.

"When Jack told me he wrote off Will and banned him from gambling with his company," he says, "and that all other bookies would be following suit, it was hard for me to understand why Jack was at peace with his decision. He'd just bought Will for eighty thousand dollars. That's what Will owed and bullshitted paying him, like some junkie shacked up in a crack house after stealing his mother's wedding ring. That's all it took for Jack to buy someone and never have to deal with him again."

THE HILLS HAVE ICE

When Rich Jardine called Robbery-Homicide Detective Koman and spoke as a confidential informant, he stated that he had been victimized by Darnell on three separate occasion—once at the North Cañon offices and twice at his home—although he failed to report the last two. The second time, they took everything he owned: "Pool table, couches, flat-screens . . . just to make a point," says Darnell. He also gave the names of six other possible victims: Richard Jardine (once again resorting to the third person), Tommy Alastra (the home invasion and "beatdown"), Chuck Pacheco (the beating outside his club), Parrish Medley (the financial analyst who shared Jardine's offices and was also the victim of a home burglary), Paris Hilton (whose sister Nicky's home on Hollywood Boulevard west of Laurel Canyon where it snakes into the hills was robbed while they both attended a party at Jason Shaw's house across the street), and "Cody?" The latter was almost certainly Johnson & Johnson heir Casey Johnson, who was reportedly robbed while she was vacationing in Mexico. Jardine also stated that Darnell may be affiliated with the Russian Mafia. What he didn't say is that Will Wright was with him when he was robbed, was out with Medley on the night he was robbed, kept the party going across the street from the Hiltons by sending out for more cocaine, and was rumored to be dating Casey Johnson just before her burglary.

According to news reports, Darnell's rambling scenarios, or the odd jagged facts that broke off when I started turning over rocks, that victim list would eventually grow to include director Wes Craven, Koi owner Dipu

Haque (both of them owned guns that were seized at Darnell's arrest), actor Frankie Muniz and musician Nick Carter (another Paris ex), Los Angeles Clipper Cuttino Mobley, Andrew Belchic, Holt Gardiner (twice), Jared Merrell, and Ozzy and Sharon Osbourne. Many of these crimes remain unreported to the police—aggressively so, even when I zealously pursued the principals for interviews—and, outside of Koman and whatever federal probe may be coming down the pike, no one in law enforcement appears to see them as part of the same pattern.

And in the case of the Osbournes, it's unclear that a crime even took place. Darnell claims that on the same night of his rendezvous with the San Diego Grizzly Adams Nomads at LAX, New Year's Eve 2002 following a Clippers game he attended at the Staples Center with Shelly and Jim Epstein, he accompanied a girlfriend to a party at the Osbourne home, where diamond jewelry wound up missing from an upstairs bedroom. (As always, Darnell discusses active crimes in the passive tense.) "I look back and I have to be thankful that I never fell off a ledge, with all the scaling of buildings I've done," he says in our conversations.

The problem is that the Osbournes hosted a party at the Beverly Hilton Hotel that night, where a diamond necklace donated by Asprey and raffled off for charity was won by ICM agent Rene Tab (who was peripheral to Will's biopic and first pass at Hollywood). Later, Sharon Osbourne claimed Tab was not an invited guest and demanded the return of the jewelry, the situation culminating in a physical altercation at Koi in April 2003, all well documented in the press. Sharon Osbourne says there was no after-party at the family's home. The couple *was* robbed of $2 million in expensive jewelry, but at their estate in England in November 2004. (Darnell nonetheless claims that he attended the party at the hotel, then privately made his way to the house, where he had once visited Jack Osbourne with Brandon Davis.)

"Joe Francis alleged that I broke in his castle with the help of Erin Naas," writes Darnell. "Paris Hilton thought I did it along with another person. Casey Johnson, the baby oil heiress, had her house broken into, and millions of family jewels were stolen. Investigators claimed that I pulled this off with the help of a *Playboy* Playmate. Tommy Alastra was burglarized and suspected that the Incredible Mr. Riley was the culprit, assisted by Erin Naas and model-actress Kristen Williams. Frankie Muniz's joint was knocked over, and again, I was the suspected villain, along with several other models. That string of crimes led police to believe I was the infamous

Bel Air Burglar. Like I've said before, I never met the guy. Investigators later stopped calling me the Bel Air Burglar when they captured the real Bel Air Burglar on camera. He was an older white guy. I assure you, that's not me." He even may improve on O.J.'s *If I Did It*: if I had done it, it might have gone something like this.

Take the case of Mark Wahlberg. In December 2003, before the Erin Naas incident that led to the Joe Francis incident (at least on the chain of cause and effect), but after Darnell says he attended the *Simple Life* premiere—Paris Hilton's first public appearance after the original sex tape was leaked online—with Erin (who denies attending), Will, and a German model friend named Helena, Timmy got his ass handed to him by Wahlberg's crew for mouthing off. By the time Darnell got wind of it, Timmy was licking his wounds at Kristen's Sunset Plaza apartment. ("I think maybe I do remember Timmy getting beat up," says Kristen, although she remains vague about the details.) As a parting shot, Timmy fired a final threat at them in the form of Darnell's implied retribution. Attempting to broker an armistice between warring parties, and maybe rattling a saber for effect ("Timmy is definitely a bitch, but he's my bitch."), Darnell says he took the liberty of slipping unseen into Wahlberg's apartment (how, he doesn't say) and left a note that read simply, "Get at me."

After the matter had been amicably resolved, a member of Wahlberg's entourage told him about some videotapes in a private safe that might prove lucrative in certain quarters.

Months later (and well after the excitement of the Joe Francis incident), Darnell describes in detail how he targeted the home in the Hills, which he termed a "clusterfuck": slipping over the five-foot iron gates, negotiating a catwalk along one edge of the roof, avoiding line-of-sight perspectives from the neighbors to the north and south, cracking a massive safe that turned out to be a movie prop, and finally pocketing two mini-DV tapes. Outside, supposedly keeping watch, Timmy managed to let a nondescript dark blue Mercedes get past him, and Darnell had to beat a hasty retreat, swinging from a tree limb over an ivy-covered chain-link fence into a neighbor's yard and safety.

According to Darnell, the first tape showed heiress Casey Johnson cavorting with actress Tara Reid and Simon Rex, the ex-MTV-VJ, actor, rapper, and gay porn star who allegedly made and costarred in the rumored *second* Paris Hilton sex tape (never released), filmed at the Bellagio on Hilton's twenty-second birthday with Playmate and former roommate Ni-

cole Lenz. The second, says Darnell, featured Vin Diesel filming himself
with a woman. Darnell claims that the first tape was returned to Johnson.
For the second, he says he met with Diesel's longtime associate Gordon
Bijelonic in the Dominican Republic, on property owned by Darnell's mentor. Darnell singles out Alex Vaysfeld as one person he showed the tapes to,
which Alex confirms.

Bijelonic laughs when I describe the extortion attempt and its cloak-
and-dagger resolution, although he does confirm that he and Diesel have
traveled to the Dominican Republic before, where Diesel owns property.
He also expresses bewilderment about Darnell himself, claiming "I don't
even know who the dude is," despite Darnell's purportedly having once
gotten him in to see the band the Queens of the Stone Age at a taping of
The Jimmy Kimmel Show, the date of which checks out. Shelly describes a
phone call from Darnell's mentor during which he said something about
them having brokered a deal in the Dominican Republic concerning a videotape, but she is unclear on the contents of the tape. When I called him
and asked him about it, he denied it, but in a particularly curious way: "I
cannot confirm the Darnell-Vin Diesel thing in the Dominican Republic. I
will not even discuss that." Neither tape was available for me to view inde-
pendently.

Months later, Casey Johnson's home was robbed of a reported $750,000
in clothing, handbags, accessories and, especially, expensive jewelry. When
I initially asked Ron Richards if his client was responsible for the Casey
Johnson break-in, he wrote back, "Nicole Lenz is believed to have committed that burglary and we believe is currently being charged for it," although
when I interviewed him in person, he said he didn't know who Lenz was.
Scott and Giovanni told me that Sale Johnson, Casey's mother, would tell
anyone who asked that Nicole Lenz, who had been living there, was responsible, in conjunction with Will Wright, although this isn't technically
true because she wouldn't talk to me.

"Nicole Lenz—that's who Casey Johnson was blaming for her robbery,"
says Kristen Williams. "Because she lived with her for a little while. But it
was probably Will that put that into her head." Imitating Will, she says,
" 'It was Nicole. She took all of your Birkin bags. All of your Kelly bags.
Thirteen-thousand-dollar handbags.' She had like thirty of them or something. I heard that Will had an affair with her, so I wouldn't be surprised.
He had been over to her house." (Lenz has not been officially connected to
or charged with the crime in any fashion.)

As evidenced by the public record, Johnson is no shrinking violet. At one point, her Friendster.com profile listed her interests as "sex, pole dancing, licking lollipops and making fun of desperate debbies," and the feud surrounding her suspicions of an inappropriate relationship between her boyfriend, Johnny Dee, and her aunt, Libet Johnson, merited an entire feature in *Vanity Fair* magazine.

At an MTV party at Club XES on June 6, 2004, Johnson's friend Bijou Phillips punched Lenz in the face and dragged her across the floor by her ponytail. Based on this and a later incident in which Phillips allegedly called Lenz a prostitute and a thief at a charity event in the Pacific Palisades, Lenz filed a $1 million lawsuit against Phillips, which was met immediately by a countersuit. According to published reports, Phillips eventually settled out of court for $250,000, which Lenz donated to charity.

Of the break-in at Johnson's home, Darnell claims, "That was Nicole Lenz. I reaped the benefits of it, but that was completely her gig. It happened twice. The first time was mentioned, bullshitting around with Nicole while we were doing other stuff—running around, running around. She was like, 'Hey, I swiped this!' 'Wow. Cool. Look out.' This was way before Casey ever knew. A month or two later, that's when that situation happened [with Bijou Phillips] at the club. That's when she went back. But she had keys. That's why the cops never looked at it as a break-in. It was more or less a civil dispute over property."

Darnell later identified the house where he burglarized the two tapes as that of Parrish Medley, who shared the office suite with Rich Jardine and Frank Mancuso Jr. on Cañon Drive. And in fact, a description of the house matches to a T, down to the prop door, the hidden safe, the layout of the property, and the ivy-covered fence in the back. But Medley knows nothing about the videos. He doesn't have a roommate, and he doesn't drive a dark blue Mercedes. Moreover, he *was* robbed later—on August 27, 2004— and he's happy to talk about it, down to the smallest details. This includes the theft of a video camera and microcassettes, including compromising videos made with his girlfriend. Just not those videos.

Parrish is forty-six, buff, and tan (he founded Mystic Tan in his native Dallas) and entering his distinguished gray period. A successful entrepreneur and venture capitalist (he took Davi Skin, a division of Mondavi Wines, public), he worked as a stockbroker for five years in Palm Beach, Florida, before relocating to Los Angeles, but still carries traces of his Texas

drawl. Due to the combination of savagery and capriciousness in the circumstances of his home invasion (sideways hearts were scratched into
expensive flat-screen monitors, water faucets were left running, an eight-
foot painting was slashed and ruined), police believed early on that an
ex-girlfriend was involved.

It's a theory that Parrish has only belatedly come around to, in the person of an ex-stripper and live-in girlfriend named Joella, whom he first met
in Las Vegas in late 2001. Both were from Texas and lived near each other
in Los Angeles. On their third date, she confided she worked as a stripper
(she once worked at the Spearmint Rhino in Las Vegas alongside Kristen
Williams), but wanted to get out of it. Within six weeks they were living
together, at one point leasing a second residence in Vegas. According to
Rich Jardine, she also dated both Timmy and Will (as well as Darnell, apparently: he says he took her to Las Ventanas, the Cabo San Lucas resort
that shows up in the fourteen hours of stolen Paris Hilton footage). At least
the Timmy part was confirmed by both Holt Gardiner and Andrew
Belchic. (Belchic confirms hearing Timmy brag about robbing Parrish,
whom he identified only as "Joella's ex-boyfriend.") After the break-in, police questioned Parrish about her, but as far as he knows, they could never
locate her to interview her.

Oddly, on the day I spoke with him, Joella had just called him after a
two-year absence and told him she was a successful art dealer now, and they
were scheduled to meet for coffee as soon as she got back from San Diego.
She later canceled. When I reached her by cell phone afterward she told me,
"I'm not a part of that. I knew them from back in Hollywood and that's it."
She took my number and agreed to get back to me, but never did.

"There were things that Darnell, or someone like him—a man—would
not take," says Parrish about his burglary. "I had a book that my name
comes from: *Parrish*, by Mildred Savage; my mother named me after that.
There was a picture of me and Joella that wasn't up; that was sort of tucked
away in my closet, and it was gone. A four-thousand-dollar Versace comforter."

A year after the break-in, Parrish learned from a mutual friend that in
the months before he was robbed, Joella, whom he was no longer dating,
had been calling asking about Parrish's whereabouts, or whether they
planned on going out that weekend. Around the same time, Will began
aggressively calling Parrish.

"We knew each other, but we weren't good friends, per se," says Parrish.

"We met through his girlfriend Kristen. Each time we'd run into each other, we were kind of getting chummier. 'Can I get you a drink?' I didn't think much about it. One night he came over to my house after being out. He stopped by and brought this girl over; we ordered some pizza. But ever since then, Will was calling me on the phone every day. 'Hey, I'm going to New York! Why don't you come up to New York with me?' 'I'm in Vegas—there's a big party!' It seemed rather odd."

Deciding on the spur of the moment to go to Prey on a Thursday night, he called Will; he felt mildly guilty about always turning him down. "He goes, 'I'll meet you there,' " says Parrish. "He was real quick and perky, with a different attitude. I'm literally walking out the door and he beat me to the club. We go in, got a table, and everything was on him. Just balling, right? We had a great time. And in hindsight, I can understand that he's keeping tabs on me. He's actually a very crafty guy. I'm the guy who is usually getting the table and footing the bill for everyone at the bar, and feeling like an idiot at the end of the night [because] I didn't even know who was on my tab. But Will got a table and he ordered a bunch of beer—they were all in an ice chest. And he took the bottle opener and kept it in his pocket. In other words, he controlled the drinks to make sure that no one was coming to the table and getting at it. Watching it, you could tell that he was cunning, even about that.

"He had a complete agenda that night. It was all at my service. The mission was for me to have a good time. We stayed there until closing time. At two a.m., he says, 'Hey, c'mon man, I got an after-hours party for us to go to.' I told him, 'I don't want to go to any after-hours party, but if you want, you can stop by my house for a little bit.' " I was kind of feeling grateful for the evening, I guess. Once again, Will was headed to an after-hours party, yet he beat me to my house. I had to stop and pick [my girl] up, and when I get there, I'm surprised to see that he's in front of my house. He'd rather hang with me than go to this after-hours! I have some front gates, and I had left the garage door open that night, but the gates were closed. As soon as I open my front gates, I notice that my Harley [a silver Flatboy] was gone. I walked in the front door, and my floors are full of water. What they had done was they stopped up all the sinks, all the bathtubs, and turned on all the water. They were flooding my house. If I had stayed out all night, my whole house would have been demolished. Will was the first to say, 'Oh my God, I can't believe this happened. We've got to call the police and make sure they fingerprint. Don't anyone touch anything.' He says, 'Hey, listen, man, you know I'll stick by you, and if you want me to stay, I'll stay, but I'm on probation.' In retrospect, it was Academy Award–winning stuff."

When Joella called him after the break-in, after some initial pleasantries, he said to her, " 'Let me ask you a question: Will Wright?' And she said, 'Who I fuck is none of your business.' And I said, 'Yeah, you're right—unless two of the guys are the guys that robbed my house.' The next time I heard from her was last week."

Cherchez la femme.

"Joella was Timmy's girl," explains Darnell. "That's his ex. They were with each other, but separated. Then Medley was with her when he lived in Vegas. After he moved here, he used to take her out in public." Darnell says she told Timmy that Parrish beat the shit out of her. "Timmy takes the comforter, because he makes love to Joella on the comforter—as a way of bolstering himself with Joella. All [Parrish's] underwear, we put talcum powder all over it. Just stupid stuff like that. Turned the water on and let everything dribble out into the house. The main thing was the Warhols and this whole collection of fine watches." Of Will, he says, "He was the fluffer: 'Take him out and get him drunk.' "

Darnell identifies the ultimate recipient of Parrish's Harley-Davidson as a sometimes host of programs on the E! Channel. Another item taken—a sculpted cross made from the compressed wood chips of a West African tree that he bought for $6,000 from Chrome Hearts—shows up in Darnell's personal photos (among the very few that were returned by police, an issue over which Darnell is currently suing). Parrish readily identifies it when I show it to him, and says police had shown him the same photo.

"The reason they never indicted me for the Parrish Medley burglary based on the photo of the cross is because it's just a photo," says Darnell. He won't identify its current whereabouts, but he does claim elsewhere that Joella is holding several Warhols of indeterminate provenance for him. He refused to return the cross to Medley despite my urging. (Parrish identified Darnell from police photos, but isn't certain how he knows him.) Kristen says that Will showed her a $1,000 Chrome Hearts doggie bed that he insinuated came from Parrish, but Parrish claims he didn't have a dog at the time of the robbery. He is certain that Will was involved, though, and points out that his house is the last house on a cul-de-sac above Sunset Plaza—one way in, one way out—and exactly the kind of locale experienced burglars would avoid, unless they could be certain they wouldn't be interrupted.

Parrish also vehemently denies ever hitting Joella, and thinks this was just business for her, even as he has to stop the interview a couple of times to regain his composure. "The bottom line is that she was a stripper hanging around to get paid," he says. "After the relationship was over, the break-in was her justification for not getting paid in the first place . . . She knew what I had. I don't know how women think, man."

Eventually, Will and Darnell showed up at the Hamilton-Selway Fine Art Gallery in Beverly Hills with Parrish's blue Warhol Paramount logo—the twin of the one belonging to Frank Mancuso Jr. taken during the Cañon Drive burglary and later returned to him—that Parrish initially purchased through the gallery. According to dealer Ron Valdez, Will claimed he had a buyer in Florida and needed to authenticate the painting. Valdez was familiar with the painting and could easily vouch for its authenticity, but insisted they fill out pro forma legal documents verifying chain of title. When they refused, he declined to issue them a certificate, and he says Darnell threatened him at gunpoint. Valdez told them to "get the fuck out of my gallery" and contacted the police. The painting was eventually recovered by the LAPD Art Crimes Unit, but without a clear trail that could have led to indictments. (Parenthetically, Valdez told me he once saw Will "destroy a guy in a fight outside of a nightclub.")

Koi owner Dipu Haque reported the theft of several guns, including the Smith & Wesson .357 chrome revolver found at Darnell's residence, on July 24, 2004, along with a Rolex, a laptop computer, and some Mont Blanc pens. Heather says that Haque once confided to her that he held Timmy responsible. Darnell, who says he and Timmy used to refer to Dipu and his brother Nick as "Indian Muppet Babies" behind their backs, says that he actually won the gun in a poker game at Haque's home a year earlier, and that Haque's claims of being robbed were a ruse to hide the gun's disappearance. This would have figured into Darnell's legal strategy, as Joe Francis identified the silver .357 at the preliminary hearing as the gun that was used against him in January 2004, which Haque didn't report stolen until six months later. (Darnell also claimed that a Sturm Ruger .22 caliber pistol traced to film director Wes Craven had been a gift from Bolo. That gun was taken in a burglary of the director's home in mid-2003 in which assailants smashed a glass sliding door with a rock.)

According to Gordon Bijelonic, the home of L.A. Clippers star Cuttino Mobley, whom he knew as a fellow investor in some of the same restaurants, was also burglarized in similar fashion on January 28, 2006. Once again, according to a second source, Will was out with the victim Mobley when his house was hit, and according to the West Hollywood Sheriff's Department, Will is still a formal suspect in that case. Mobley refuses to comment.

Not that there haven't been more than enough robberies to go around. As per Darnell: "Once Timmy and I came into possession of a huge safe and I couldn't crack it at the place we were at, and I couldn't drill the safe because it was in a residential neighborhood out in Dana Point, so we took it with us. We hoisted it up onto a truck at four a.m., after me trying for two hours with just a stethoscope and hair touch. So we get it to my boy Jerry's gym; we used the alley entrance and had the garage for our use. I forced it open in thirty minutes. Sawed through and got the loot inside: antique guns and a couple hundred thousand. I gave Timmy his cut and took care of Jerry for letting me use the place. This safe weighed close to three hundred pounds, if not more. It stood five feet high and three feet wide. It took Timmy and me to hoist it onto the truck after sliding it down two flights of stairs in this palace of a home that overlooked the ocean. Once we finished with it, I asked [boxer] Desir [Alexis] to help me put it back on the truck, and this animal picked the safe up like it was a lunch pail. I've bench-pressed three hundred fifty pounds without a problem. I'm no wimp. But he picks it up without a grunt."

Even Andrew Belchic, Timmy's one-time employer, was robbed of artwork in a 2005 burglary following Darnell's arrest, although apparently it didn't occur to him that anyone he knew could be responsible until I asked him about it, even though the culprit would have had to have been known by his dogs, as according to neighbors they failed to bark.

And investment banker Holt Gardiner was robbed twice—once at his home off Hollywood Boulevard in 1998 or early 1999, either right before or right after Darnell's release, and once on April 23, 2002, at a storage space in Van Nuys (while he was in between residences and working in Sacramento) in which he lost virtually everything he owned, a loss he estimates at $700,000. Darnell's friend Susan Yannetti, who got him work as a production assistant on cable TV shows, worked as an assistant to both Holt and Frankie Liles. (Darnell met Holt through Frankie Liles.) Timmy and Frankie organized Holt's thirtieth birthday party in Las Vegas (the one where a guest's casino winnings were stolen). On the day of the first break-in, Liles showed up unannounced and offered to drive Holt to the birthday party he was hosting for a friend at the Foundation Room at the House of

Blues. He says that Yannetti—whom he claims he later fired and is currently embroiled in a business dispute with—"was the one who called me and said, 'Oh, this is all gone . . . how could it happen?' "

Holt also claims a prominent Beverly Hills pawnbroker named Yossi Dina of South Beverly Wilshire Jewelry and Loan (whose brochure reads "One man's misfortune can be another man's gold mine") tried to sell him back his own merchandise following the second burglary.

"This guy had some of my stuff in his possession, so I called the cops," he continues. "Within about an hour, I had two thugs at my house. I said, 'Dude, I really don't care. I mean, what are you going to do—kill me right now? I'll call the fucking cops again. Don't push me around.' And then suddenly the guy laid off, and when I went down to check the stuff out, it wasn't there, and the guy said, 'I don't know, I never heard of that.' "

I visited Yossi in the company of Rick Doremus, who acquired the nickname Shrek for a reason, and would at least give him pause if he tried to get rough. "Play your cards carefully, one at a time," Doremus counsels me while we wait out Yossi's return at a nearby Starbucks. "Do not put him on the defensive." Back in the store, we watch as a tall, bald Israeli is buzzed in, barking into his BlueTooth headset: "I'm going over to pick up the check . . . He didn't like being followed—he didn't like the pressure." When I introduce myself, he stares me down and asks if I'm a detective. As a concession to get rid of me, he offers to run two names through his computer database—I give him Timmy Iannello and Darnell Riley—and he returns to tell me that *one* of them (he won't say which one, and he won't let me guess) hit positive: "I bought a watch from him for fifteen hundred dollars, and the police have a lien on it." Darnell later claims it was him, the watch was a Bulova sports watch that was a gift from Louis Ziskin to Kristen Williams, and that she had sold it to him when she needed money. The lien was because Darnell was now a felon. This was all confirmed by Louis.

After the second incident, Holt hired a private investigator, who told him, "It was this fucking kid Darnell"—a theory confirmed to him by Tommy Alastra, who after his own home invasion and putative physical assault would volunteer his story to anyone who appeared to have been similarly victimized.

Darnell pins the storage space burglary on Timmy, working with one of Holt's girlfriends, despite the presence of some of the stolen items showing up in Darnell's photos. He adamantly exonerates both Liles and Yannetti.

"It was Timmy and the whore, looking for a score," says Darnell. "Lowlife shit—robbing his friends. Holt took care of Timmy plenty of times." (Holt doubts this explanation, since the woman in question, despite a subsequent drug problem, gave him back his expensive gifts after they split.)

"I told Timmy, 'Go pick up the shit from Yossi that you got from Holt,' " says Darnell, having been contacted by the pawnbroker. "He nearly shit his pants. He tried to explain but I told him, 'You ain't got to explain to me— that's *your* friend.' Holt and I were casual."

Holt identified several of his possessions from Darnell's photos: a Rolling Stones album cover signed by Keith Richards, a framed poster for *The Italian Job* that was a gift from Vin Diesel, a nude sketch. Darnell explains that they were collateral for a loan to Timmy, but again, he refuses to return them.

Several days after I interviewed him (but before I subsequently spoke to Darnell), Holt received a mysterious phone call at six o'clock one evening on his home phone number from a male voice that sounded like it was distorted by a vocal scrambler. The number was blocked, and the phone company later could provide no further information. It said simply, "Hey, you need to stop talking about Darnell Riley," and then the line went dead.

"When I'm not whacked out of my brain drunk, it's pretty easy to see stuff," says Holt in retrospect. "They try to sell your own shit back to you." But out of all of them, it's Darnell he blames the least. "Some of the people that Darnell has fucked with are real douchebags, you know?" says Holt. "He has never blatantly claimed to be my friend, and then gone and done something, as far as I know. Whereas Timmy has claimed to be my very good friend and set me up over and over again. And Will I've never been anything close with, other than I know he was doing the same thing. Darnell has a little bit more redemptive quality, from my perspective, because even though he may be the worst of them and did the most evil things, he never tried to schmooze me about it afterwards."

"Will Wright *is* the connection between all of these people," says Rich Jardine, in an e-mail to me summarizing some but not all of the above, when he declared himself formally done with the whole WhoIsWill Wright.com universe. "He has avoided the law because there is no proof. Because he was not physically there stealing people's things: instead, he was *with* them (keeping them busy) while their houses were getting robbed. He uses people's fear of Darnell to scare them into not talking. Will was out with Nicky Hilton when she got robbed. Will was out with Richard Jardine when he got robbed. Will was out with Parrish Medley when he got robbed.

"Will and Darnell are best friends. He was the one who brought Darnell into those circles. Will actually got Darnell his attorney, Ronald Richards, because he figured if he (Will) is close with Darnell's attorney, Darnell won't tell on Will in exchange for a plea bargain. The other sex tape of Paris is real, and Will has it. That's why Paris doesn't want to testify, because if she does, they will release the tape.

"Bottom line: Will is the one common denominator in all of these robberies."

"I'm telling you this, I've told you over and over again," says Ron Richards of his prize classroom speaker, following the end of Will's parole in September 2007 (at which time he was finally free to travel without restrictions): "He never had anything to do with any robbery or burglary. That's not his game . . . He has no criminal cases anymore. I got his release terminated. He makes movies now. It's a pretty unbelievable turnaround."

For the disparity of crimes that seem to have come across Darnell's desk—brainstormed in the field or phoned in from the home office—the same artifacts show up repeatedly. Everyone wears a real or fake Rolex, and it's an ongoing game of rock-paper-scissors trying to figure out which is which. Picasso sketches and a Louis Vuitton steamer trunk stare out from the corners like *Gatsby*'s enormous yellow spectacles. Pricey Patek Philippe watches maneuver through these stories like schools of pilot fish. And everyone has Warhols; they come from Ron Valdez and the Hamilton-Selway Gallery and always, ultimately, find their way back home.

At least with the last one, it's easy to see why. Warhols are virtually mass-produced—more brand name than art object. They're commercially interchangeable, the next best thing to printed money. And then, Andy Warhol was the guy who said, "In the future, everyone will be world famous for fifteen minutes."

FIFTEEN MINUTES

One last legacy that Paris Hilton leaves us is the celebrity sex tape: not so much infamy through indulgence, or even a kind of inspired improvidence, but rather the maxim that sexual conquest is a route to power like any other. She's hardly the first in these environs to come up with that formula, but she did invent a better mousetrap: (1) Paint a target on anyone more famous than you are; (2) Take their picture, capture their soul.

Holt Gardiner, whose bank has dealings with *AVN (Adult Video News)*, the official bible of the porno industry—or the show-it-all business—stands closer to this observation than most. "I hear about all that shit," he says. "Ninety percent of [rumored sex tapes], there's usually a grain of truth to them. I would imagine that there's probably twenty Paris sex tapes out there. But I don't know what the value is."

And of course, any new industry needs its facilitators. Given his history, Darnell was perfectly positioned to help. He claims to have made such a tape with Anna Nicole Smith, just then living with Charlie Pope, and offered it for sale to Larry Flynt, who declined. Of course, both Flynt and Pope deny this.

But Pope did live with Anna Nicole Smith for nine months in Playa del Sol, was involved with her on and off for a decade, a fact confirmed by Brandi Young, and he appeared on newscasts after her death as a grieving friend. He admits to knowing Darnell, but is adamant they never made a tape with Anna Nicole. Moments later, he amends this to claim he and

Anna Nicole never made any tapes at all, and that, "Darnell Riley and I have never met." When asked if he ever supplied drugs to her, he is less emphatic. "I don't know if I want to answer that right now," he hedges. "Anna Nicole and I have done a lot of drugs together. I had mine sometimes, she had her own sometimes. It was back and forth. But was I Anna's drug dealer? No." He does volunteer, however, "She *loved* Demerol. She had tubs of that—literally. And tubs of methadone. That's heavy shit. She had grand mal seizures, but that was a lot of drugs for anyone." He suggests I might be interested in helping him write his Anna Nicole book. "She was pregnant with my kid before Dannielynn," he says. "She bought my Tahoe to give to her son. We did make sex tapes together, but we erased them all." And we're back where we started.

Darnell also claims to have attempted to broker staged provocative photographs of actress Christina Ricci in bondage gear before Ricci thought better of it. These are among the materials he claims he cannot get back from the LAPD. In a British newspaper in August 2006, discussing her efforts to land the hypersexual lead role in *Black Snake Moan*, Ricci told the interviewer, "My agent started inundating [director] Craig Brewer with photo shoots I had done that are pure sex shots!"

And in the connection that runs the furthest afield, Darnell claims that three or four levels removed, he was able to help broker a sex tape involving a controversial pop star. Without forensic tools, this seems like a game of gossip run amok, or perhaps the six-degrees version of Parrish Medley's Warhol, run repeatedly through false fronts and fake passports to mask its origins.

On the same trip in which Darnell visited Milan and Lake Como (and Munich, Prague, and Switzerland), Shelly got wind of the pop star tape when she happened upon his plane tickets. "I just had a sense that he was hiding something," she says. "He claimed it was business, but since I didn't know what kind of business he was into, or any of the people in that world, I questioned it. I got more and more distant with him after that."

Estranged from Shelly from July 2004 on, the one stabilizing influence in his life, and possibly emboldened by the apparent success of the Joe Francis home invasion, the next twelve months—his final year of freedom—proved to be ones that in retrospect seem increasingly out of control. Rich Jardine left the country in March after his partnership with Darnell turned problematic. At the same time, Will went off to Las Vegas. On April 4, Darnell "tripped and fell" on Stevie Wonder's property. In June, Darnell punched a guy out in the parking lot of Shelter after he squared off against Will for hitting on his girlfriend. Darnell and Will were handcuffed by security, and both were banned from the club for a month. Around the same time, Casey Johnson's home was robbed. On June 19, Tommy Alastra was bound and brutalized in his apartment. In late July, Dipu Haque reported the theft of his guns. And on August 4, Nicky and Paris Hilton's house was robbed in the middle of the night, with them not more than fifty feet away.

Darnell claims both he and Will were out to dinner with a group that included Paris Hilton. Afterward, they went to an after-party at the home of Jason Shaw, another Paris ex, who lived across the street from the house Paris and Nicky shared on the residential part of Hollywood Boulevard west of Laurel Canyon. At 3:15 a.m., Nicky Hilton and Kevin Connolly returned to the Hilton home to find the screen door cut and Paris's room alone ransacked, then went back to the party to tell the others.

"Paris kept screaming that she thought Nick Carter was to blame, and Nicky kept nodding her head in agreement," says Darnell. (Carter and Paris had just broken up after dating for eight months.) "Everyone was calling the cops, so I figured it was time for me to leave."

Kristen Williams had recently broken up with Will, and people would routinely keep her informed of his movements (whether she wanted them to or not). She says that Will, Darnell, Paris, and others were at dinner and the after-party together. "Will was partying with Paris and Nicky across the street that night at Paris's ex-boyfriend model's house," she says. "And he made them stay over there. He even went to get more cocaine to make sure that they would stay later." (That's just Will trying to buy his way into the party, Darnell says.)

According to police reports, at 2:15 a neighbor saw two black males standing by the Hilton sisters' mailbox, apparently taking photos. Paris claimed the theft of watches worth $200,000, additional jewelry worth $47,500, and a laptop, for a total of a $250,000. A box of photos was also picked through. She later revised that to include a purse with $20,000 cash hidden in her closet."

Following the break-in, Darnell claims that Paris summoned him to her home convinced that Nick Carter had been behind the break-in, and determined to recover video footage she thought he had. Soon after, Paris showed up with apparent bruises on her face at Concorde, the ensuing paparazzi photos serving as a not-so-subtle message to Carter that she could control his destiny as easily as he could hers. Darnell says the matter was resolved with his intervention. "There was a little B&E," he says. "Carter had a little place on La Cienega a while back."

As luck would have it, Darnell wasn't through with the matter.

"About a week later," he says, "I got a call from one of my boys at the gym, and some guys wanted to talk to me about some videos they had of Paris. The guys were two Russian kids. They weren't in the Hollywood crews. They hit her house not knowing it was Paris's house until they were inside and saw all of the photos of her around the house. They snatched whatever they could get their hands on, including the tapes in Paris's room at the bottom of her panty drawer. Without seeing the videos, I said I'd buy them sight unseen for fifty thousand dollars. I already knew some juicy shit was on them, how Paris was crying to Rick about what she thinks might be on them. The Russian kids went to their house to get the goods, and I had my guys follow them without their knowledge and they brought me the tapes back. I had the cash. My boys broke in their house. I had them take everything. The Russians came back to the gym, I gave them the fifty thousand, and they gave me ten mini-DV tapes. My boys brought four extra tapes, and once I reviewed them, they had all the juice on it. I reviewed the footage—every second of the fourteen hours. I called Timmy every time I saw something good."

Jerry Rosenberg confirms this version of the origin of the tapes in broad strokes. Darnell provided the address where the Russian kids were living: North Kings Road, just north of Hugo's Café on Santa Monica Boulevard in West Hollywood. "An old man lives there; they used the house as a crash pad," says Darnell. "You'll see a Jeep Cherokee in the driveway." The house was for rent when I went by, and neighbors didn't remember a Russian crew living there. The Realtor said the same family had lived there for the last twenty years.

When Darnell reviewed the footage, he found the following:

- Jason Shaw and Paris in the back of a taxi: "The taxi ride is with a Sikh driver with the turban. You can see Times Square in the background. They pass a billboard with Jason on it. Paris holds the camera on herself as Jason fiddles [under her dress]. She pans down as she is reaching climax. The cabby is oblivious to what's going on. The camera pans back up so you can see how flushed her face is, indicating she was enjoying the ride."
- Paris and Nick Carter at the Las Ventanas resort in Cabo San

Lucas: "The video opens with Nick holding the camera as Paris opens her luggage. She pulls out a huge ziplock bag full of weed. She flew drugs *into* Mexico. Unbelievable. Nick comments on how this tape must never get out, and Paris says, 'Yeah, the Paris Hilton Tape, Part Two.' She breaks the weed down, and rolls a fat joint. They smoke for about ten minutes, go out to the pool, talk a little shit. They have lunch poolside, go back to their room and Paris shows a tattoo on her ass of Nick's name, and he shows one of hers on his wrist." (They also spot Kelsey Grammer having lunch with Nick Lachey and Jessica Simpson, as well as Dennis Rodman pool-side, and Paris makes a joke about his endowment, possibly from experience.)

- Horsback riding: "Paris talks a little shit about how Nick's cock is like the horse's. Waiting to get the horses, still in the SUV, Nick pulls out a bag of Viagra and does a stupid impromptu commercial: 'The wonder drug!' "

- Paris and Jason Shaw in a smoke shop in Amsterdam: "This part of the video was a splice from video I had taken when we were in Amsterdam. I happened to get on film Paris ordering weed from a menu and packing the pipe/bong like a pro."

- Her grandmother's funeral: "Paris is sitting in the church shooting video of herself. She is paying no attention to the eulogy. Meanwhile, Brandon Davis, Nicky Hilton, and Nicole Richie sit next to her dumbfounded that Paris has the camera on, stuck in her own face. Paris has Brandon film her when she gets up to say her good-byes to her grandmother."

- And finally: Paris and Brandon Davis are approached by two effeminate black men at an MTV party who invite them to an event for singer/actress Eve's new clothing line. Davis initially asks if there will be any women at the party, before they exchange phone numbers. Then, according to Darnell, "On the way to the Jeep, Brandon says, 'Stupid fucks,' talking about the black guys, and Paris says 'Dirty niggers,' and they start laughing and jump in the Jeep. You could tell that Paris had tried to erase the tape, because that part had a blur in it, but the words were clear."

Perhaps the centuries of inbreeding between wealth and beauty have caused this selective gene pool to fail, as a means to redistribute wealth.

Maybe every third generation or so, these genetic virtues must express themselves as broadly as possible, to ensure the continued survival of the species. How else to explain Brandon Davis? Like hemophilia among nineteenth-century European royalty, his unique blend of boorishness, imperiousness, and petulant weakness is guaranteed to disrupt the lines of inherited power as efficiently as the destruction of the bridge on the River Kwai disrupted the Japanese supply lines. I would be hard-pressed to name a person who seems to hate himself more than Davis. Even David Reich has had about enough of him:

"Yeah, well, I have a lot of thoughts about him because I know his father is a horrible guy," says Reich. "But he borrowed money from friends of mine in Vegas recently; as you know, he lived with Will for a while, and he was fucked up on drugs. I was there when he was going to rehab, and he hid three eight-balls in a shoe, and Paris and I were just sitting there going, 'Are you kidding me? You're going to rehab and you're hiding blow? Why don't you just skip rehab?' He said, 'Because my mother will cut me off unless I go.' " Reich refers to inherited wealth as "the Brandon Davis sperm donor program."

"His mom, Nancy Davis, has multiple sclerosis, and every time Brandon does something fucked up, she gets stress that she should not have to deal with in her condition," says Donald Thrasher. "If he didn't have all that money, Brandon Davis would be Will Wright."

So it pains me to have to defend Brandon Davis in this context. I haven't seen the footage, but I've had it explained to me in great detail. And Paris Hilton's use of the N word, with Brandon Davis flagging her on like a demented courtier, is the same joke as calling Lindsay Lohan "fire-crotch": trying to appear as outrageous as possible for the cameras, which are ubiquitous in your life, as a private joke with your friends. That's why their hijinks escalate the longer the tape rolls. It's like the backstage moment in *This Is Elvis* when he mentions a girl from last night who gave great head: he's playing to the newsreel cameras. Probably not the best media strategy, but not overt racism either.

Two weeks after the break-in, on August 15, Nicky married Wall Street money manager Todd Meister in Las Vegas (the marriage was later annulled), and on August 27, Parrish Medley was robbed. Darnell was in Moscow sometime in September when Joe Francis entered town on a whirlwind and Alex Vaysfeld sent him packing for home.

"Alex had to let him know that they ain't in the U.S. and he had already seen the tape," says Darnell. " 'You ain't that tough with a dildo in your ass, so cool out.' Joe Francis was appalled and tried to buy the tape from Alex. That's when he knew [it was me]. Everyone around town saw the video."

Then in mid-September, Carole Aye Maung, a British tabloid reporter for Rupert Murdoch's *News of the World*, accompanied her boyfriend to Tru Gym where he regularly worked out, and Jerry Rosenberg introduced her to Darnell, who was just then editing the highlights of the fourteen hours of stolen Paris tapes into an eleven-minute highlights reel.

"That's what really fucked it all up," says Jerry. "I told Darnell, 'Don't even say nothing to that bitch. I'll talk to her for you.' Because they can say whatever they want about me, you know what I'm saying?"

A week later, "I had Carole meet me at the Grove," says Darnell. "I had Timmy posted up at the outdoor patio section on the third floor of the Star-bucks inside the Barnes & Noble. I escorted Carole up there while Timmy looked on to see if we were being followed. I had my guy Bo posted at the door to see whoever followed us in. Timmy had the video loaded on his laptop." She told them the video was useless to her, since she was a print reporter, and asked for five stills. She offered £5,000, and they came back with £90,000. Presumably, they met somewhere in the middle, and two days later they met again and Darnell turned over memory sticks with photos of Paris and Nick Carter together. Maung immediately contacted Paris for a comment, and spokesperson Fred Khalian ("fucking Fred" whom she takes a call from during the *1 Night in Paris* video) contacted police, claiming that, according to a report by officer Kenneth Scott, "The two individuals that are attempting to sell the footage were Darnell Riley and William Wright. Both are personal friends of the Hiltons and have frequented the Hilton residence in the past. Wright was also in the wedding of N[icky] Hilton that was held in Las Vegas shortly after the burglary. Maung met with police and picked Darnell out of a photo lineup. She also identified an individual named Tim or Timmy who had been present at the meetings, and named 'Ronald Richardson' [sic] as the lawyer whom Darnell claimed was cur-rently negotiating with Larry Flynt to sell the footage."

"Paris was about to start filming another season of *The Simple Life* on Fox, as you can see by her text messages to me, and she had billboards all around town of her Guess advertisement," says Darnell. "So me showing Carole the video of Paris Hilton was just to get the buzz going to drive up the price, and it worked . . . I had no intentions of selling, I just needed them to start the fire, and then we made our move."

Richards takes extreme exception to these last allegations. "I'm not in the business of selling tapes, and I didn't represent Darnell or anybody else in connection with the selling of a tape," he says.

Even Joe Francis weighed in on the Paris tapes, claiming that he had seen excerpts—presumably the teaser reel with the N-word clip—and that if released, they would ruin her career. Of course, by doing so, he as much as admits that he knew Darnell before his arrest, since Darnell's entire leverage with the tapes depended on him not making copies or letting them out of his possession. Darnell says he eventually brokered them back to Paris through Rick Salomon, for which Darnell received a payment of $20,000 a month, diverted directly from her ongoing *1 Night in Paris* profits. This is in addition to the $10,000 a month he says he already received for his part in the original tape, a claim supported by the check from RSTT Enterprises.

In October, Nicky Hilton had her birthday party at the Hard Rock Café in Las Vegas, where Darnell first met Jack and Heather, and Will told Paris of Darnell's involvement in the Joe Francis incident. In November, Darnell flew with Will and their girlfriends to Hawaii for Thanksgiving, where he was just about to propose to Ruby, when Will spilled the beans about Darnell's prison history during dinner, dousing the mood. In December, Paris told Joe Francis what she heard, and he notified authorities. Darnell spent New Year's in Japan with Frankie Liles, and subsequently went to work for Donna Antebi.

On his police record, there's an odd entry for February 8, 2005, two days after the Super Bowl, which is always Darnell's busy season, and which he spent in Vegas. On that date, Darnell filed a report claiming he was the victim of a hit-and-run in Coldwater Canyon while driving a 1992 silver Mercedes 500 CDL with Will in the car. That is, a week after the *Vanity Fair* article on the Bel Air Burglar came out, two days after the Super Bowl—the biggest gambling event of the year—and two and three weeks, respectively, before a tracking device is placed on Will's car and a warrant is issued for Darnell's arrest, he contacts police as the *victim* of a crime. As with the Stevie Wonder story, I asked him if the real story was more complicated.

"Crazy, isn't it?" he says. "I was getting rid of my Mercedes." When I ask him why, he says, "Paranoid." Months later, he confided the real story.

"The hit-and-run was a friend's old-school Cadillac," he says. "She needed to get rid of it. Will had broken his ankle riding dirt bikes with

Jared [Merrell] months prior and needed his ankle reset, and he didn't have insurance, so why not say he was in the car when he wasn't? It was staged—duh. So yeah, the real [story] is much more interesting. In fact, I had Jerry drive the Cadillac into the car we had. He loves bomber car shit. So the girl needed to get rid of a car, and Will needed surgery and didn't want to pay. Here I come to the rescue."

There were other activities: counterfeit RFID ("Radio Frequency Identification") poker chips with a line into one of the casinos; a gold coin scam on eBay with Alex Vaysfeld; fake passports; dealings with Alex's friend from the old country.

When I called Alex to get his version of Darnell's latest international intrigue, I learned that Alex himself was now headed for a multi-year bid in the Big House: first a layover at Wayside, and then probably Taft Correctional Institute. (Maybe he can have Louis's old bunk.) It seems that Alex was facing a half-million-dollar restitution after some stolen construction equipment worth several million dollars was seized on the Russian docks with his name on the return address, and the D.A. wouldn't accept the deal. And so another confidante joins my list of sources who are either mobsters, pimps, party girls, drug dealers, drug addicts, fugitives, or convicted felons. And they all want me to help them write their book.

Mid-February, Paris's phone book was posted on the Internet. By sometime in March, Darnell says he was officially cashed out of all criminal enterprise. And on March 28, he was arrested in his driveway.

EPILOGUE:
I Want to Live Forever

My mother died when I was two. She was twenty-eight. Later, in my early juvenile life, in a fit of justified rage, I remember my father telling me, "You inherited one thing from your mother: the gift of con."

I skirt the line. I live as close to it as I can, and on occasion I have snuck over to the other side. I think the difference is that I know I don't belong over there, and I can always find my way back. In Lake Tahoe, there's a casino called the Cal-Neva Lodge. Sinatra owned it during the Kennedy years, although that was just as a favor to Sam Giancana and Fat Tony Salerno. It's built right on the state line, so that half of it is in Nevada where gambling is legal, and half is in California, where it isn't. Used to be, if you walked by that part of it any decent hour of the day, there would be a gang of kids crowded together on the California side, and when the security guard wasn't looking, they'd run across the line and drop a token in the nearest slot machine.

That's me. I've been a junkie, a liar, a thief, and a cheat at various times in my past, and I feel comfortable among those who still are. Comfortable because I can see myself in them, and comfortable because I don't have a problem calling them on it. You know why people do drugs? Most people would tell you it's because they're weak, that they can't help themselves, but actually it's the opposite. People do drugs long past the point of contraindication because they are too strong, impervious even: they can easily see the price in human wreckage on everyone around them, and yet they're also able to see past it. If they can just get high or get over, just this once, then—blah blah blah. Doesn't matter what. Everybody has their reasons. So I live among the criminal class, professionally, but I'm not of them, and unlike Jerry Rosenberg or Charlie Pope or Alex Vaysfeld, I could never make that transition. Consequently, someone like Darnell could survive in my world, and did—impressively—for six years, while I wouldn't last till dinner in his. "You want to know about me, just look at yourself," Darnell once told me. "We're not too different. You would do well in here. Nah, I'm bullshitting. You'd be cleaning someone's dirty drawers." More likely, I'd *be* dinner.

"You live on the edge," Koman told me.

But also, maybe, it makes me susceptible to someone like Darnell. The story he tells is fantastic—and I've tried to follow the ant trails that emerge from the welter of detail. Except behind every door that Darnell opens stands another one waiting for me to peek behind. Darnell almost certainly has a story to tell; I've seen the reflections and shadows of it cast upon the faces of everyone I've spoken to. I'm just not sure that this is it. For all the master crimes attributed to the Incredible Mr. Riley by himself and others, his greatest haul may have been people's secrets that he got close enough to steal, and the strongest element of his narrative is its proximity. Yet he can't tell the stories of those around him without in part revealing his own, much of which he must obscure out of self-preservation, and which emerge as sinkholes in his landscape, conspicuous by their absence. Consequently, telling his story is like unwriting a novel: it's woven together out of a million colored threads, and there's no way to follow them without them unraveling in vibrant snarls.

It's a world where the eyewitnesses rarely speak lest they be ejected from the party. So Darnell may be like Keyser Söze, the criminal mastermind at the end of *The Usual Suspects* piecing together an elaborate cover story out of the increments of what he finds in the corners of the frame. But there is truth in that as well, if only you can reconstruct the original image—like those women in Eastern Europe, fortified by infinite patience, who are piecing together the lost historical record out of the shredded documents of a collapsed police state. Maybe the characters in his story were all ones he knew intimately, in ways he could leverage, if necessary, to create the story strands he desired, without fear of intervention on their part. But there were real crimes committed, with real victims and real loss. Work backward from the crimes, and these tendrils will eventually intertwine with the yarn he is telling.

Motive was thornier than either method or opportunity. Maybe he just wants to be rich or famous, control his own story, augment his destiny, the same as everybody else. Jaime Weinberg, his ex-girlfriend, told him he set goals as a challenge to himself, including possibly his entire segue into crime, because he became bored too easily. Maybe his bone to pick is with me: he didn't like my original story, he doesn't like being called "Dildo Dude," and he's got time to lay out the whole story—the combustible elements of his opus set to explode upon contact with the open air.

If Darnell's story proved too daunting by half, then I found an unanticipated ally in Darnell himself. In a letter he wrote me soon after my first visit, he said, "I tell ya, sometimes I feel like a man who has died, then sets out in the afterlife in search of proof of my own existence. Trying to get confirmation from others of events and hard proof in the form of photos and audiovisuals when I'm behind these walls is a motherfucker. As you can now see, many of the people commenting are doing so with half-truths, which turn out to be full lies, and are angling to put themselves in the best light possible, and at the end of the day, they know they've got to see me again. And a lot of them are complicit in the many acts that have been attributed to my 5'9 frame . . . No one is gonna want to admit that I've slapped the shit out of them, or that I've fucked them. These people got lives right now, careers, trust funds. Who wants to be attached to the bad guy? No one wants to go on record and box themselves in, or piss me off and inadvertently put themselves in harm's way. I've got to verify everything I say and do. I've never been one to have to justify or explain my flow. You'll get pieces from different people, because that was my life. Welcome to my world."

"Any time someone has a book coming out, people get freaked out," says Brandi Young. "But I think Darnell is more forthcoming and more straightforward when it comes to telling the story—his story—than it would be if you asked anyone else. Especially Will, Timmy, or Joe. In a way, Darnell—because he's already doing his time—is the one person who is untouchable. He has nothing to lose. Of all people that you've mentioned, Darnell is the one person who never drank, never smoked, never did any drugs—he was always clear about what he was doing. Whether it was the right thing or the wrong thing is a different question altogether, but he was always aware of what he was getting himself into."

"They need Hollywood more than Hollywood needs them," says Darnell. "Who are they? The Kristen Williams, Will Wrights, Chuck Pachecos,

Rick Salomons of the world. Someone who ain't got their own world going on. Someone who feels unfulfilled if the camera ain't on them. The Parises and Britneys. Look at me. I'm the obvious bad guy. I'm locked up. But a Lindsay or Britney is one DUI test away from being in here with the boogeyman. As long as they can look at my kind as cast off to no-man's-land, then the closer they will get to no-man's-land themselves. Prison is a reality for everyone." He's quoting *Scarface*: "You need people like me so you can point your fucking finger and say, 'That's the bad guy.' "

Of Timmy Iannello, Darnell says, "I let him walk around town once Mark Wahlberg's guys whipped his ass. He would have been punked without me, and he threw me to the wolves." Of Will, he says, "If the Feds don't have Will Wright now, I don't think they'll ever get him. If he's smart, he's closed up shop. But he may be one of those junkies who just can't stop. Even if he's not personally the one packing the drugs and putting it on the plane, he may have some sort of detached investment in it . . .

"Knowing that I could have gotten a better deal had I turned Timmy and Will in just let me know that once again, I was the only one playing by these archaic gangster rules and protecting my boys. It was like my juvenile case all over again. I took the fall and protected my boys, and I get the finger in the butt when it's all over.

"Fuck, I played myself, hanging with stupid fucks like Will. What the fuck was I thinking?"

Late in the writing process, I got word that Mario King, aka Mario Good, aka Ocean, had been arrested on a robbery beef in Orange County and was scheduled to appear in court in Murietta Hot Springs in Riverside County, about an hour down the coast from L.A. On a boiling hot afternoon, I drove down to the Southwest Judicial Center, where among the meth-addled white guys and handful of cholos, I finally located the name Mario Goode on the electronic roster, just as the bailiff directed a nattily dressed, heavyset, bald black man in designer sunglasses toward the clerk's office. When I inquired with the bailiff about Mario Goode, he told me to "follow that guy." I caught up with him in the hallway.

"I'm looking for Mario King," I say.

"I'm Mario King," he says, adjusting the Bluetooth headset in his ear and studying his BlackBerry. I told him who I am and that I was interested in what happened in Pasadena back in 1993. His eyes twitched slightly, but there were no other outward signs of alarm.

"So you want to talk about Darnell and Bonnie and Chris and all that?"

he asks, his head tilted down and cocked slightly with his eyes looking up, like from underneath an overhanging ledge.

"I do," I say. "Maybe I could sit down with you sometime."

"As long as I get paid on that," he says. "If I tell you that story, I *better* get paid, because it's deep. You came all the way down here to find me, huh?" Veiled suspicion was boiling off, leaving just amusement.

"It's the only way I could get face-to-face with you," I say. "Pasadena is done—I'm not trying to rope you back into that."

"Well, you *can't*," he says, cutting me off. "I'm *clean* on that." He makes a smooth, flat hand gesture, like an umpire calling safe.

"And how about this?" I ask him, looking around the courthouse hallway.

"Aw, this ain't no big thing," he says. He asks for my card as we reach the clerk's office. "Which name was I under?" he asks.

Back in the courtroom, as he waited for his case to be called, I could see him in the back row texting on a BlackBerry hidden in a baseball cap. When his name was finally called, a public defender joined him at the front of the courtroom, and he agreed to waive time and remained free on bail. The whole procedure took less than thirty seconds. I followed him out of the courtroom and into a crowded elevator, and then out into the sun-blasted parking lot.

"What are you doing for a living these days, Mario?" I ask him.

"I've got some investments here and there," he says. "Where's your car?" I point to the clunker that managed to get me the fifty miles down here and hopefully back. "I get it," he says. "You're saving your money. Where you keep your money—you invest in real estate?" He seemed very interested in investment strategies.

"Are you going to stay out of jail again this time?" I ask.

"Yeah, I don't know what this is all about," he says, one more victim of life's circumstances. I compliment his strategy in the 1998 Pasadena trial, bringing in his fellow Muslims to pray in open court. He points out that he represented himself *pro se*, only bringing in Peters, the attorney of record, at the very end. "We had nude pictures of Bonnie with that bailiff, and we also knew that he put her and Chris together so they could get their stories straight," he says. "I asked Peters to show the video that would prove I wasn't there, but he thought it would be too hard on the people to see that. I almost cried when they said not guilty." About playing the race card, he says, "So what? I was a convicted felon and a black man standing before them."

"You've got nine lives," I tell him.

"And that kidnapping in Santa Monica: First trial, hung jury. Second trial, acquittal in less than an hour."

I ask him what happened with Darnell on the stand. "He took a deal," says King. "That was life he was looking at."

"That's not what Darnell says," I tell him. "He says he never named you on the stand."

"Named me for what?" he asks.

"Giving him the gun."

"Yeah, I don't know about that," he says.

"Really? You were there, right?"

"Yeah, I was there," he says. All pretense of small talk has gone out of it now, and his eyes bore into me, daring me to push him any further.

"Did you speak to Darnell afterward?" I ask.

"I haven't spoken to him lately, but he did call me wondering if I was going to do anything to him," he says. "I wasn't going to do anything. By God's grace, I was free. I was looking at paradise or freedom, and I am free. I'm done." He smiles a Cheshire Cat smile and walks off into the blinding glare, swinging his keys.

Then, just before the book went to press, Will made a surprise reappearance as well. On August 18, 2008, Will was involved in a bizarre showdown with Chris Paciello, the former mobster and sometime Erin Naas flame, and Reza Roohi, co-owner of the night club Villa. That day was Will's 31st birthday, and Al Maimon, the convicted ecstasy dealer who Louis blames for turning state's evidence against him, was scheduled to throw Will a birthday dinner at the trendy One Sunset restaurant-lounge. Both men were clients of Ron Richards, and all three had been spotted recently dining in public.

The incident began on the evening of August 17, when Will happened across Clippers' star and unsolved burglary victim Cuttino Mobley, who was drinking with Paciello and Roohi at Café Les Deux. Going on the offensive, Will accused Mobley of disparaging his reputation in public by suggesting that Will was responsible for the burglary of his home. Instead, he blamed the break-in on Darnell (who had been in custody at the time). Mobley reportedly called Will a piece of shit, told him to take a walk, and tough guy Paciello sent him packing. (Says Louis of Paciello from prison: "He's no punk. And he knows how to use his hands. He clipped me pretty good in Miami.")

According to a source who talked to Paciello immediately afterward, Will tried unsuccessfully throughout the night to get Paciello's phone number, until finally, in the early morning hours of the 18th, Ron Richards finally patched Will's call through to Paciello's cell phone. Will told Paciello to meet him at the corner of Sunset and San Vicente, around the corner from where he lived.

Paciello and Roohi showed up in Roohi's black SUV and Paciello got out of the car. At that point, Will allegedly pulled a knife and began threatening him. Paciello punched him once, knocking him down, and Will scrambled into a nearby gas station convenience store. Richard Simmons, the night clerk on duty at Sunset Oil, says that at approximately 3:15 a.m., Will entered his store and told him to call 911, saying, "There's about to be an incident." He then lifted his shirt to reveal a large fillet knife wedged in his belt. When Will exited the store, a black SUV idling at the pump gunned it and drove directly at him. Will backed up onto the elevated curb and began slashing the front of the SUV with his knife, as the car stopped short of hitting him. At that point, both Paciello and Roohi chased Will back into the convenience store and Paciello administered a savage beating. The police, having already been notified, were there within minutes and all four (including the store clerk) handcuffed, although Will and the clerk were released. The whole thing was captured on surveillance video, which was confiscated by the West Hollywood Sheriff's Department. At Will's sparsely attended birthday party later that night, he showed up black and blue in a skull and crossbones T-shirt. He told TMZ in an update that Roohi had run him down, leaving a gash in his head that needed fifteen stitches. In the days afterward, he told those who asked that he'd been in a car accident.

When contacted a day later, Ron Richards, who said he represents Will, the club Villa, and Reza Roohi, defended his actions putting impulse control-challenged client Will Wright in touch with Paciello at three in the morning, saying, "I did not think they were meeting because Chris told me he was going to follow my advice and go home. Instead, without telling me, he picked up Reza and took him to meet Will." Asked about Will in all of this, Ron predicts, "The matter will be going away. I obviously know how to do my job." And, in fact a few weeks later, charges were dropped against both Paciello and Roohi.

Like Ocean, Will never seemed to be in the vicinity when crimes were being committed. People committed home invasions, boosted Rolexes, pocketed expensive jewelry, tied up victims, and fled in their luxury automobiles—either with their complicity or at their behest; accounts differ— and yet every time it doubles down, the criminal justice system has been ineffectual in dissuading him.

As Koman continually points out whenever he gets a moment alone with Darnell, if it hadn't been for Will's slip of the tongue to Paris, and Paris's Good Samaritan debriefing of Joe Francis, and Joe Francis's sudden revelation as to Darnell's identity, the police would never have known he existed. Of the hundreds of things he could have eventually been arrested for, he considers this one of the least likely.

"If Will has a grand plan, I can't say with any certainty," says Darnell. "He is stupid. He knows he is as complicit in the Joe Francis situation as I was, so I doubt if he would have put himself in the line of fire—his possible arrest because of his part in the Joe Francis incident. I truly don't think he's that smart. He was just trying to get laid, and bolster his credibility as a heavyweight." But then, isn't that what he'd want you to believe?

Darnell was always the guy who came in and did everybody else's work. Gambling, drugs, loan sharking, prostitution, extortion, "beat-downs"— lurid autobiography: this stuff takes enormous effort, and he was always the one willing to expend the labor. This may be a sign of character, or it may simply replace character—the distinction between seized opportunity and simple opportunism. But this is Hollywood, after all, where gossip passes for wisdom, and personal obligation rarely exceeds the limits on Daddy's credit card. The honor among thieves he had learned to expect from a life in the criminal arts did not apply to the class of people he met inside the bubble. Once out of sight, he was easily out of mind—yesterday's diversion.

We all have confessions to make. This is mine. The last time I visited Darnell up at Corcoran, I broke down and cried. I worry about what will become of him. I've consistently throughout asked him about redemption, and he's always quick with a reply. He says he's out of the life, that he's too old, that the past is difficult to judge and the future is bright with promise.

"I understand how I played myself by justifying smacking a guy like Joe Francis around, or Will for fucking me over on a deal, or robbing a dope dealer because it was illegal business anyways," he tells me. "They were into crime, they weren't civilians. I bent reason to justify my position that, as long as I wasn't robbing civilians or legitimate citizens' businesses, it was alright. Because it was all illegal, I had to act within the system of street justice. But I got no more left. I'll still kick some ass, but the ethical bending of reason has run its course."

I wish him luck.

As F. Scott Fitzgerald says in *The Great Gatsby*: "Reserving judgments is a matter of infinite hope."

ACKNOWLEDGMENTS

The author is grateful to the following people. Some provided research assistance or interviews; others provided help with the manuscript or provided moral support during the writing process; and others have simply inspired me or this project in some fashion, even if I've never met or spoken to them:

Herbert and Mary Ebner; the Enright family; the Hughes family; the Spring family; the Just family; the Calvi family; the Ott family; Dan "Danno" Hanks of Backstreet Investigations; Lisa Derrick; Lisa Ullmann; Shawn Schepps; Christian Logan Wright; John Connolly; Paul Cullum; Christian Darren; Tucker Max; Donika Miller; Luke Heidelberger; Jordan Golson; Ben Corman; Anna David; Richard Rushfield; Ryan Holiday; Davia Deakin (for the DVD of *Mister Sterling*); Holt Gardiner; Andrew Belchic; Eric Rayman; Ursula Cary; Jennifer Bergstrom; Patrick Price; Joseph Menn; Becky Kershman; the Wednesday Night Poker Crew—Vince, Dino, Mike, Mikey, John, Jim, Keith, Chris, and sometimes Solo; the Silverlake Rounders; Eric Schaeffer; Jessica Allen; David Simonds; the TruTV Believers; Terry Danuser; Mickey Ramos; Bill Bastone and the Smoking Gun Crew; the Kaiser Permanente Emergency Room staff; the Venice Family Clinic; Nick Denton; Ellen Meister; Detective Steve Koman, LAPD–Robbery-Homicide Division; Deputy D.A. Hoon Chun; Detective Mike Vanags; Detective Thomas Delgado; Jack Ninio and Heather Bernardcyck; Kristen Williams; Elizabeth Jawhary; Parrish Medley; Gordon

Bijelonic; DJ Morty Coyle; Tamer Ibrahim; Jerry Rosenberg and the Fortune Boxing Gym; Alex Vaysfeld and Union Bail Bonds; Corcoran State Prison; Taft Correctional Institute; Ben Wallace; Coerte Felske; Brandi Young; Louis Ziskin; Shelly Wood; Donald Thrasher; E. G. Daily; Giovanni Agnelli; Scott Bloom; Donna Antebi; Jaime Weinberg; Joe Carnahan; Ruben Hernandez; Rick Doremus; Claire Hoffman; Alex Guevarra; Frank Mancuso Jr.; Christopher McQuarrie; Catherine Keener's mom; Dexter, Humphrey, Judy, Tuck, and Cooper; Bill Wilson and Bob Smith; Susan Leibowitz; John Guare; Heavy D; Retired Deputy D.A. Sterling Norris; Jim Epstein; Pat Grubb and Jack Kintner at *The Northern Light*, and the good people of Blaine, WA.; Julien Nitzberg; Max Wong; Ross Johnson; Chris Reilly; Freddie Roach; Christopher Tennant; Maer Roshan; Mim Udovitch; Larry Flynt; Karen Foshay; Bill Weedman; Dolores Schaeffer; Roy Lee; Penny Marshall; Thomas DeTrinis; Tricia Boczkowski; Jeremie Ruby-Strauss; Brandon Boyce; Pete "The Cripple" Oddo; Tim Talbott; Charlie Black; Mason Alley; Dylan Kussman; Scott Steindorff; Gil Reavill; Andrew Breitbart; Jeffrey Wells; Harry Knowles; Jim Goad; Ken Druckerman; Banks Tarver; Anneka Jones; Maria Ruvalcaba Hackett; Mark Lisanti; Jeffrey Taylor; Andrew Brin; Jennifer Howell; John South; Joshua Leonard; Peter Elkoff; Ben Schwartz; Susannah Breslin; Xeni Jardin; Jerry Stahl; Joel Gotler; and, of course, Darnell Riley.